The highest praise for
JUNGLE IN BLACK
by Steve Maguire

"Blinded by an incident of war, Captain Steve Maguire passed through the ordeal of recovery and adjustment to win his personal battle. Today he possesses the true vision of wisdom, love and meaningful accomplishment. A moving story. My strongest endorsement."
—Major General Barry R. McCaffery, U.S. Army
Commander, 24th Infantry "Victory" Division,
Desert Storm

"I thought it unlikely, after reading *Rumor of War*, that I would ever again read an account of the ordeal of Vietnam that could match the intensity and poetry of its focus. Incredibly this has happened, and I can say with confidence that no one with 20-20 vision has accomplished what Mr. Maguire has done in telling what it is increasingly safe to speak of as The Other Side of Vietnam."
—William F. Buckley, Jr.

JUNGLE IN BLACK

STEVE MAGUIRE

DICKINSON AREA
PUBLIC LIBRARY

BANTAM BOOKS
NEW YORK • TORONTO • LONDON • SYDNEY • AUCKLAND

JUNGLE IN BLACK
A Bantam Falcon Book/August 1992

ISBN 0-553-29486-5

Published simultaneously in the United States and Canada

PRINTED IN THE UNITED STATES OF AMERICA

84952   RAD   0 9 8 7 6 5 4 3 2 1

DEDICATION

For my fellow grunts whose lives were for a time bound to that war in Vietnam, especially for those who by virtue of that took the kind of hits that must be borne forever.

Courage is almost a contradiction in terms. It means a strong desire to live taking the form of a readiness to die . . . A soldier surrounded by enemies, if he is to cut his way out, needs to combine a strong desire for living with a strange carelessness about dying. He must not merely cling to life, for then he will be a coward, and will not escape. He must not merely wait for death, for then he will be a suicide, and will not escape. He must seek his life in a spirit of furious indifference to it; he must desire life like water yet drink death like wine.

G. K. CHESTERTON

ACKNOWLEDGMENTS

I thank my wife, Suzy, for her resourceful abilities to encourage my writing and for her lively and practical interest in my thoughts and hopes. I am indebted to her unwavering support even throughout her personal crisis of cancer and chemotherapy. Her enthusiasm and dedication have more than compensated for my own losses.

To D. Keith Mano I owe THANKS in capital lettering. He was a constant resource of encouragement and well-rounded criticism.

For my spiritual guides in Ireland, Fr. Bernard O'Dea O.S.B. and Fr. Christopher Dillon O.S.B. I give thanks. Their bountiful discussions and heartwarming hospitality at Glenstahl Abbey, Murroe, County Limerick, encouraged my writing abilities to develop.

A debt is owed to my friends Diane Buck and Laurie McCarthy for their efficient and thorough typing and proofreading of my manuscript.

I direct my appreciation also to my agent, Tom Hebert, not only for his help with this book, but for all that he has done over the years for Vietnam veterans. His devotion to the *Vietnam Newsletter* and bookstore has been a tremendous contribution in telling the larger story of the war.

I want to express my deep gratitude to all the fellow soldiers and friends who are written about. Some names have been changed to protect identities, but all events are actual and authentic. Thanks to Andy Wilson and the rest of the Pit crew for their camaraderie, concern, and spirit. Even the bad times came to good. In the war, we fought for each other, and after the war, nothing had changed. Deo Gratias.

AUTHOR'S NOTE

People prayed for it, but in 1969 I did not come back safely from our longest war. I came back from Nam a hardened combat soldier with no sight to help me make my way through an emotional and object-infested jungle, where all terrain is an obstacle course. Darkness has an interminable intensity. Blindness has no aftermath. It is a constant. My jungle in black is an unalterable fact, but I must make my own way in it, or become my own worst liability.

This is the story of my regeneration following that one fate-loaded explosion. Read it and know that I am a fortunate man. I realize life is more than what is seen on its surface. Had I the chance, I would not trade my life today for my pre-Vietnam life. I have a passion for life because I found the powers of love to be fascinating, strengthening, and self-evident.

CHAPTER ONE

A few black grease-penciled markings on a clear acetate map cover told the whole story. My name, E-66, shepherding a series of arrows, randomly pointing, a cluster of feathered dart tails. Each arrow nosed a letter, A through I.

"Nine insertions?" I asked, dismayed. "We just got back in this morning."

Captain Hanney, the S-3 Air Assistant Operations Officer, pushed up from his desk. Coming around it to stand next to me, he placed a muscled arm around my shoulder. It seemed to accentuate his considerable height. "I'm afraid so, Steve," he sympathized. "The colonel agreed with Major Caldwell. We're short on birds and it's the only way we can do it. The bitch is, it's going to be another three-day humper for you."

"What the hell's out there anyway?"

"Intelligence has it that the second Long An battalion crawled out from under a rock. A lot of civilians are reporting bad shit to their district headquarters."

"So why not the ARVN?" I interrupted. "Or people at Tan Tru? It's a long way for me to be going."

"Well, most of the ARVN Twenty-fifth is concentrated around here now, securing all these towns and villages"— he swept his finger to my side of the map and flittered it across a dozen grid squares—"and their recon units

1

don't have access right now to the choppers that it would require. The Second of the Sixtieth is completely committed on a big operation in this region up here." His finger pocked another part of the map.

"Yeah, right, nine insertions. But stay out for the night? And two days beyond that? Our feet've been in water for three straight days already."

He gave a leery shrug. "I know. But you've managed this kind of thing okay before. It's basically the same ol' shit—hopscotch until you make contact or run out of daylight. Alpha and Charlie companies will back you up."

"Shit, it'll take over an hour to get them out to me." I bent down, inspecting for some clues or terrain features, as if there were any; hell, this whole Mekong Delta read virtually the same—rivers, canals, rice paddies, woodline— variations on the theme of water and mud. "What about this bush along here?" I made reference to some dark green running in a border along the blue of a river that wound a cordon around part of the target area. "Have you been out there?"

"Yeah, yesterday on a V.R. Nipa mostly. Not that big tall stuff like out in Phuc Lam, but still thick enough to hide bunkers. There's some banana . . . usual crap. We'll suppress with gunships on your flanks on Bravo and Foxtrot. They look like the best bets to rustle something up."

"All right. That looks good." I began copying all the coordinates.

"You'll be flying out with Hornet this time, slick leader is Hornet one-four."

"Gunships?"

"Right, Stinger five-five, light fire team. You're okay with arty as well. There's no one-o-fives that can reach you, but we've got some eight-inch and one-five-fives at Tu Twa; only two tubes each. You should be all right with that."

"If they can crank it out fast enough when I need it."

The sound of tramping turned our attention to the

doorway. Major Caldwell, the S-3 Operations Officer, entered the room.

"Whadayasay, Mack," he grunted through a soggy cigar clamped in his teeth.

"Not bad, sir, considering Echo six-six's assignment."

"Uh-huh." Caldwell nudged himself between Hanney and me to mark a few more details on the map. He stooped down to write on the bottom, a sheen of sweat glistening on his thick black neck, funneling into a dark wet V down the back of his shirt. He mumbled a few curses about the heat; his calling attention to it seemed to instantly raise the temperature ten degrees. The entire building was one huge bunker divided into half a dozen rooms or offices, and this one was completely without outside ventilation. Three ambitious little fans swayed their heads back and forth, droning . . . endlessly blowing the same hot fetid air up, down, and sideways, as if hoping desperately to pull just a trace of clear cooler air in from the hall.

"I'll bet that cigar died two days ago," Hanney quipped, changing the subject.

"Three," he winked my way, "and besides, I don't like the smoke, I just like the juice."

"I'd rather chew on a dog turd."

"I know you would, good buddy," Caldwell said, straightening up his burly form, "and enjoy the hell out of it too."

Hanney chuckled and we backed off from the display of a huge section of the Delta, from Saigon to My Tho.

I scuffled over to Hanney's side of the room on the way out and fiddled with a field telephone that sat on the edge of his desk. It was a lightweight Russian model and had a handy pad and pencil holder attached. I toyed also with bitching to the major about back-to-back three-day patrols. My men needed to dry out their feet, which were rotting from the constant immersion, but at the same time those targets goaded me. Lots of NVA in the open, choice opportunities. Hell, he would only tell me that my recon platoon was the only one that could do it, flattery I was eager to accept. Behind Hanney's desk hung a number of mementos of his months as Bravo Company C.O.: a Swedish Gustav 9mm, a Chinese carbine, a large NVA flag. I strolled around to have a look at something on a shelf, but was caught by a small picture tacked to the center of the flag's yellow star. A nude, spread-eagled. She looked at me with a particularly hungry expression. With similar hunger I stared back. Next to me on the shelf two live mortar rounds, one 82mm and one 60mm, stood on their tail fins like squat sentinels. Chinese characters ringed the waistline of the larger. My name in gook? Nah, I'd be dead already if it was. Probably samples from a bunch that I'd brought in myself. They had not and would not kill anyone.

A long sign ran along the top of the flag in block letters: FUCK COMMUNISTS. Red, white, and blue striped the first word. Red and yellow colored the second, its C forming a hammer and sickle.

"I doubt if their broads are any better than ours," I said, contemplating the picture again.

"Never fucked a communist," said Hanney, ". . . not to my knowledge anyway. I found that sign the other day in a map locker—must have been left here by the Third of the Seventh. It might work as sort of an amulet to ward off newsmen."

"Yeah, those A.P. guys took my picture this morning. I let them have a few bloodthirsty comments. Sure to be quoted."

"Don't know why the Army lets so many in," he muttered, "they've seen the enemy and they're us. They don't care about what we're doing, they just want stuff to fan the fires back home."

Caldwell began to leave, and Hanney and I tagged along, out to the muddy street. We lingered in desultory conversation before I headed off in the direction of my hooch at the other end of the base.

Can Giouc, home of the Sixth Battalion, 31st Infantry, Ninth Infantry Division, lay snarled in the barbed wire around me. The usual fire-support base was surrounded by dirt bulldozed into a berm with bunkers dug into a ringed perimeter. Ours, though, lay exposed, belted with a wide swath of open space. Due to the monsoon rains, acres and acres of it shone as vast shallow lakes. The base seemed more like three low-lying islands connected by thin isthmuses of mud attempting to act as roads.

Seeking out dry crusty ridges around the deeply rutted muck, I zigzagged along the road that led to the troop area as the mission and my people's reactions consumed me. They were expecting an easy one-day operation nearby but were getting three, held together by night ambushes. They'd complain like hell, and I'd be left to sell them—on the possibility of less mines and booby traps, and a solid crack at an NVA unit. The Can Giouc A.O. had become lean, containing only tattered remnants of the Viet Cong, and they were so tight in the wainscoting that they no longer mattered. We'd all appreciate an unhindered grapple with the enemy.

I cursed. Ahead of me a deuce and a half slogged forward straddling my path, waddling from side to side in the wheel-spun ooze. I stepped aside, and both shower tongs sucked off in the gummy laterite. The rains had begun to let up now that we'd entered November, dry days spaced the rainy ones, yet the volume could still be awesome. The day before, I'd seen a parked, unoccupied three-quarter-ton sitting in a downpour so torrential that the footing under the tires dissolved, sending the truck off the road and into the pond as if winched by an invisible cable. Tomorrow we'd be wet the entire time out; our feet completely submerged.

Ahead, I could see Alpha Company's first sergeant giving instructions to a few guys who were attempting an expedient shoring up of a blast shield. All around me rickety conglomerates of timber, plywood, corrugated metal, and sandbags collected like shanty houseboats; our quarters. With any luck the enemy would spare this place a mortar attack, with still more luck, the rains would subside and spare it real destruction.

The first sergeant leaned against the railing outside his orderly room, watching his men's awkward efforts at straightening the list in a wall of sodden top-heavy sandbags. A large piece of unsecured plastic sheeting flapped annoyingly in their way.

"Put in a bunch of engineer stakes behind it," he called, "then push the back of the truck into it. Slowly!"

"Well, ain't you the cute one, sir . . ." He smiled at my bush hat, aviator sunglasses, bare chest, trousers cut off at the knee, and bare feet—shower tongs now dangling from an index finger.

"Best I can do, top. Serves me right for choosing this place for my vacation. And I was just thinking as I came up the road, you'd better not have a police call, they'll shitcan your whole company. Mistake it for a cigarette butt."

"Now I know just what I'll do." He glanced at the guys lethargically milling around the sagging pile of stubborn green bags.

"Got any cold beer?"

"Not cold. I sent a couple of dudes into town for some ice, but they're not back yet. I'll throw in a couple of cases when they get back."

". . . A couple of cases of V.D.?"

"Not with those two dildos I sent."

"See you after chow."

I chuckled and went on a few paces to the end of the road. Echo Company. The road terminated in a mire caused mainly by runoff from the shower—an airplane fuel pod on joists, which looked like an aluminum cigar on stilts. In front of the orderly room a jeep and three-quarter-ton sidled each other like mother water buffalo and calf. Wallowing motionless after a ponderous frolic in the slime, their grills seemed surreal and toothy.

With a pull at the railing post, I climbed up onto the elevated porch of the orderly room. The heavily timbered and sandbagged structure was outranked in sturdiness only by one other in the entire base, the living quarters of the first sergeant and his clerks. It shouldered from behind as an impregnable redoubt. Impressed gangs had long labored to fortify his days and nights.

Inside the door a pair from my platoon stood importuning at the first sergeant's desk. From behind the desk he spoke to me without looking up. "Do you want anything, Lieutenant?" he asked as my men clumped off.

"No," I clipped. He deliberately substituted my rank for sir at moments when he felt his arrogant best. Between the top next door and Heulen E. Hughes lay an army of difference. The former was an older brother to the joking and kidding about the ordinary foibles of men in military life. Hughes, aloof and austere, acted out Charles DeGaulle as a sergeant; tall, gazing over the top of men's heads. Hughes sharpened one characteristic that top kicks in general shared—a keen dislike for lieutenants, and in Echo Company there were only two.

As I scooped up a new copy of the *Army Times* from a chair, the company C.O. strode in, a scowl creasing his pudgy face. His head jerked to the side, toward the duty roster, as if he'd caught something there in motion, the list of names and numbers on the acetate sheet suddenly breaking into a dance.

"Where's Nep?" he barked in a tone that implied he knew something I didn't, something I could be sure the first sergeant had planted.

I stared at him, screening the possibilities, my options. Captain Donald Ritchie, the perfect staff bureaucrat, stumpy, disinclined by nature for the field, stared back. He needed to be teaching eighteenth century literature somewhere, not dressing up as an infantry captain in my war.

Tossing the newspaper, I went over to him. Tran Van Nep, ex-Viet Cong, I thought, Tiger Scout extraordinaire and pain in the ass supreme. For the C.O. to be asking about Nep, it would have to mean that Nep would not be bunked out on his rack. He would have been seen on the road, and that meant AWOL, a problem for me and a little pleasure for the first sergeant, unless of course I went out on a limb again.

"I let him go out on a pass, sir."

"Beautiful! He just had a four-day pass last week . . . and he only gets three days a month. Besides, I'm supposed to sign those things."

I glanced at Hughes, who shuffled papers from one side of his desk to the other, pretending to organize various piles, his expression a Mona Lisa of internal serenity.

Ritchie stepped outside, beckoning me to follow, to chew me out in private.

"Look, sir, it was an emergency," I said. "You weren't around, so I authorized it. He'll be back before we go out."

"You didn't sign my name, did you?"

"Hell, no, I signed my own." My tongue crinkled the words as though I'd called him an idiot. He would take it that way.

"What is it with these Tiger Scouts, anyway? You've got four times as many as you're supposed to, and you bring them in and lop them off without a word to me. I'm the C.O. of this company."

"Yes, sir, but the S-5's in charge of all scouts' assignments in the battalion."

"What happened to Sang? He lasted two days. I lose a man and don't even know why."

"I didn't trust him. The other scouts came to me with the same idea, so I gave him five minutes to pack his shit. He's been sent to the ARVN."

"I *am* interested in the fluctuating strength of this company," he said sarcastically.

Part of Ritchie's annoyance with being left out could be blamed on E Company structure. Its only two platoons were not under his operational control; four deuce mortars were under artillery, and my recon took its orders from the colonel. Yet he constantly tried to regain something he'd never had, by the age-old salvation of the rear area officer—"chickenshit." He had not joined me in the field, not even to observe the easiest of missions, and I had grown to hold his need to be safe in contempt. Yet on my efficiency report he would rate what kind of officer and leader I was. I needed to be nice to him . . . but at every chance, I forgot.

"Did you know they're sending me out on another three-day bushwhack?"

"Do you have a problem with that?" he replied indifferently.

"No," I said thinly, "just thought you'd be interested."

"Right." He turned, and his crisp fatigues and baseball cap disappeared between bunkers as he headed back toward his hooch.

"Fung goo," I breathed audibly. He had it rough, I thought, commanding a muck hole and a roster of names, an accessory to a war, with his tidy papers and proper headgear—while the end of our lives was just a chopper ride over the horizon. I lounged against a pile of sun-warmed sandbags and looked out over the wide expanse of paddy to my front. Prickled strands of wire cut stark broken patterns across a perfect reflection of the fluff-clouded sky.

In one direction beyond the half-submerged crochet of metal lay the paddies and dykes. They expanded, unbroken by woodline, for nearly two kilometers. A funnel of low forest gathered at the limits of my vision, a coincidental path pointed like an arrow in the direction of the morning. Anticipation budded from my noticing. I pulled my folded map case from a thigh pocket and studied the target area, converting by reflex its abstract of grid-lined pastels of green and blue into gelatinous mud and waving nipa palm. Those hundreds of tiny black squares assembled naturally as groups of thatched hooches, the dwellings of thousands of delta people. It was the benign, bucolic venue of most combat in most wars. There were other places I'd prefer, and still others I wouldn't.

I drank in the unfamiliar area and its symbols, mulling

over their real images in my mind. Just after dawn, when the choppers would lift off, I would know as always that raw intensity of kinetic energy. The ineluctable feel of weapons would subdue all apprehension for that lethal land. In the morning, standing knee deep, reality would convert again into six-digit coordinates, a language that artillery howitzers could understand.

I glanced back to my right and caught sight of First Sergeant Hughes staring at me from the orderly room. That same smile, or rather nuance of contentment, held his lips. One of his clerks stood next to him hoisting a can of orange soda. Self-consciously I looked away and slowly lit a cigarette. This little flap over Nep could only have been inspired by him.

Barefoot, I ambled down the springy steel planking that served as a catwalk over the mire. It's my fucking army, my fucking infantry, I thought, and my good ol' army will rectify it all with change soon enough. No other institution could possibly rival the Army's upward and lateral movement of men, and that was something I liked. Ritchie and Hughes were like mosquito bites; they itched now, little welts that would be gone before I knew it.

In three weeks Captain Ritchie would be going back to the States, and after nine months in the field I'd get a rest by taking his place, becoming E Company C.O., a plum job. I'd have Hughes out so fast—everyone'd think somebody'd shot a star cluster up his ass. His sycophant clerks and drivers would be hooking in behind him. Preemptory self-protection.

Another Airborne Ranger lieutenant like myself would take over recon, and with a little finesse I might talk A Company's top into coming over. And being that I was well disposed with battalion headquarters . . . yes, sir, I'd have one beauty of a muckhole and one fine roster of names.

Without windows, a permanent dusk occupied the platoon bay. Blast shields in front of the doorways caused entering light to turn right and left, confused; it seemed to give up. Smells huddled in a fug of sweat and moldy socks. Random young mosquitoes floated from between the cracks in the rough-hewn flooring, borne on the stale wafting from the larvae-filled water underneath. The whole bunker, sleeved inside a larger rusty corrugated building, had one good point. It didn't leak.

"Dat," I called out, my eyes squinting in the unaccustomed gloom, shower shoes flip-flopping along the space between parallel double bunks.

"Yes, sir," came the reply from a small figure sitting on the edge of a bottom bunk, incongruous in a black net T-shirt and red silk briefs. Drong Van Dat; a tough soldier and my best Tiger Scout.

"Where the hell's Nep gone?"

"Him go him wife, Rach Kein."

"You mean she's come up from My Tho? Why isn't she staying here in Can Giouc?"

"No same-same My Tho. Him got two." He held up two nicotine-stained fingers to represent the two women, then, continuing the motion, forking long strands of greasy black hair over one ear.

"Damn Dat, I can't have that dude taking off everytime he's got an itch. Especially not to way the hell out there. Sanders," I barked at a lifeless form lying on a bunk nearer the door. A head looked up from a paperback. "Go over to A Company's top and get me a blank pass, will you." I lay on my side across someone's air mattress, parallel to Dat to wait Sanders's return. "Three more weeks, Dat, that's about all the time I've got left," I said tiredly.

"Three week. That how many day?"

"About twenty." I held up both hands and flashed the fingers twice.

"Then you go States?" He looked down at the floor.

"Hell, no, you know me well enough by now, I'll be around here as long as you—maybe even longer. You said you might go back to the world with Robby when his time is up."

"Ya, but me got girl in Cai Lay." He fumbled through some of his belongings and handed me a small photo of an ordinary-looking Vietnamese girl.

"Uh-oh," I teased, "number ten trouble for sure."

"Maybe get baby-san," he amended.

"You mean like . . ." I patted my stomach, and he nodded.

Sanders thumped in with a pass which I quickly filled out for my number-ten trouble, Nep.

"Duc," I called, and another scout came over. I stuck the paper in his breast pocket and buttoned the flap. "Go to the front gate and give that to Nep when he comes in. Wait there until he does. It'll be dark in about an hour. He'll be along for sure. If anyone wants to know what you're doing, just say my name and make off you don't know a pussy from a pole." I couldn't trust Hughes not to stop Nep for his pass, on the hunch that I had lied. Information that he would readily drop on Ritchie.

That small matter settled, I sauntered out of the bunker and around to the platoon bar. About eight feet long and well-battered, the bar occupied space between the bunker and the outside wall of the metal building. Reputed to have been built by some artillery unit a couple of years before, it served as the center of all platoon activity during the brief but frequent times we were in the fire base.

I placed a five- and a ten-cent note on the broken linoleum surface and adjusted a tipsy shell box under my butt; a bar stool. "Give me a beer, will you, Skinner," I said with a glance to my side for who else was present. He dipped his arm in the muddy water inside the battered cooler and churned. Ice chunks and barely visible cans rolled near the surface. The blurred colors of a root beer, and a Coke, then blue. He fished out a Hamm's.

"You know where we're going in the morning yet, sir?" spoke my platoon sergeant, Randall.

"It ain't so much the where, it's how long," I answered. "Another three-day mother humper."

An undertone of mumbled curses stirred from turned-down heads as my map case opened on the bar. The squad leaders clustered around for a look, puzzlement creeping onto a couple of faces.

"It ain't nowhere around here," commented one of them.

"One map sheet to the left and down one, southwest, about fifty klicks."

"Could be mighty lonely out there," Randall mused soberly.

"Here's the intell sheet I got from S-2. You can all read it. It's good. It's fresh and not from Brigade, but from ARVN recon. We got it only because they couldn't act on it."

"Man," said Forbes from over my shoulder, "We're gonna have to go heavy." He drew the words out slowly in a sullen annoyance that only practice can perfect. I twisted around to look at him.

"Right, machine guns . . . and two thousand rounds, fifteen claymores."

Chewing on a splinter of wood, toothpick style, he commented under his breath, pursing the thing between his lips sourly. A rusty crescent of a mustache hung oddly on its dark surroundings, the spike of wood waving like a gun barrel from a duck blind. Forbes, like Randall, was black, with the similarity ending there. Randall, a laconic pro, was the only other declared career man besides myself. He performed every duty as expected. Forbes, although intelligent and capable, seemed to continually test me, often resenting what I said, taking my instructions personally, as if they applied only to him.

"We'll have most of that dropped in to us on our last insertion," I added.

"There's one thing that looks good," Randall said, still perusing the map, "that's if we do run into them out there, they'll have a hard time breaking contact. Vegetation's pretty sparse in most places.''

"Right, the gunships will be able to blow their shit away,'' I added.

"And at night?'' Forbes snipped.

"You new in Nam today?'' I asked sarcastically.

"Well,'' Forbes began, ''my bitch is that we're supposed to run around out there like we usually do, right? Except out there, we can't get away with no machine guns and boo-coo ammo.''

His point was well taken, normally speed was our game. We traveled light, carrying only magazines and grenades, and faced a foe armed similarly. New main force NVA units fresh from Cambodia, however, could outgun us with rocket launchers, 60mm mortars . . . and they'd certainly have machine guns of their own. It would be a precarious situation for my platoon to attempt a night ambush against unknown odds. "The colonel will just have to suffer with a slow recon platoon,'' I said.

The other two squad leaders, Smith and Beddows, copied down the target coordinates for their own maps without comment, unbothered. Morale in the platoon really depended on only two things: not being told to do crappy jobs by the first sergeant when they were in, and killing gooks without taking casualties when they were out. Lately both things were in our favor—in the former case because I had been intervening, in the latter because luck had.

A promise of choice action motivated the platoon like nothing else. Each man had volunteered for this unit's assignments from a regular line company, and each had his own personal reasons for deciding he wanted more combat, more chances to kill and be killed. I only knew my own, a professional infantry officer's, the Airborne Ranger, wanting to command the best unit around. Second, the war itself needed fighting, it needed winning, but wouldn't be won without people like me. I felt I was the best there was.

*   *   *

My own bunker had the look of abandonment; grass and weeds grew through the weave of sandbag fabric. A former perimeter defensive position, it now quartered both Ritchie and myself. However, a center wall separated us and permitted no passage. Pierced steel planking bridged a complete moat around this listing derelict which seemed to slump a little more each time I looked.

I unlocked my door and plunked two spare cans of beer on the makeshift desk, then plopped onto my deluxe vinyl swivel chair, the product of a very slick swap. The walls of the hooch were covered entirely with map sheets except for the contrasting topography of a collage of nudes next to the desk. I stared momentarily at the organized jumble across from me, deciding priorities, looking over a long shelf that had once held two air mattresses and two G.I.'s and which now lay heaped in a wearying disassortment of infantry equipment. At the near end were a couple of ammo cans full of cleaning solvent surrounded by the pieces of a partly disassembled AK-47. Loaded magazines were piled as if in stacks against a siege. Black cardboard grenade cylinders stood alongside, looking irresolute with half of them lying on their sides.

Jotting on a piece of paper, I began making a check-list of equipment for the morning. "Lieutenant Maguire, sir," came a voice and a knock at the door. I glanced up with astonishment, Sergeant Mike Pawa.

"Well, I'll be dipped in shit! What are you doing back?"

"Get my squad and go back in the field."

I whistled. Some weeks before, I couldn't actually recall how long, Pawa had been stabbed through the lung by an ARVN soldier in a brawl outside a whorehouse. The long stiletto blade had actually grazed his heart, and the platoon had expected never to see him again.

"Are you in good shape?" I asked. "You could figure on a good rear job with no sweat."

"Man, sir, I didn't come all the way back here to be a

fuck stick for Hughes. They fixed me up real good at Tripler.''

"You mean you got all the way back home to Hawaii only to come back here?''

"Sure, there's a few more gooks I gotta blow away. Besides,'' he added in mock astonishment, "I had nightmares about Beddows being in charge of my squad.''

"I think you were seeing the wrong kind of doctors.'' I tapped an index finger to my temple.

Suddenly somber, he added, "The guys told me about Wilkie.''

I nodded my understanding. Two weeks before, Alpha Company had made contact with a sizable NVA force. Outnumbered and suffering quite a few casualties, the gooks tried to escape across a river where gunships, hovering over bobbing heads, had drilled many more. However, visibility had quickly been lost in darkness, and the colonel decided to insert my platoon on the far side as a blocking force. When the choppers dropped us in, I moved the men to the nearest dike with orders to curl up at the edge and hold still. I had no intention of moving one inch in the dark in that area. Beddows's squad, like the rest of us, just fanned out in the paddy and took the right-hand dike on line. Wilkie had crouched down on a trip wire. Mike Pawa and he had been close friends.

"If you had tried to move up the river, you probably would have hit a couple more,'' he said.

"Yeah,'' I grumbled, "I let about thirty NVA slip through the gap. Couldn't get artillery clearance because of a village behind me. Couldn't convince them that it was safe with me being in the middle.'' I paused. "Are you sure you're ready to go out tomorrow? You've probably heard where we're going.''

"Ready as ever, sir,'' he said, swelling his chest and giving his wound a thump. "I eat plenty of pineapples. I eat plenty of other things too . . .''

"True, you're so ugly, they couldn't bear to face you.''

"But they all cry when I leave." He waved his hand near his hat in a mock salute and clumped off down the planking toward the mess hall. He looked as mean as ever in spite of the green recruit look from new fatigues and boots.

My regular field gear lay in a mound behind the chair, dropped a few hours earlier, Hrunting and Nagling, my two favored weapons, dumped on top. I lifted the CAR-15 submachine gun and Star 9mm automatic and began unloading and breaking them down for cleaning. Dropping grimy parts into the can of solvent, my thoughts converged afresh on the morning, as if the solvent marked a refurbishing for tomorrow, not the dissolution of today. Only three weeks left, I thought. There wouldn't be many more chances to blow their shit away in a big way; scarce enough that tomorrow could even be our last good chance. I would have to make it count.

Fatigue from too much adrenaline pumping for too long hardened my desires to inflict something large and devastating on the enemy, to the extent my one platoon could. There had been many skirmishes and encounters during my months in the bush. They counted. It was just that the few handfuls killed here and there, the calling for gunships and artillery to kill a few more, didn't add up to the solid battle, the ingrained hope from years of training in and dedication to things infantry. It wasn't some heroic, bad-ass situation with half my men gunned down that I wanted. I wanted one substantial harvesting of enemy corpses—not these mini episodes sandwiched between a landscape strewn with inanimate mines and booby traps, buried, hanging, hidden. I was tired of them, bone-crumbling tired of this unrelenting and deadly Easter egg hunt. But a few more days in a row were nothing, and a surfeit of very animate NVA would see to that. Just like I wanted.

CHAPTER TWO

They slogged past me, grizzled beasts in the blotched greens and browns of camouflage. Flopping brims of bush hats obscured their turned-down faces. In single file each man alternately depressed strands of barbed wire for the one behind, then slipped through the gap in the springy coils of concertina. A drab, booted caterpillar pulled its somnolent body through the entanglement and up onto the dry road bed beyond . . . then segmented into five equal parts.

I drank one last cloying gulp from a can of warm Coke as I passed Forbes's group, which lounged, talking complacently in the grass. Muddy water trickled from my trousers and squished audibly in my boots. Damn, we weren't even off yet and all thirty of us had soaking feet! We'd been out too much lately, or rather not in long enough to be able to air our dishpan feet. Another day or so and there'd be problems—staph infection would bore into rotting, cheeselike skin and take people out as easily as shrapnel.

Our brigade had pretty much pacified Long An province with its four occupying battalions. Contacts continued to fall off at all but its periphery. Enemy soldiers still fed into other parts of the delta, a stealthy siphon from Cambodia. Pressure for a body count pushed our operations west to the Plain of Reeds.

The colonel was squandering my platoon's dedication while allowing the rest of the battalion to still fart around in the local A.O. I looked hard at my men's faces, at their dusk-ringed garret eyes. They were tired. I grimly anticipated humping the quagmire all day and backing that up by a night ambush position in the bad bush. I tussled with polarized feelings. Even if they look tired enough to embrace an eternal rest, I thought, they can do it. Isn't that what recon's all about?

Fatigue by accretion had eaten into us, yet somehow we could give flight to it in moments of danger. The Airborne Ranger in me amplified that. In the slow burnout of adrenaline lay the problem, the accelerated seeping toward exhaustion. But we could overcome weariness.

I shook off these dark thoughts with a purposeful stride toward my men. I'm dedicated to this, I thought. No conditions. I'm absolute, hell, just look at me—submachine gun, grenade-slung, avatar for the Queen of Battle, confronting an enemy worthy of defeat. Without apology, I had re-created my person from a romantic war novel.

Joining the second group diagonally across from me and twenty meters on, I glanced around for a comfortable spot. As I sat, I fondly noted a nearby hat with small black lettering ringing the brim. HAWAIIAN SOUL—PINEAPPLE PAWA. One of the radios, Spiderman's, squawked with routine chatter from other units, themselves readying for a variety of morning operations around the battalion A.O. He reached up to me with the handset.

"Echo six-six, this is Dark Planet eight-niner, over." The colonel.

I pushed the button and spoke. "Echo six-six, over."

"Eight-niner, you got your people all set?"

"Six-six, affirm."

"Okay, the birds should be along real soon."

I thought I could hear the sound of choppers in the distance, but could observe only a single helicopter whooping over the woodline to the west, probably the colonel. Squinting a bit keener to the northwest, I could see them, tiny black gnats on the horizon about three miles away. The Mekong could accommodate that way. Flat as water. A road bed vaulted, a virtual promontory at two feet above sea level.

The five choppers inched along, not directly at us but obliquely, closing the distance. The staccato of their blades changed suddenly to jet turbine whine as they swung to the south of us. Finally, in an east-southeast direction, they dipped their noses and plummeted in staggered left formation.

Pulling the pin on a smoke grenade, I tossed it into the weeds on the other side of the road. It popped with a kick, and a genie of dense violet smoke expanded rapidly from the small canister.

"Hornet one-four, roger victor smoke." The pilot's voice stabbed through the pummeling sound of the aircraft.

Spiderman confirmed his call as the last of the men got to their feet, creakily, with the reliability of old pack animals. Commands were unnecessary.

About five hundred meters out, the choppers slid into trail formation, single file for the road pickup. The first three dropped smoothly, their skids touching almost simultaneously; the next two humped cautiously in the backwash of turbulent air, tails canting in a dexterous hover before hitting the ground. Instantly, our groups of six disappeared through the wide open doors as if fleeing the transformation of quiet humid stillness that had erupted into a swirling storm of blade-driven wind and mechanical fury.

Climbing on the second chopper, I gestured a greeting to the pilot as he half turned in his seat to watch us clamber aboard. I dropped my butt to the floor and spun my legs outside. Immediately we heaved upward, the full pitch of the blades pulled with powerful circular strides. Small children, our regular morning friends, waved us good-bye, momentarily squinting in the gale and the tinnitus-inducing screams of five jet turbines. We quickly rose and turned, leaving the watery fire base and the disheveled town of Can Giouc far behind us. My feet dangling above the skids, wet trousers rippling fiercely, I relaxed back to back against Dat, the cool wind buffeting a massage through the door.

For the first thirty minutes, I charted our progress over familiar landscape, river configurations that bent and twisted themselves into names—the Snake, One Hung Low, B.J.'s Nose, the Pipes, Melissa's Tongue—of origins both obvious to the eye and unknown, names pinned by men the first time as jokes, then as curses as friends of theirs took their last steps near them. From this altitude it all looked benign, umber swatches of varying thickness, random ellipses laid flat over green . . . green nothing. The semi-regularity of paddy dikes like the "canals" on Mars could only be fully understood by standing on them.

I slid my map case from my thigh pocket and began to orient it to the new terrain coming up on the near horizon. Spiderman tapped my shoulder with the handset. I took it and pushed it hard against my ear, covering the other ear with my palm to block out some of the noise.

"Mack, I'm putting you down on Tango Bravo first." It was the colonel's voice, faint but unmistakable, over static that sounded as loud as a thousand strips of frying bacon.

"Six-six roger over." I referenced target B on my sheet.

"We've spotted some recent activity—a few bunkers, but can't tell how big a complex it might be. I want you to bust in there and move as far as the river, then sweep November Whiskey to that open area five hundred meters upstream. Call me when you're ready for a pickup."

I gave him a roger and noted his command and control chopper dipping down over the target. Red smoke indicated wind direction, and our birds dropped in rapid descent, a pulling roller coaster down toward a near woodline. With our stomachs still hauling at rib cages, we hit treetop level. The machines shuddered near full speed.

The men around me cocked their legs underneath as if tightening springs for a catapult. Safeties on weapons clicked off. Outside, fifty meters away, the same styptic tension repeated itself in the two choppers flying in tandem, diagonal sidecars to our line of three.

The iridescent jungle and gleaming water blurred below the skids. My eyes darted back and forth across the muzzle of my weapon, culling blocks of green for instant analysis, for any nuance of my foe.

No matter how many assaults like this I'd been on—and I had over 180 of them—they never became routine. In spite of the fact that on the vast majority of occasions, we assaulted "dry holes," the excitement lay in the potential—potential for disaster. A single heavy machine gun could reduce a whole flight formation into cascading balls of burning jet fuel. The escaping wounded, dazed and floundering in the paddy, could then be worked over with light weapons; the accidental landing on a greatly superior force. The worst of all possibilities, I thought, that mythical "hot L.Z.," tracers so thick you could get out in midair and walk on them. Any ground resistance at all could kill. What I had seen of it taught one thing: vulnerability, hanging like bull's-eyes, clothespinned to a line.

Our own five were at that treacherous point, lofting into the wide open paddy next to the woodline, fanning back hard to slow down. A sharp blast erupted in the bush and chunks of dirt and trees arched in slow tumbles into the sky. Another succession of explosions sprang ahead of the Cobra gunship and stunned the woodline along our flank. Simultaneously the ten door gunners opened up.

This covering fire lifted instantly as we leapt from the choppers into the paddy where flattened rice stalks rippled in the blast of wind. The choppers lurched upward as we splashed madly across the open, in toward the only cover there was—the enemy bunkers. The platoon spread out along the edge of a woodline on a hundred-meter front. They crouched, weapons poised as if pent up. I rapidly checked out the terrain ahead for the best point of entry. Squad leaders glanced my way anticipating a signal. The sound of the helicopters had faded completely. Silence . . . life scared off, leaving only droplets of muddy water to drip from the tattered leafy curtains, and our labored breathing from our dash through boot-swallowing muck.

I motioned for Skinner and Voss to move in straight ahead of me. Smith's squad would flank to the right. The two pointmen pulled themselves up a small bank and slipped into the tangled veil. A gunshot barked. Heads turtled into shoulder blades with a jerk. The shot echoed hollow, from somewhere in the interior.

"Fuckin' sniper," I whispered peevishly. Dat's M-16 erupted next to me. Short bursts of automatic fire punctuated squawks of Vietnamese. He ceased firing but still froze in a hard squint down the barrel of his rifle.

Some of the men hit the prone at the sound of Dat's weapon, although Tiger Scouts reacted to his imperatives and moved up. I mounted the bank, CAR-15 held high, on full automatic. Next to one of the bunkers a shock of black hair tucked into view. I fired two fast bursts, and hard dry bits of dirt skittered from the bare mound. Surprisingly, the head popped back into view; and with a third jolt from my weapon, it was vanquished in a puff of clay dust. The head seemed to come apart like the scattered crumbs of gravel. At thirty meters I could see little and was sure of nothing.

From the far end of the line, Robby Smith's squad suddenly opened up. They concentrated on a single bunker. Two grenades whumped in the undergrowth. No resistance, but we seemed to have something here. Were these only a couple of stragglers seeking concealment in the bunkers when the choppers came down, now finding themselves trapped by infantry? Or a trap for me?

"Stinger five-five, this is Echo six-six, over."

I could still see him far in the distance, prowling on the horizon. Skinner tossed in a yellow smoke and in less than a minute Stinger bore in level, the compressed energy of a dragonfly incensed. Two pairs of long slender rockets sprang from their pods and vicious bolts slammed in among the bunkers. A fine mist of debris fell on us as the

Cobra jerked around. Its blades sliced upward like a turning boomerang. Glare across the dark-tinted windshields lent it a gaze as if from the eyes of a green bottle fly. Its six-barreled mini-gun swiveled, restive as the gunship slowed in an agile hover; with a chainsaw rip, a thin stream of tracers and lead studded a pocket or two in the thickest vegetation.

"Echo six-six, this is Stinger five-five. On my first pass I spotted one who appeared to be wounded. I've lost him now. I'm out of ordnance—got to go back and rearm."

"Echo six-six, this is Dark Planet eight-niner, Mack . . ." The colonel's voice, transmitted in the audible snow of somewhere distant. "Need artillery out there?"

I reassured him that so far it was only a single shot and not the enemy company we hunted. I told him to hold off, then, yelling to Smitty to take his squad straight in, I slithered up the bank ahead of the pointmen to lead off our entry. At a low crouch I approached the bunker, which rose from the dense thicket like a massive gray-brown wart. My eyes darted to either side. Stealthily I edged around and checked behind, so connected to the sight and sound before me that if a single leaf had moved it would have been as if it had pulled the trigger of my weapon itself. Perfect stillness. A couple of rockets had struck in the mud, splintering, shredding, bathing everything gray. I peered inside the bunker's opening. Empty. The handle of a shovel protruded, half submerged in water. I thought I hit a dude. Where was he? I took hesitant steps, wading past my knees into a crater of muck, my sight fixed beyond the torn fronds farther ahead.

"Em-Bee-Ay!" Dat shouted, coming from the other side of the bunker. My body contracted in reflex. This time he wasn't firing. I turned. He pointed down, directly behind me. There he was, all right, legs half buried, body coated in a film of slime. I had stepped over him without noticing. Partially on his side, he had one arm looped over his head in a kind of swimmer's stroke, drowned between breaths. He was bare-skinned except for a pair of blue nylon NVA shorts. I wedged the toe of my boot under his unusually tall lanky form, and with a lift the face came up. A few red licks of hair matted a fringe above an ear, where a display of something like moldering yogurt exited. Dat levered the outstretched arm, and the face became totally visible. The left eye was gone, as well as the entire side of his skull. Chunks of brain hung outside.

The platoon consolidated and began moving deeper toward the river. Robby Smith had reported that his earlier firing had also produced a kill. We ambled forward, slow and cautious, but less tense in spite of the fact that neither body had produced the weapon that had fired the single shot.

When we reached the river, we swung parallel with it and followed a well-worn trail northward. About fifty meters upstream Skinner called back. He'd spotted a patch of blood. At once he and Voss tore off. I hustled after them, passing blood dribbled on the smooth ground and streaked on long blades of grass. My heart muscle clenched as automatic fire shattered the air from just out of sight. Ambush? I hurtled forward. Comforting. The sound was M-16s.

Around the bend, Voss knelt on the trail; lazily clicking in a new magazine and chambering a round. Skinner stood a few paces beyond, smiling.

"Got to be that one the pilot said he saw. Got him coming out of the water." Skinner pointed across to his trophy lying slung with a bag and a weapon on the opposite bank. "Just like popping off a muskrat back home in Tennessee. Wounded fucker, made the river, but that's all he made."

The rest of the platoon bunched up around us until Sergeant Randall spread them out again for better security.

"Okay," I began, "who wants to go over there and pick up that stuff?" I spoke to the pointmen plus Forbes and Pawa, who were nearby. They glanced at each other then back at me without saying a word.

"You got to be shitting me, sir," answered Pawa after a pause. "It's a long way there and back."

"I've got to know what's in that bag. Could be documents. In any case, we can't leave his weapon just lying over there."

"I think I forgot how to swim." Pawa made a spastic floundering motion to demonstrate.

"Sir," said Forbes. "If somebody goes over there, they've got to take their weapon—the gooks can see you and try to come up on you because you can't cover all that good from here. Then you gotta come back with both of them. You can't swim back with everything."

"I guess I'm gonna have to be the one, then," I said. "After all, I am the only Ranger here."

"You crazy, sir. You gonna be the only dead Ranger here." Pawa's tone worried for my safety, although resigned as usual to my ideas.

I removed my web gear, extra magazines, shirt, boots, socks. "It's a new twist to the riddle of the farmer trying to get the fox, duck, and bag of grain across the river," I told them, sliding my Star 9mm from its holster.

"The fox has friends," Forbes quipped drolly, "with AK-47's."

"Okay," I instructed, passing a length of cord through the trigger guard and looping it around my neck. "Put the machine guns over there, and down there. I want the M-79 to start popping rounds on the front edge of the wood. When I get a little more than halfway, shift the fire back a bit, then fold it back to the edge when I'm on my way back. The MGs are for just in case." I entered the tepid brown water with the first crash of a 40mm round in the treeline on the other side. The muddy bottom squirmed beneath my toes as if a live thing. My feet were sucked deeper than with boots. A few more concussions from the M-79 and my cockiness and invulnerability grew, but in a moment were gone again. The pistol hung heavier than expected, thumping annoyingly on my chest as I breaststroked through the water. My baggy fatigue trousers dragged like a sea anchor, each kick a message that I should have done it by the book, completely naked.

Covering fire dropped back as I reached the far bank. Bellying on the mud like an alligator, I checked the body without having to leave the water. The poor bastard had been hard-core. One leg was completely blasted off below the knee and left behind. A grizzly image of him kicking it free to swim across made me grimace more than the thought of the ragged bullet wounds that laid open sections of his anatomy for inspection. I hugged low, close to him, sifting through the plastic bag which he'd slung with a string. Although mostly rice, it had a larger packet of papers lying at the bottom. Dumping out his rice in the mud, I grabbed up his AK-47 and chucked the magazines behind me in deep water.

Figuring that the plastic bag could be used as a float, I scooped it against the water to trap air. I passed the muzzle of the AK through the loop of cord around my neck and clutched the stock in close to my body. With my free hand I sidestroked with strong deep arcs. It was no good. I was barely moving, expending all my energy just to stay on the surface. My legs kicked forcefully yet felt as though they moved only inside my pants, failing to churn any water outside them. I increased their scissored arc, snapping my feet feverishly. Although the bag had a drawstring at its neck and could be easily held with one hand, bullet holes kept appearing as if new, causing me to grope awkwardly to scrunch it to save air. The gook's weapon took me under. Shit, that one-legged bastard, I thought, seeing his revenant form looming over me, poling me down with the elongated butt of an AK, shoving just when I gasped for air. To save myself I would have to drop the stuff as my guys stared from the far bank. Voss began to strip to come after me. I let the bag drop from my teeth and breathed in, tilting vertically, pulling in a near panic. My toes scratched bottom. There was more of it than I expected, chin deep when I'd thought it was still over my head. I pushed myself forward with the soft ooze. That gook behind me had probably felt a lot like I did now, just before that beehive swarm of bullets had torn after him.

"Guess we kind of messed up that dude, huh sir?" Skinner asked with a forced malevolence.

"Fuck him if he can't take a joke," I said offhandedly. It was the kind of reply he was looking for.

The platoon threaded along single file through uneven tropical scrub until it split into three groups upon entering open ground. Our plan was to head north half a kilometer to check out a group of hooches while waiting for the choppers to ferry some other units back at Can Giouc. They'd have to refuel before returning to hopscotch us up to another target. Refreshingly behind schedule, all nine insertions wouldn't be possible. We walked at a comfortable pace along low dikes patted smooth by many bare civilian feet. These dikes would be free of mines; well-used trails this close to a village always were.

There were acre-sized paddies on either side holding wizened rice. The crop had the pale, exhausted look of just trying to stay alive rather than grow. We were on the periphery of the Plain of Reeds. A few kilometers farther west and land would support no rice at all and be virtually uninhabited.

Three women transplanted young shoots beside us, folding and tamping them into much clay and too few nutrients. They bobbed relentlessly like small oil dereks. I caught their surreptitious peeks, averted under conical straw hats in motion, the pretense of taking no interest, as if inured. In this area it was possible that we were the first U.S. troops they'd ever seen close up. I was reassured that they continued to stay at their work despite having heard our recent shooting. Firefights for them were not a spectator sport.

Although not close by at the moment, we could count on the enemy to have been in regular contact. It would not be a comradely relationship; at bare subsistence, there was nothing to share, yet with one NVA unit after another

trekking in from Cambodia, they would press these people
to do just that.

In spite of the fact that civilian women always said to
us that their men were away with ARVN in this part of the
delta, you could toss a coin. Since the Tet offensive the
year before, the Viet Cong numbered few. But Viet Cong,
ARVN, or dead really didn't matter in this small, unpacified
hamlet. It mattered only that NVA were here in strength
and that these villagers could point to where.

"Pawa," I called, "take your people down there and
set up some security on the woodline." I pointed to a
slender peninsula of vegetation that hooked around and
connected with three of the hooches. He and his men
veered off and filed onto a dike that skirted a wide gulf of
rice paddy. "Smith! Set your guys up with the machine
gun on the other side of that big hooch."

I glanced at Nep then nodded at another hooch. It
would be ours. In the field Nep was my twin in black tiger
stripes. He slinked as effortlessly as my shadow, yet at a
safer distance. Of all the scouts, he had the least pidgined
English, but his typical advice was silent. A glimpse of
those malignant ex-Viet Cong eyes patrolling for clues of
former familiarity told much; the gold dog teeth, concealed,
said calm. His strange flattened nostrils, unflared, said that
he was not about to pull the trigger.

Forbes's squad dispersed and automatically began
checking the hooches in the middle. There was no need for
conversation. From the nearest doorway, ours, a small boy
gawked at us. He propped a dusky infant on his hip like a
comforting teddy bear, a good sign; they weren't clinging
to their mother's side. I could see her in the dim interior.
Her uncertain eyes surveyed us intently but without fear.
We would reassure her, allay her uncertainty with the
bummers from our C-rations as gifts, and perform for her
children like Captain Kangaroos in camouflage. We were
puzzling curiosities, not the brawny miscreants the V.C.
would have warned them about.

Ducking through the entrance behind Nep, a quick

eyeballing of the interior took a second. Nothing, so I slipped off my web gear, equipment, and extra magazines and rolled my shoulders around in grateful relief. Spiderman appeared at the doorway, wrestled the radio from his back, then perfunctorily unfolded the long whip antenna and poked the tip through the roof.

Here the thatched nipa roofs granted us a stay from the executioner sun, and the vast open paddies barred unexpected visitors. Delta dwellings gave up few interior decorating ideas. No furniture except an occasional slender pedestal-like table with oil lamp and incense, a shrine to their ancestors, no color, no flooring save a dampish clay under foot. A bunkered sleeping area occupied a full quarter of the interior, its hands-and-knees opening making it look like a transplanted bear's den. The family would ordinarily sleep on planks and rush mats laid across its top, but inside if the war ventured near.

The woman turned from us and squatted at her indoor cooking fire. Half a dozen children descended toward her as evenly as keys on a xylophone and watched our every move. Their alert little eyes swung back and forth at the striped and mottled giants that so casually filled their home. An old man sat placidly among us on the bed planks. His gnarled legs dangled in front of me, stained a mahogany from half a century of plodding in the manured ooze. His veins were illustrations to the text of his life. Gray varicose lumps mole-hilled around his knees and headed for the shinbones. Less rumpled blood vessels did an aimless burrowing toward the feet, looking like dead worms under the skin. He stroked a sparse wisp of his goatee and nodded his head at us repetitively with a bemused affect of questions answered in advance. "Yes, sure, okay."

"We gonna bag it for a while?" Forbes asked from outside. It was his favorite question.

"Yeah," I replied, "the choppers have gotten tied up with Bravo Company. Have to go in again to refuel before coming back to us."

"Hey... we won't get nine insertions now."

"No."

To the colonel's knowledge, we were still in the woodline busting in his "November Whiskey direction," looking for now evaporated gooks while doing a sixty-booted exploration for mines and booby traps. There were times and not times in this war. As long as I was the officer on the ground and not far off in the safety of a helicopter, I would decide which was which. To beat the enemy I would have to make these distinctions forever error free. Chuck could die every day and leave his dead behind; he numbered more than I could kill. I numbered but one. The margin of error favored him.

No mistakes, I thought. Two purple hearts already, how many chances do I get? You won't zero in on me, you fuckers, I taunted inside myself. Turning back around, I pulled at a C-ration pack of cigarettes. Taking one, I handed the other three to the old man. He studied them with intense concentration, holding them at different angles, sighting down their length and tapping at the filter.

"I can roll one hell of a tight smoke, hey, old man?"

He looked at me and pertly nodded another affirmation, as if both understanding and believing. He thumbed the wheel of an ancient lighter, sucking flame from an oily gout of smoke. He did not smile, yet somewhere in his face broke a small craggy contemplation. A serene thought about my peacepipe? About me? About this big ball of shit that he and I had found ourselves in? "Nep, ask him if he knows anything of those three NVA we blew away."

I left the hooch to check security. My men lounged near their weapons in and around half a dozen other dwellings. Some heated up cans of C's while grunting a few syllables for conversation. The scouts roamed about chatting with the people. While Dat and Be talked to a mother, Duc whispered questions to a young child of about four; one too young to know about not giving away the secrets of another's army.

After a bit I called the scouts together to develop

some consensus on the local situation. It was consistent with the S-2's report. The day before about fifty NVA had passed through the vicinity. Helmeted and well-armed, they were not like the three we had shot up. Those were also NVA, but part of an earlier unit that had left them behind to build bunkers and act as guides in the booby-trapped areas. The present unit was commanded by a first lieutenant and one other officer. Although understrength from malaria contracted in Cambodia, and hungry from shortages of rice, they still sounded ominous. They carried many rounds of rocket-propelled grenades and several machine guns, in addition to individual AK-47's.

I ambled among the hooches in a pensive funk. Outgunned and outmanned . . . and we're hunting them . . . in their very own mine garden. I sat down next to my sniper's M-14 and picked it up. Using the scope as surrogate binoculars, I scanned the woodline in the direction we'd come. I snooped along the vegetation at the paddy's edge without expectation. Another group of hooches lay at a distance to my right, and I swung the muzzle toward them. The scope lent a sinister element to the view as I gathered an old woman into the cross hairs. She laid tiny strips of fish on a drying rack.

"What we gonna do about those fifty gooks?" Forbes asked. He plopped down against the hooch next to me.

I put the rifle across my legs and squinted his way. "We're going to surround them, then call them names until they cry. Loosen up, Forbes. That's why we're sitting tight right now. On the other insertions, we'll have the gunships. After that we'll bag it. If we really need it, I don't think we can get support fast enough out here either."

"So what about tonight? It'll be even worse." Forbes always asked me things like he represented a delegation. He was a squad leader and did represent those men, but his style insinuated a whispering conspiracy. He liked it that way, particularly when he was right. He asked because his life was potentially in another man's hands. Mine. What decisions would I make regarding it? Would my mission pivot on getting him out alive or killing as many NVA as possible? His tone indicated his doubts.

"We'll play it cool, Forbes, take up a secure position for ambush, put out all the claymores. If they come along, we'll just kill as many as we can straight off then dee-dee back to a safe spot. Remember that time before we came up from Dong Tam when we got those gooks in that big banana grove? We chewed 'em quick, then got out."

He nodded and seemed satisfied, but did not get up and walk away. Looking at me for a while, I thought he might ask me something else. He didn't.

"How come you're out here, Forbes?"

"What?" An eyebrow went up, like a dog's ear.

"Why are you here in Vietnam?"

"I got drafted."

"Into the infantry? Into recon? Noooo. I think I know why the others came here, a lot of different reasons. None of them fit you."

"You mean me in particular?"

"Yeah." I wanted to say especially you, too cynical to be putting your life in danger at all, much less like this. Too cliquish with the "bros" in the Soul Tent to trust whites ever. "Most of us are in the Army because we got drafted," I said, "but we're here in recon, here in the worst A.O. in the delta at the edge of radio contact for..." I looked at him; he seemed to deliberate while looking out over the paddies, yet said nothing. "Most of us seem to be here to prove something—"

"I ain't got to prove nothing to nobody," he cut in.

"That's my question, Forbes: Why are you here?"

"I got to prove somethin' to myself, I guess," he said, "that sometimes you just got to know how bad you are. The pussies in the rear, to say nothing of the ones back in the world, don't pay it no mind, they just accept that they are that way, but some of us got to know, got to know just how bad."

"Why?"

"Same-o, same-o, accept it."

"I accept it, Forbes." I wasn't sure if I did. I accepted that we were here for ourselves, but what about the reason for the war? That the communists were nasty bastards was a convenience. I thought about some of the meanest dudes I'd ever known and how some of them were already the deadest dudes. My attention scudded into an obscure crevasse in my mind, from a barely overheard conversation or some scrap of reading. God! Something about the best chicks, and how candy-asses were inheriting them from dead heroes.

"Aw-right, you guys!" I yelled. "Saddle up!"

By late afternoon four more insertions cast my men into disheveled hulks of mud and sweat. I hoped that they looked more tired than they were; gauging myself, I was unsure.

Each of the assaults had produced no contact with the enemy, yet more information from civilians helped me focus on my quarry of fifty. During the afternoon I had become increasingly preoccupied with my map. From the air and the ground, I studied one lonesome hamlet.

CHAPTER THREE

The rubber eyepiece of the Starlight scope cupped my left eye, exposing a strange world, a landscape glowing in a greenish haze of dancing phosphorescent photons. A minute oil lamp burning in a distant hooch filled the lens with shimmering light that etched the village in an eerie desolation. It wasn't ever perfect. Just good. Closer to the woodline there was a better site for an ambush, but this one was safer. We were too far out to take extra risks. If we got in trouble, help would be too long in coming. I swept the scope again along the woodline, a long slender island of glowering black jungle. Most nights of my Vietnam tour had been spent this way, lying on a paddy dike, beside a trail or canal, eyes bulging in a vain effort to gain an advantage on the vaporous ink. I passed the Starlight to Spider with a poke.

I had scratched our last insertion to sacrifice speed for stealth. With the sun a vague memory, the greasy black as always rose up victorious. Equipment taped to prevent clunking, we slid without a splash into three prone groups. Our ambush location, selected during daylight, lay astride several paddy dikes. Two perpendicular mounds of grass-covered mud formed a machine gun position that looked to a corner of an adjacent paddy. Another nearby dike became the position for the other group as they settled in their reed hiding. A path, worn from a millennium of footprints, departed an eight-hooch village, tarried through the middle of our ambush position, then ran two hundred meters toward the nearest woodline.

My bet was that tonight, sometime, the NVA would use this trail, believing that the U.S. troops that had shadowed them during the day had returned to their base camp. Earlier, in the grainy misperceptions of dusk, I'd called five choppers in to feign a pickup. The NVA units would feel comfortable now, easy about moving men anywhere; like into this village and on their way . . . into my ambush.

After checking the alignment of machine guns and claymores for a maximum kill zone, I hunkered up with a radio to register artillery. I wouldn't follow the common practice of firing a white phosphorous round to burst in the sky as a marker. That did only one thing—told any enemy around that he wasn't alone, told him some G.I. unit was marking reference. I used the delta's advantages, its open terrain, its rivered and canaled landmarks, for accurate plots of location, and called for one round of H.E. on the deck. Fifteen minutes and a large blast erupted from deep in the woodline about four hundred meters away. That angered me. "If I'm in trouble, I won't have fifteen minutes," I whispered acridly to the anonymous cowboy, Lone-Seven. "Left one hundred, drop two hundred."

The next one crashed right at the edge of the wood-line, its concussion splitting the night. Spider, lying near me, fitfully scrunched his body lower to the ground, conscious that our bodies were the highest things around.

Satisfied that the NVA troopers would probably take the rounds as no more than random harassing fire, I relaxed. Spider and I lay close to keep each other awake, hopeful that four other pairs were doing the same.

The platoon was fine, all except for Forbes's group. When I checked his squad's position he'd moved all his people. Where he had placed them or allowed them to be, their dark forms showed up against the background. It was the most comfortable spot, but comfort wasn't one of my priorities. Security meant everything, and Forbes knew it; even so, he reacted to my instructions with hushed venom. Maybe my lack of tact with him didn't help, I thought, but this isn't the place or time to coddle hurt feelings.

Rice paddies were not quiet places at night. Darkness revivified a biological menagerie of chirping, peeping creatures which, never seen, go at whatever it is they do, then vanish at first light. The whole earth resounded with the plangent croak of millions of them, a throbbing lullaby for a tired man. One identifiable creature was not shy. No matter where, they descend as if suddenly collected from diffuse trace elements in the cool calm air. A squadron for each man, they cried like tiny little Stukas; slow and screaming before diving one by one to gorge themselves on repellent-soaked ears, an annoyance that helped keep you awake by breaking soporific watches up into tiny periods between sorties.

When the first watch was over, I crawled to Randall and tapped him on the shoulder. His head jerked up as if in a preoccupied daydream rather than sleep. I dragged myself back with the effort of a slug for my two hours of benumbed escape.

A blast stunned the night, slamming my head and sleep like a hammer smashing fingertips. Close. I felt the whip sting of a piece of shrapnel bite into my right buttock. I pointed my CAR-15 at the kill zone with a somewhat impotent feeling. The explosion had been behind me. A commotion of splashing broke in the paddy to my right. Another blast from someone's M-79 shattered the night . . . followed by an instant battle of unknown M-16's and AK-47's erupting in return.

Whooh! The gooks were between our positions; a gut-clenching feeling. We were being overrun. Bullets zinged past. Bitchy. My boys on the other side were shooting into the middle and their rounds were coming across. I flipped to the far side of the dike for cover, towing at my bandoleers. Everyone was yelling in the dark and no one near me knew what the hell was going on.

Two more claymore mines went off with a deafening crash. Flashes. From the bleary darkness men scrambled from the paddy in front of me. My ears caught panted Vietnamese syllables. For an instant my finger froze in the trigger, a reflex against shooting a Tiger Scout.

My God, a banzai! A body and pumping thighs hit and spun me, wrenching my weapon away as he drove over me. I lunged and bear-hugged him around the waist. He seemed to explode with animal fear in an attempt to twist free and we both crashed headlong into the mud and water of the paddy on the other side. The aqueous pitch suffocated me, its humid foreboding pressing on my face like a mask of lead.

I sucked, frenzied, for air. "Aahrrrrr!!!" I roared, expelling my own fear and driving it into a mad rage. Grabbing for his throat, I checked my action. His arms were free, and he fumbled with his rifle. I parried the muzzle with one hand and pinned it underfoot. I hugged him again, squeezing his arms inside, a tourniquet of pressure. A hand moved. A knife? I clenched his wrist and pressed my weight more heavily on top of him. Now! Bite. Rip out his throat with my teeth. *I* would not die.

A large hand pushed in the way. I saw the glint of a blade just before is disappeared flat into the man's mouth with a sickening choke. I fell back, one hand grasping the iron-hard forearm of Randall. Propping on one elbow, half submerged in water, I watched him pull the broad bowie from the man's skull and ram it in again under the rib cage.

The quiet struck me as though something essential to the world had been removed. Even the night creepers were stifled, perhaps holding their breaths in an airless vacuity. I breathed out forcibly in self-reassurance. In the back of my mind I couldn't recall any firing since I grabbed that gook. I spun through the possibilities while hauling myself up and back toward the radio

"Get them out of here," I shouted to Randall, and pushed the talk button to call Cowboy one-seven.

"Echo six-six. Reference Alpha, six rounds. Fire for effect!"

I swung on my gear. Randall squatted next to me.

"Everything's okay. Five gook KIA. Long got a sliver of shrapnel in his elbow from the first seventy-nine round. Band-Aid job."

"I got one in the ass . . . Take Forbes's and Smith's squads and move to the hooches. I think we only bagged their point team."

The men anticipated moving. It was standard procedure and they were ready. Our fears were confirmed as two rocket-propelled grenades came in from the woodline. One landed wide to the left and beyond, and the other was nearer but a dud.

"Smitty," I called, trying to shout in a whisper. NVA knew where we were, but I didn't want them to know exactly where. "Get your people out of here." Charging into the paddy and toward the forward dike, I called for machine guns. Two more RPGs exploded somewhere behind me, closer. That convinced. The main force would be in the woodline, and they weren't waiting for the point team anymore. Having given them up, they could pop a few RPGs. *While they maneuvered?* Maybe the machine guns could pin them long enough for the artillery to allow the rest of us to get out of there. Otherwise we'd be running along the top of the dikes with RPGs breaking at our heels. They'd get us.

"Hey, Segar? You got any C.S.?"

"Only two rounds."

"Get them out there, either side of where those rockets came from. Follow it up with some H.E. You're too damned high," I growled at Norcross, whose machine gun bursts had begun to climb. His tracers threaded red arcs over the woodline and far into the night sky. Another rocket screeched directly overhead yet blew up near the village. Nervously, Norcross overcorrected by blasting towers of water into the air in the adjacent paddy. I kicked him out of the way and took the gun myself, pulling yammering bursts into the woodline.

"On the way," Spider called from the radio, with what we were all waiting for. *Not bad, four or five minutes.*

A few seconds later the unmistakable sound could be heard—the quavering whisper of artillery shells passing invisibly through the darkness overhead. The first two, 155s, boomed with shocking blasts right where I wanted them. The best followed, two rounds of eight-inch seemed to lumber in. Inherently exciting, these beauties impacted with ear-splitting fury. Even at a distance the sodden ground convulsed like bowling balls dropped onto a waterbed.

"What the hell happened back there?" I asked Randall, lying down next to him on the dry thatched bedding of a pig's hooch.

"Shit," he hissed softly. He was angry. A sheen of sweat on his black face capped the prominent features with a fierce gray pallor. The stars had come out, joined by a quarter-moon. He didn't say anything for a few moments. "Damn bastards could have gotten us killed."

"They were asleep, weren't they?"

"Hell yeah. Mullens and Alverez. Gooks must have walked right past them, claymores and all. Maybe they noticed something—that they were smack in the middle of a G.I. platoon. One of them talked out loud and Segar heard them and got a look at them with his Starlight, then let loose with his some seventy-nine. Got his whole position to open up on them. Three got loose and tried to dee-dee-mao over our asses. Nep dropped two straight off, and me and you took care of the other . . . Fuckin' luck was all. They could have blown away Forbes's entire squad."

"Well, we won't see any of them tonight. There's way too much open ground for them to cross."

"We can cut back watch to twenty-five percent."

"Yeah, hey Jim, you like pigs?" I asked, nudging him with my boot as I rose.

"Back in the world, it used to be all I liked."

"I meant the sweet-smelling, two-legged variety." I sat, leaning back. He uttered some unintelligible thing as I settled with my equipment and radios on the other side of an indolent hog who gave only a dyspeptic snuffle to my presence.

I thought about luck. Fuckin' luck. Of how many times had it played a part in what happened. Too damned many. A couple of times my own luck had been incredible. In my pocket I carried a lucky bullet. A gook had once pulled the trigger on me from a thicket only a few feet off the trail. His weapon misfired, and the man behind me blew him away. I ejected the round from the dead man's chamber, removed the bullet from the cartridge, and carried it, a talisman. It had some power on the recent occasion. A lone gook had walked up on me, sauntering like he was back in Hanoi. I froze, holding only an unfolded radio antenna. Lifting his lowered muzzle, he unloaded half a magazine in a single burst. Point-blank and he missed, but during that instant of stone terror, and of resignation so intense and compact, I swore to myself that I could actually feel the impact of the bullets ripping through my chest. He was diving before he needed to. I was diving before I realized I was. He dove into the bunker I had just wired with C-4. I dove for the detonator.

The luck of those incidents was diamond pure, but this little ambush tonight certainly wreaked of it. If the two men had not fallen asleep, they may have prematurely sprung the ambush on that five-man point team; resulting in our platoon getting pincered by the rest of their unit. The gook point man had been alert, yet *they* were dead.

For the soldier who made no mistakes at all, a wide margin still existed, the consequences of which decided everything. On one jungle trail a man could step with his left foot and plunge a hidden mine's detonator that would rip off his legs. Yet with equal chance he could step with his right, unknowingly missing the same detonator. That right step, insignificant among millions, would lead him to the steps of the plane that would take him home. Relying on luck or having faith in it was like rappeling with cobwebs. The idea that you could control or get it to work for you was gossamer. Maybe chairborne commandos, like Captain Ritchie, had the only smart solution after all: take as few steps out here as possible. To keep a career in the Army, you did have to be alive and whole.

Morning appeared around the hooches like a slow chemical reaction, light neutralizing dark in the catalyst of liquid humidity, mosquitoes evaporating.

Standing outside the door of a hooch, I stretched. Whiffs of haze poised suspended, motionless around us, smelling like moist fetid breath. I scanned the still obscured woodline and noted only the movement of a scuzzy rat nearby, skittering home after a night's coursing. In a few moments I could make out one of last night's bodies, sprawled over a dike. And the rest of them, I thought, are laying out there in bad fuck-ass luck.

Soon all the men had broken out something for breakfast and arranged their gear for the day. The civilians stirred from their bunkers and mingled timidly amongst us in their morning putter.

"What are we going to do today?" Spider asked.

"Same old shit, airmobile out, hit a few targets, fight some bugs and mud."

"Are you going to check the woodline first?"

"No. They'd expect us to do that, to check out what arty did. Any additional bodies would have been gotten out by now anyways . . . and booby traps left in their places."

"How come," asked Spider, "it's such a big thing with them to get rid of their bodies all the time?"

"What they want is for us to fight, take casualties, and find that we got nothing to show for it. You know how we feel when that happens here; back in the world, this thing is having the same effect on the whole war. Anyways, they could give a shit about the five, they know we know about them."

"I suppose those dudes last night will lie low today—now that they know we're still around."

"We won't see them," I agreed, and lifted a can of coffee from the smudge on the ground where the lump of C-4 had burned out.

By noon we had made three insertions into "dry holes" around the same general area. However, because of our night contact, the colonel believed it was all a matter now of how hard we hit the bush; the harder we humped that ground, the more likely it was to turn into a teaming NVA stronghold.

The platoon slowed noticeably, eyes bleary from sweat and fatigue. With little sleep during the night, I was exhausted. On the first insertion my bush hat had gotten whipped from my pocket by the wind while we were still airborne. The sun had gotten mighty hot since.

I decided to head across a wide expanse of open ground where we could walk easily, taking advantage of the unhampered breezes that abated some of the heat. I'd let the colonel believe that we'd broken balls in woodlines the whole way. Ahead in the distance as we trudged, huge cumulo-nimbus towers, of which the tropics are capable, mounted higher and higher like heaven-spun floss. It gave a steadying, vertical aspect to the otherwise redundant flatness of the land. Their underbellies were dark- and cold-looking, almost charcoal where edges met the horizon, turgid with the cats and dogs of a monsoon deluge. I checked my wrist compass and determined that they were sliding to the west, oblique to our march. The direction of the wind confirmed that it would miss us, sparing us a five-minute hurricane and keeping us under a blast-furnace sky.

I swung the platoon left and entered a swath of low jungle. Our prearranged landing zone lay on the other side. My watch allowed only time enough for one more insertion before we would have to take up another night ambush position. This particular place showed no sign of human activity recent or ancient. Thick undergrowth and vines battled it out with a few variations of hapless trees, fighting not for sunlight, but for supremacy alone. Flowers in unusual profusion roared a chorus of propaganda that their death-wrap was only the beautification it appeared to be. As I wondered why the V.C. didn't or hadn't used the place for a well-concealed base, their wisdom literally hit me. We entered a clearing surrounded by walls of vegetation; it cooked, a windless, stifling bowl that seemed to make instant asthmatics of us all. Rills of sweat sluiced from our every pore, and men cursed from front to rear as the last of canteens were drained. It was as if the entire place lay under a glass bubble, a giant fish-eye lens, with the sun gone into supernova. Out of the direct rays the mosquitoes took over. A small, gnatlike job that worked day or night rose in fuzzy light explosions from the dank thickets. We breathed them and cursed again; a thirty-man blood donor unit transfusing an entomological nightmare.

Ants sallied for the uppercut, red fire ants, pound for pound the most hostile and aggressive life forms on this planet. Lodging in overhanging branches, they willfully dropped off to rain on passersby. Scrambling and biting all the way, they go down the collar inside the shirt and into the pants, vicious and obsessed with their goal—the crotch. Alvarez had sounded the warning by becoming the first victim; with spasmodic gyrations he left the trail bucking and throwing his gear aside as fast as he could get it off. In an insane dance, he swatted his body with one hand while fumbling to remove his shirt with the other.

The next two guys ducked away quickly, catching only a few each. We had occasionally skirmished with these ants before and as an experienced platoon, the rest of us knew enough to detour their territory. As I watched Alvarez still twitching with paroxysms of a neurological disorder while trying to put his equipment back on, I scored this with pleasure, a part payment for his snooze the night before. Nearly hundreds of red savages still scurried around in every direction, fuming hot anger. Many had already assaulted a tree, hoping for a second frenzied chance.

They dripped onto the empty trail, the biological mechanism of attack as yet still unextinguished. One solitary trooper, mounting the toe of my boot, stood on his head and chomped his horny mandibles into scuffed leather. I crossed my other foot over and crunched him.

About twenty-five meters from the L.Z., more damning shot back from the point men. Walking third, I could see nothing unusual. Then, engulfed in the invisible, I knew. We would have to cross chin deep in a canal whose water had not been disturbed since the time of Yao. Its skin broken, a terrific stench bellowed up. Pure black organic rot, halfway to becoming crude oil, it clung with desperation, as if needing us for itself. The platoon gasped in this giant feculent fart.

The choppers soon picked us up for a cool reprieve in the upper air, albeit temporary. We swung in a half orbit on our last target. It was nearly four o'clock in the afternoon, and the countryside below looked as serene and untroubled as it always did. The rivers and the greens shone smooth and glossy as a postcard, displaying gentle tilled patches. Comforting, like farmland anywhere. Hell, come dark this place would spill with an army mean as red fire ants. Terror worked, and from exasperation I envied their power. I knew I was a better soldier and that's all that really mattered. Yet they had the edge; the consummate principle that the revolution justified anything and is to be advanced by whatever means are necessary. Civilians must either support them and their ideas or by definition be an enemy. . . and all enemy must die.

All of us had a list of things, either determined by the Army or ourselves personally, things that circumscribed our conduct in war. The gooks had no such list.

Dropping in for the assault, our flock of clattering ornithoids passed over an improved dirt road, and a hundred feet below something caught my eye. An ARVN two-and-a-half-ton truck lay on its side in the middle of the road, a large gaping hole at its nose. Half a dozen ARVN soldiers stood there looking at the truck and into the hole.

A routine enough job: plant a mine in the road at night, run the wires to a good concealed spot, and wait. Let all sorts of traffic pass over it until just the right moment, say an ARVN truck full of soldiers. A single dumb-ass could do it. Still, the wreck below tightened me up. And from Spider's face I could tell it had the same effect on him. Some kind of enemy was close.

Our gunships had not been cleared for suppression fire, and the L.Z., about five hundred meters from the road, lay tranquil. Our exit and assault was less than energetic, our normal rapid thrust into the woodline becoming stillborn by a deep canal at its edge. Skinner and Voss poked around for an acceptable spot to cross, while most of the platoon crouched idly in the open paddy along a dike. Five of us crossed neck deep in silt-laden water to a grassy patch sprinkled with low scrub bushes. Beyond loomed a stockade of iron-hard nipa. Thirty-foot spires shot upward to feather brush the sky with waving fronds. Dense, with cut stumps at their base, they somehow rooted into waist-deep slime.

"We're not going any further," I called out to the point men. "We'll only get stuck in there."

"Stuck and fucked."

"Hey, look at this, sir," Voss called while studying something on the ground. "A whole bunch of dudes spent the night in here."

Pressed grass impressions indicated about twenty men. "By the look of how they're laid out, I'd say they were here for resting. Ain't no place for an ambush . . . ARVNs?"

"Not around here," I said. "Not us either—it's NVA, all right, but there's not much we can do now— they've been gone since morning."

"That truck out there on the road's only been blown an hour or so ago."

"Hmm," I agreed. "But they probably left a local V.C. to sit with the detonator all day. Okay, I want Skinner and Voss to check it out a bit further down. Pawa, turn your squad around and back out into the paddy. I'm going to try to get the choppers back, and maybe we can move to our night location early . . . there's nothing we can do in here."

Everyone duly registered my words and began acting on them. I stood for a moment, staring at the swamp with my mind in neutral. Turning to observe Pawa's last two people reenter the canal, I mechanically followed, hesitating for a moment before plunging in. I considered again the grassy impressions where dragon's teeth had been sown, where hard soldiers had risen. The redolent decay seemed to hold all life in a languorous intoxication. My eyes wandered over this cavity of green around me, automatic, perfunctory.

The point men were intently studying what appeared to be a trail I had not seen before. It ran directly into the nipa. They're going to call me anyway, I thought, and headed over. Never can tell, it could always be something interesting. "Can you guys see where that goes?"

"It goes nowhere, sir," Skinner answered, as though he accepted it as remarkable.

"Let's find out where nowhere is. We might even meet the people attached to the feet that made those prints."

"There's a booby trap over there," Voss added, pointing to the dried crossed palms that the gooks left as a marker.

"It's got to be right there," I said, motioning them to look at a tiny hummock on the side of the path. "In those leaves—it's the only place they could hide it."

"You want us to go through there?"

"Sure, I want to get a better look at that trail. So we might as well scuff up that booby trap on the way. We can join the platoon around this way." I pointed.

Skinner deftly picked his way through the palm fronds, prudently scrutinizing each leaf for a trip wire. I moved up to add my eyes to the scene, the tall grass being thicker than it appeared from a distance. Skinner cautiously took two steps; Voss followed.

"There it is," he said matter-of-factly.

"Yep," I added likewise. I crouched low to see where the green monofilament ran and noted how, inexplicably, it was wrapped around Skinner's heel.

A shocking blast burst from the ground upward; everything came apart just in front of me and disappeared in a watery blur. The concussion stunned, but the shards of steel leapt in a howl of pain. My riddled body felt seared with fire. My hand jerked instinctively to my face. *My God, the eye's gone. Splattered.* A strange feeling of calm and dark came over me, and I sank back . . . as if to welcome death.

I rolled to my side and tried to call for help, but my mouth gritted with burnt powder and dirt. I spit feebly. My call for help gurgled only drool. The guys, already there, pulled at my limbs, barking words. Consciousness hung a tenuous grip on my torn meat. A wicked hatred of myself fumed . . . *The war is over . . . and damn it to Hell, I'm not done with it! It can't be. . . . not me . . . not this way!* I cried out in agony. The anger swelled into an amazing fury that centered in one maniacal spot. *Got to stop it, put an end to it . . .* My CAR-15 still swung on its sling around my arm. I fumbled for its pistol grip. The weapon flopped awkwardly, my right arm useless, but I managed to bring up the short muzzle.

"I'm going to blow my fucking head off," I proclaimed hoarsely. My hand grasped at the magazine rather than the trigger, and I concentrated desperately, to make the fingers do. The weapon pulled away.

"You bastards, fucking sons of bitches! Let me!"

My body lifted, a makeshift litter. Consciousness drifted like some ethereal vapor . . . memories of other medevac wounded suffused my body into images of theirs. A voice bellowed above the others. Attending to the words was impossible, barely sorting its presence from a surreal radio transmission, I heard Lt. Col. Walter B. Conners. The call for a dustoff from Randall meant, I, Echo-66, had been hit. Conners had come down, taken the platoon, tried to comfort me. I recognized only his voice.

The sounds of the medevac. Nothingness. Movement. Raging pain. Litter clamped inside.

We lifted off and I felt swallowed in a black vortex of annihilistic noise. The aircraft shimmied violently as the pilot pushed speed to its limit.

"Oh God hurry," I moaned, words sucked into oblivion. "Somehow! Somewhere!" I called out, half in pain . . . and despair.

CHAPTER FOUR

The seventh of November 1969 did not exist. My corpus-cum-corpse lay somewhere, the I, the me, drifted on the swells of nether reaches, those far Elysian Fields, yet the distance between the crisp sheets of intensive care and the crinkle of a plastic bag in graves registration could often be measured in angstroms. Sometime on the eighth some doctor, some pair of hands, effected a fusion of soma and spirit . . . brutally. The world burst in an explosion of dormant uncontrollable neurons, firing then glowing white in my bed. The hands had scalpeled an incision in my left side to jam in a piece of tubing. I spasmed, a motorized man attached to a faulty power cord. Hands screwed the tube deeper, into the lung. My body arched in a rigid jerk, a scream frozen in a paralyzed diaphragm.

"Sorry about that, you were supposed to stay unconscious." The words came with a pat on the shoulder. "Your lungs were filling up with fluid . . . a guy in your condition doesn't need pneumonia. You'll be all right."

Awareness flooded in a sharp treble of pain, rippling over me like echoing discordant riffs. The prick of a shot hit my upper arm and shortly took effect as if wires had been yanked from the jangling tweeters, leaving only the dull throbbing of the bass. A space cleared in front of my head, enough to think and make some assessments. My head and face seemed swathed with gauze and tape and I couldn't see at all.

Lying flat on my back, I felt squashed to the mattress as if the earth had suddenly increased its gravitational pull. My extreme weakness surprised me, but I did satisfy myself that movement was possible and that everything was still connected. The right arm, bandaged to some kind of board, was immobilized. I reconned with the other, its IV tube hanging freely. Islands of gauze yelped at the touch. There were more tubes. Locating one just below my navel, I was startled to find it rooted deep in my abdomen. A curious wiggle set off Promethean torments. Another tube skewered my penis. It issued from my innards and with others ran out over the edge of the bed and beyond my reach.

My legs seemed all right, twin columns of pain that ran down toward the end of the bed. Feeling through coarse wrapping around the right foot, I checked one foot with the other. I tried to scrutinize individual injuries, but they blended into each other as if after a shotgun blast someone had played connect-the-dots with a razor blade.

With my fingertips I studied my face. Bandages and tape covered the right eye. I remembered the left's complete mutilation, and the lack of any light was easy to account for. Clipped ends of sutures bristled from tender skin between nose and left "eye." With my fingernail I tapped a hard plastic disc, installed where my eyeball had been. Sliding my finger around it, the consequences of what had happened, of its permanence, began a stark stare in my imagination. One little Orphan Annie eye. I had known the eye was fucked . . . but gone!?

Concentration, simple thought, exhausted me, and with the overtaking drug, I succumbed to sleep. After some unknown interval, I awoke with a vicious headache, as if the process of thinking had torn ligaments from inside my skull. My head felt encased in some cruel medieval implement of torture—"the Devil's Diadom" . . . Kerist, the fucking Death Helmet. A dungeon fantasy seemed nearly real, with my body still whimpering from punishment exacted earlier; and the weak moanings of my comrades, in total darkness, chained to the far wall.

On the third day, Colonel Conners spoke from my bedside, saying he had already been around a couple of times but I was always asleep. We began a typical conversation as if I had just come in from the field and nothing had happened except the usual battalion business. Though a struggle to talk, it comforted me except for one piece of information. Burns of Charlie Company had taken over as recon platoon leader. An experienced Airborne Ranger like myself, he had been earmarked to succeed me for some time, but I felt emotions churn. The war's still going on, he's had me replaced, I thought. I'm out of it and taking everything I know along with me. Others will relearn it but might die in doing it. That thing out there belongs to me! Damn it to Hell, I'm not with them.

The colonel told of the last three days. I envisioned one of the squads moving in a file along a paddy dike. In a labored trudge, their baggy fatigues and equipment burdened shoulders distorted into squat Oriental figures; blurring into watery ink sketches on a nonexistent background. I observed from behind, both them and myself fading at the edges, wisped away by a zephyr on the tips of rice stalks, erased by the discomfort of watching myself watch; no longer in charge.

"Mac, you shouldn't have been out there," the colonel said, fidgeting, half stating something that was bothering him.

"Shouldn't? You mean didn't have to be."

"No, you shouldn't have been." I knew he was thinking of my standing in front of his desk listening to unwelcomed instructions two weeks before. I'd been grazed in a skirmish. "The doc says that leg wound of yours is still not completely closed. And since it needs time to heal, and I need someone to take our four deuce mortars,

I'm taking you out of recon. You've been out there longer than anyone in the battalion anyway, and you're the only one I've got who's qualified for mortars."

I had argued. The alternative I wanted was for a second louey from B Company to fill the mortar slot and to leave me free to take command of Echo Company. Colonel Connors, who treated his officers as junior partners, all engaged in a collective effort, saw merit in my scheming and gave his reluctant consent.

"All right, Mac, but if that leg of yours gets infected, I'll put my boot square up your ass." His gentle admonishment seemed ironic now that the punk lieutenant who told him what to do lay before him half blown apart because of it. Maybe he had regrets, but they were nothing like mine.

Already I'd thought plenty of what I would do if I could do it all again. The same mostly—change the part where I'd followed Skinner and Voss. That single scene, just those few frames, had gripped my available waking time like a single corrosive spot in the entire rerun of my life, that singular moment of casually turning from the platoon to follow Skinner and Voss, to lend my eyes for a look. Even then with the wasting rush of steel spit, there was room. If my head turned just an inch or so, I might collect only a few superficial wounds in the face. I moved my body while keeping the pattern of shrapnel stationary like marked targets on a map overlay. Straightening the body, the eyes came damage free, but lower—a piece from the abdomen eliminated something else. I'd be bright-eyed with a hairy cleft between the legs. A sideways movement impacted chunks that had zipped by now punched out my heart or something equally unhelpful. Entertaining this stupid game was like playing pinball with dead flippers.

"Look, sir," I said at last, "I begged you to let me go back out there, it's my thing, you know it, that's why you let me. You were wounded in Korea twice and went back both times."

"We had heads full of beans in those days. Full of notions of glory left over from the Big War. We took much higher casualties than we do today because of it."

"We've had the same number, just more years. Staying in the field's what gets the job done."

"Well, true, but we can't really go around with those ideas of glory anymore. They're kind of an embarrassment."

"I know combat's different now," I said hoarsely, "probably for the good. The Marines still have beans in their heads, and more of them are dead because of it too. But that's not what I mean . . . nowadays glory is no more than stomping around out there until you find your way into a world of shit, just to fight back out again. That is, if you haven't already stomped on all the mines and booby traps in the area. I fought *those* kinds of ideas, sir, every damn day."

"I know you did, Mac." Connors got up and cleared his throat as if to add something. My voice became gravelly and I scrunched to get more comfortable but couldn't. "Hey guy," he said, "it's time you got some rest." His tone had changed the subject. There was something not quite decent about talking to a freshly fucked-up soldier on the philosophy of getting fucked up.

"Don't go yet, sir. I wanted to say something else."

"I'm still here," he answered. He was only inches from me, but I lowered my voice. "Did they tell you I tried to blow myself away . . . the rest of the way?"

"Your medic did."

"It wasn't because of the pain. It was because of the dishonor."

"Dishonor? What do you mean by that? You thought you failed?" he asked with a touch of surprise. "You didn't even trigger that charge."

"I knew it was there. I had no business making such a mistake."

"We were just talking about old ideas of glory. The Japs used to do things like that when they thought they had failed. Don't be so hard on yourself. I'm putting you in for a Silver Star. What you've got to do now is rest and take it easy.''

"My men wouldn't understand, but you will. I wanted to kill myself because I knew I was bad off, bad enough that I won't be able to stay in the Army. It's all I ever wanted, all I can remember wanting. If I was going to bc out, then I wanted the Big Out.''

"You don't want that now, do you? You've already given enough.''

"I haven't thought of it since. I'm not sure . . .''

"Don't think like that, Mac. It's not like you. Just hang in there. The doctor told me that you'll be all right. Every tough thing I ever asked of you, you did. Now it's time to do something tough for yourself—hang in there.''

Time warped into fat bulges of marauding pain, then stretched into languid pools of sweaty ague, defended always by my faithful concubine, Sister Morphine. I could understand how one could become addicted. If it made me feel good when I felt so bad, how would it do if I already felt okay?

In the small moments of unhazed waking thought, I daydreamed for exercise. Lying in a shallow unlidded box packed with half a gross of young angora bunnies, my mind free and billowy with the condensed Guernica of my war, stimulating blasts and gunfire swam in the whirl of chopper blades. Men danced in frenzied motion choreographed by fluid tracers. In a never-ending, body-high orbit of the earth, they came with the merriment of a grand finale. The men ducked and twisted in a palsied fandango, wide-eyed, blinking in a glowing pyre of red lines . . . and somewhere I heard Dat's voice. A shakeout. My arm. Right, Dat, I could always count on him. Best Tiger Scout in the world.

"You awake, sir?''

"You okay? We come to see you." Pawa, just like he was here.

"Sure, totally." He was. "Pawa," I rasped, "you don't know good pussy from a prickly-ass pineapple."

"It don't matter, I eat 'em both."

"What are you goldbrickers doing here? Captain Ritchie will have you filling sandbags with a spoon."

"He went up to Tan An," Smith said. "We borrowed a couple of jeeps and commenced to troll Saigon streets for some snatch . . . and since we was in the area . . ."

"What are you using for bait?"

"Dick heads, it's their favorite food."

"In this town you can use a bare hook. Who's here anyway?"

"Norcross's talking to Skinner, Hannibal and Zonker are with Voss, Lieutenant Torro is rappin' some nurse."

"That figures. You say rappin' or raping?" I tried to pull myself up a couple of inches. "Hey, Dat, see that guy next to me? NVA dude." Connors had told me about the poor bastard in the full body cast and all. I jerked my thumb at my former nemesis. "Tonight I go in dark, ka-kee-dao him."

"You no can get up," he informed, as though taking me quite seriously. A Vietnamese ward maid mopped between the beds, and Dat exchanged a few words with her.

"She say him boo-coo bad. Maybe die tomorrow or next day."

"If nobody's looking, he might just go in the next few minutes," Smith quipped in a stage whisper.

"No one come now, I ka-kee-dao," Dat said.

"Give him a break." I attempted a laugh. "He's my buddy, minds his own business, drains his own pus, real quiet dude."

But I knew Dat meant it. I could tell from the tone of his voice. I knew the look he would have, the boyish face etched in the hot animus of a personal vengeance that was a secret part of his having left the communists.

"Dat, you must get out of this place, this country," I said gravely, trying my best, in those few hoarse words, to convey the urgency that I suddenly felt for him.

"If you don't get going, you're going to get same as me, maybe dead—understand—you *biak*?"

"Me *biak*." I believed that what I said had passed over him. He changed the subject.

"Nep gone, now him go to ARVN. You gone—him say him no work G.I. no more."

I was deflected; Dat knew I'd take it as flattery. He knew he'd never find another officer who'd protect him like I did. The platoon will be a lot *smaller* with him gone. What a *pisser* he was.

"Took eight cartons of cigarettes when he hooked up," added Pawa.

"Dat," I said turning back. "You've got to go back to the States with Robby—forget that girl in Cai Lay, she'll be all right. You won't." I felt unable to express myself beyond those words.

When Greg Torro, the four-deuce platoon leader, came over, Dat and Robby Smith said good-bye and swung around to Skinner's bed. I wouldn't hold him with talk of leaving his country, even though he and Smith talked of it plenty. I knew he wouldn't go. His private vendetta, that slow burn, would keep him fighting for a long time. He might have to, I thought; the gooks will keep things going until they win or haven't a man left standing—he can't make that pledge. He's got to get out. Fuck the war. My own vulnerability, so painfully evident, corralled the obvious; of how vulnerable he was, of how little his toughness and experience mattered, of how soft the flesh really was, and how inevitable was his death.

"Dat!" I called after him, a thought springing as in reflex. "You take my Star, my pistol! Take the holster too—wear it under your shirt." Instinctively I attempted to demonstrate with my right hand, but its immobility restrained me. I switched to an awkward backhand with my left hand and drew the imaginary 9mm automatic from a shoulder

holster. Not wearing a shirt, I wondered if he understood.
"Under," I motioned again, "so no one will try to take it
away."

"Thank you, sir," he said softly, his Oriental reserve
failing to hide his surprise at receiving the gift, an officer's
private weapon.

"Wear it for the rest of your life," I said heavily.

"I could of gotten you about two hundred bucks for
that thing," Torro whispered when Dat left.

"No, Greg, make sure he gets it . . . and if that
Ritchie or Hughes tries to vulture it, go to Colonel Connors.
Dat saved my ass more than once. I want a bit of me to
stay with him and work out when I'm gone."

Torro and I discussed what should be done with all
my gear and belongings, a considerable collection by now,
and none of it ready for this eventuality. He promised to
bring my captured SKS to my home in Connecticut when
he derosed in a month's time.

Pain had been consolidating for a while, but I put off
asking for a shot. It would put me to sleep, and besides, it
wouldn't look good—getting it in front of them.

Hamblin, the hugest man in the platoon, the one we
called Hannibal, spoke at the end. "From all of us,
sir . . . we all liked you . . . and just wanted to let you
know."

I was in no mood to doubt his words, I wanted to hear
them, wanted to be remembered well, wanted to be
remembered at all. They are really heading down that dike
now! I thought sorrowfully. Leaving me behind. I stuck
out my left hand and they filed past, each grasping it.
Paying their respects to a specter who couldn't see them—
with a stupid tube up his nose . . . trying to smile. I cursed
myself, embarrassed at being so inert, so incapable in front
of the men to whom I had once been so significant.

"Hey, do you guys know that Saigon is off limits to
grunts?"

They answered with a couple of puzzled no's.

"Do this, when you go out of here," I said. "Leave

the jeeps in the lot, walk out through the gate, turn
left . . . about half a block up is a whole slew of cathouses.
The M.P.s aren't likely to fish you out of that place."

"You wouldn't be sending us into black syph country,
would you, sir?" came a wry query from Hamblin.

"Hannibal, it's the only place I'd send you."

"Shit man," taunted Pawa, "what you worrying
about—you don't catch it . . . you give it out."

"When I was here last month, I went up there
myself."

"You mean it's officer stuff?!"

"No, like I gave President Thieu's daughter a ring
but she was already fixed up for the night. She had to go
visit her sick grandmother. Now get out of here, you've
been disturbing my sleep for the last five months." A
quick flash of memory brought a smile to my face. Only a
month before, on another ward, I'd met a captain who had
gotten smashed in the face by a chunk of tree that was
shorn off in an explosion. We had gone up the road
together, he with his eyes so blackened he looked like one
of the Beagle Boys, and me stitched up and striding like
Chester. In new fatigues, like a pair of E-1's, we walked
past the girls' cooing monkeyshines and erotic enticements
behind wrought-iron gates. In a shop further on we'd
donned our proper rank and insignia and ambled back. At
the first portico a pair of glossy-haired things in baby doll
nighties mocked with the equivalent of Oriental hilarity at
our instant promotions while hiking up negligees to pout
their twats between the bars. We surrendered.

I thought of the last time I had been with my men. I'd
tried to put a bullet through my brain. That desire to shoot
myself, the passion of that moment, had passed. It seemed
an overreaction. Introspection began to distill distinct drams
of emotion. Taken out of the war—that was the reason for
my anger. I continued scarring myself . . . I've been beat-
en, I thought, the sons of bitches got me.

It wasn't really those soldiers who had reared from
the ground; who made my anger rise. It wasn't the ones

who had set the booby trap but the ones who would eventually have died if I'd stayed in the field. Those lousy bastards got off. I thought of them as safe as mice up a sleeve, somewhere in the vast sodden reaches of the delta . . . laughing. Those fuckers probably know that this time I won't get patched up and come after them. Turning myself to the left, I leaked some excess venom at my fellow sufferer from North Vietnam. "Hey, you gook piece of shit, why don't you croak and make my fuckin' day?"

"Is something wrong?" asked a sympathetic nurse from nearby. I was knocked off balance at having an audience.

"That guy just pisses me off."

"But we've just moved him to Ward Five."

"Ah, fuck," I let out under my breath, my face flushed with the fire inside. "Fuck him, fuck this whole place, fuck everything!"

As days passed, I became more conscious or aware of activity beyond my bed. But the intensive care unit still existed only in sound, a collection of them, where I used every bit of experience and imagination I had to construct and comprehend it. The whole staff of nurses and medics moved as diffuse matter, disembodied voices, which traded bandages and injected my arm. Some sleep accomplished, new voices would float past the tiny squeaks of rubber soles indistinguishable from each other. Less activity meant night.

Occasionally the monotony broke with a touch of drama across from me. A guy, apparently in an oxygen tent, would give some sign of leaving us, the emergency sounded, a flurry of doctors arriving to labor intently around his bed, a contingent of nurses zipping to and fro to the abbreviated instructions. In unison they would blow on the spark. The pilot light set, the ward quickly settled back into normal routine. I witnessed this crisis about once a day. Hell of a dude, I thought, communicating with vital signs alone. When I left, his life still dangled at the end of a wheeze, still threatening to depart and leave that battered, useless body.

On the ward the usual description of fighting for life generally lacked evidence from my vantage point. Nobody seemed to be conscious, all groveling in the flow of sedation, or totally passive, limpid flesh taking substance with near indifference. I need to get moving, I thought, and find out what shape I'm really in. Pushing my pillow against the back of the bed, I propped myself higher against it to await my next change of IV bottle or whatever.

"What's your name?" I asked a forthcoming presence.

"Lieutenant Schaffer," the female replied, unemotional, informative.

"What's your first name?"

"It's Doris."

She pulled back the sheet and began working with a bracing cold liquid around the drain in my lower abdomen. Supine, in full frontal nudity except for the random gauze patches, I felt very naked. She proceeded to repeat the cleaning operation on the urine catheter, the tube that shish kebabed my penis, her fingers manipulated. My cock stirred. "Damn not fuckin' now." I gritted my teeth, an image flashing of a steam job, blow-bath-massage operation in Dong Tam. From a creaky start and long dormancy it crept as if from some crusty chrysalis. *My God! The Kamasutra* of intensive care. She was finished. Turning back the sheet, her hand touched mine. I grasped at it but it disappeared. In a moment she returned with an offer of an ice cold can of Coke. Solicitously she held the can and aimed the straw. I attempted to find the appropriate expression of thanks, as I might while standing next to her at the officers' club bar.

Yeah, Doris Schaffer and I are old friends, going way back. Why damn! She used to clean out my tubes.

"Good afternoon . . . and how are we feeling today?" interrupted a male voice.

"Fine," I said thinly.

"Well, things certainly are looking a lot better." He

gave a brief tip to several bandages for a peek under. "Fine, yes, fine. No signs of infection . . . coming along just—" He interrupted his ingratiating chatter to take out a couple of tools.

Turning back, he added, "I'm Dr. Burgess, your ophthalmologist and the one responsible for your general treatment." Without warning he began removing sutures from my neck. Deftly he snipped and tugged from jawline to collarbone.

"I'm sorry, but unfortunately we had to remove your left eye."

"Yes," I said.

"Now, I'm going to take the bandage from your right eye."

Indeed, the hair of my eyebrow reluctantly gave way to his jerk as the adhesive tape lifted. He didn't have to tell me what to do. From the cranked-up position of my head I gazed easily around the room. Nothing. I squinted, hoping to see something recognizable. Still nothing. Black. I looked up at the ceiling, trying to catch any overhead lights. Geez, must be some kind of temporary thing, I thought, from being covered up—probably stunned by the blast or something. It seemed there had been a similar case or two in the war movies. There isn't much of a flash, though, even at night—only a momentary spray of red sparks. Confused, I allowed the technicalities to pass. I turned to the doctor.

"Can you see anything?" he asked.

"No," I answered cautiously. "Should I?"

"Well yes, you really should."

Of course I should, I thought. Anyone with at least one eye should; but then it did seem reasonable for someone who'd just stuck his head into a blast to have come out with at least temporary blindness.

I felt a low rumbling in my gut, as low as great continental plates shifting in a grinding quake against each other. He leaned over and pried the lids open and clicked his close-held light to study the eye from several angles.

"There's a certain amount of hemorrhage in the vitreous humor . . . a lot, really. I can't actually see beyond it to assess the damage. We'll have to wait for it to clear."

"I can't see out and you can't see in. Because of blood?"

"Well, perhaps."

"How long will it take to clear?"

"It's difficult to say . . . could take up to a . . . six months."

Six months . . . anything to six months . . . and I'll see again. I made the two synonymous . . . but anticipating a prudent medical equivocation, I did not rearticulate the equation for his approval. As things were, I hadn't even thought about not seeing when bandages were removed. Black with my eye open! I thought I couldn't see because of the bandages. I had not even attended to it as a separate injury, not with the loss of the other eye and the howling of the injuries below. Now I knew there was something wrong, all right, but like he said, waiting seemed like the cure. *The blood, that's the reason I can't see, but it'll clear.* I was satisfied. *I can do six months of this.* As a postscript the doctor removed a few more stitches from the edge of my vacant left eye, a final touch to the bust of Lieutenant Maguire. I was very tempted yet reluctant to grab the doctor for odds on the right eye; he would have seen a few in his day. Expecting either to be put off or told what I didn't wish to hear, I laid them on myself, pessimistically; 100 to 1 against complete restoration. Maybe 1 to 10 on something dim or blurry, even money on a write-off.

"You told me a few things," I said, "but I've got more questions than before you came."

"Maybe it will help to know that in a few days, when your condition has stabilized, you'll be evacuated to a hospital in Japan."

Sure, that makes sense. They wouldn't be expected to do any hot shit eye surgery here in Nam—but in Japan— hell yeah.

"Also," he added, "your other wounds have to be closed. Tomorrow morning you'll be taken down to surgery."

"You mean they're still open, I mean not stitched-up already?"

"Yes, of course—in order to clean out the dirt and debris—you wouldn't want us to have closed all that up in there on the first day, would you?"

"No," I said, thinking of the implications, visualizing my own flayed meat as yawning mouths of shallow breathed pain.

"Well, Sergeant Skinner, how are we feeling today?"

That was that.

Two medics arrived at my bed and hauled me onto a gurney. I was pleased that they hadn't been issued gaffs or pikes for moving patients. Hands brought me over with the deftness of a wrestler's takedown. A nurse's shot to my butt set propulsion, a silent glide away.

Transit anywhere at Third Field Hospital, Saigon, meant going outside. The complex, a worn but pleasant group of stucco buildings, was connected by red-tiled sidewalks that were covered overhead. The change from the velvet glove of intensive care to the fetid humidity of the city filled my head.

I strained every perceptual nerve to experience and savor the moment. A soft humid breeze blew from an open garden on my left. On my right, toward the city, brawled the intense noise of Oriental traffic. Just to the other side of the compound's barbed-wire entanglements surged six lanes of manswarm. It pleased me that we were halted in the crowded central corridor. I knew exactly where I was and could visualize everything. All around us the voices of hospital personnel mixed with those of patients and their visiting friends just in off the line. Educated accents meshed with the monosyllabic patois of life in the bush, a contrast as distinct as the crisp whites and dust-caked fatigues.

With the easing of an apparent bottleneck at the door

of the PX, we rolled ahead, the source of my propulsion silent. A sharp right, a ramp, and the muffle of an airtight door brought me into a room with the crisp feel of an enlarged space capsule's atmosphere, cool as if laced with excess oxygen. Androids readied my body with sterile efficiency. Sheets lifted, replaced; IV pricked, attached.

"Count backward from one hundred, please." The sequence triggered speech. "Count backward from one hundred please." A tape loop. I wonder if . . .

"Can you hear me?"

"One hundred . . ."

Bruno Grappola, in the next room, with a blood-spattered apron, cleavered off loins and butt roasts to a metronome. He dealt inch-thick chops like stud poker and, of course, one-eyed jacks were wild.

"He's under—didn't even reach ninety-nine!"

"Ninety-nine."

Sensation dismissed the nowhere mind. I had been a stand-in for a Buddhist monk's immolation, then staked out for the rats to flense chunks of my meat. "Bruno" had me wrapped and on the scales. The wounds roared like a cast of thousands. I obviously had gotten much better, as now I was much worse, wounded all over again.

On returning from recovery the next day I found out Ray Voss had been shipped. Later the same day it was Skinner's turn. We exchanged threadbare good-byes, a fitting ending. At room's length for more than a week we had swapped fewer than a dozen words. He had been in my life or at its perimeter for only a few months, no different from any of my men, really, yet how profoundly he had crossed my path. Still, it sufficed that I knew little of him. I would have listened if he had spoken, but was relieved not to have to. I had total recall of his irritating banter back at the fire base. His silence seemed strange.

"Hey, Dwayne," I called to him. "See you in Japan."

"Yes sir!" he drawled, a rasp of puzzling enthusiasm. "I sure will . . . Steve."

Skinner's departure whelped off a new brood of feelings. A peculiar loneliness crept in. Voss, the three of us, had been displaced siblings, their silent presence alone reassured. Near them I somehow maintained contact with my unit. With the monotonous regularity of staff servicing parts of my body as the only stimulation, a pervasive boredom inundated everything. Although the hurting seemed to be rapidly diminishing, I begged shots to suppress consciousness, to bridge time.

Preparations for my move to Japan arrived with a dismantling of my tubes. The prospect of someplace new, someplace inherently interesting like Tokyo, boosted me in wobbly fashion. More hospital rooms, not the dazzle of nightclubs, were more likely; more service androids instead of steamy baths full of Japanese tarts . . .

"Are you Lieutenant Maguire?" I nodded.

She shook my arm, seeking more evidence of life.

"Yes," I said.

"Oh, I'm from the Red Cross. Would you like to speak to your parents? We have it all set up at the end of the room. We've got them on the line."

"Damn!" I whispered in surprise. It was all I could manage; this heavy bit was the last thing I needed.

"They're on the line now."

"Okay," I replied accommodating rather than agreeing. I gave in while wondering who had initiated this ambush. It seemed out of character for anyone around there to come up with ideas. They wheeled my bed to the phone.

"What do I say?"

"Tell them all about what happened to you. Tell them how you're feeling."

"Hello, Steve." I heard my father's resonant voice, clearly, somberly. "Steve?"

"Dad . . . good to hear you—caught me half out the door on my way to Japan." I was satisfied at having pushed my gravelly voice into registering enthusiasm, as if I'd just won the trip in a contest.

"How are you? They say you've lost . . . an eye and have . . . loss of vision in the other." His grief was evident.

"Oh that . . . I'm feeling a lot better really—I'm not as bad off as it sounds." I searched hard for a way to soften the situation. "I can't see yet . . . but everything else is good."

"We got a telegram a few days ago. It said your condition was stable and comfortable, although you were still very seriously ill. The next day we got what was supposed to have been the first telegram. In between, I kept trying to call the Army Casualty Office. Your mother and I were really upset . . . are upset. It's really been terrible for both of us. That office gave us the details . . . and it said how you were wounded and what is wrong with you."

"You probably know more about what's going on than I do." I laughed, relieved that my voice still held its buoyancy, belying the concentrated effort.

"They say you have multiple fragmentation wounds in both arms and legs, and in your body and . . . head," he said grimly, his voice trailing off.

"It was the only way the gooks could get me off their backs once and for all." I wasn't sure it was the right time for bravado; only silence came from the other end.

I could see his face the last time I had seen it—the solemn eyes, the face, cragged with an internal lament of a father who knew what happened to Rangers in his own war. Now I saw the premonition in his expression, his knowledge of what my enthusiasm meant. I had exacerbated their solemnity in that airport terminal with every jovial step of my shining Airborne boots and every carefree swing of my overnight bag.

My mother had shadowed us, withdrawn into paralyzed silence. There was silence between us again. I began to realize the extent of their grief, yet suddenly felt it more appropriate for a KIA.

"Hey," I exclaimed, my voice echoing as if forced down a long narrow pipe. "I'm not that bad, really! Where's Mom?"

"Steve, your mother will talk to you next time."

. . . There was another pause, and although made uncomfortable by it, I could think of nothing to say to fill it.

"Try and call us when you get to Japan."

"Sure, no sweat."

CHAPTER FIVE

Experience had given me a preview of extended sightseeing on a bus without windows; and so, shorn of any prize value, the trip to Japan ran fat with uncertainty. I would be touring alone. Isolation seemed predictable. My condition repelled rather than evoked contact, and I continually fought near capitulation. Yet the changeling was in place. "He" had for one eye a clear-disked porthole to raw tissue, and for the other a crimson bulge. "He" was me. I had to find a way to explain, to convince, that he was not me. I lay still and mute, the struggle smoldering.

I mused over a cinematic me; swathed in bandages, helped by comrades and enlivened by their reassurances. So much for film realism when the camera's eye perseveres with the lens cap on. So damn, what could the sight of my eyes mean? The eye, window of a person's soul. Dead men disturb. Their spirit-sucked eyes beg to be closed to mask that wide-eyed terror at the loss of their own soul. My eyes meant my personal diminution and the pain and desolation of passing from an envied position to a most unenviable one; a destroyer cum fly-buzzed carcass. I belonged with the loathsome and the dead, the we who traveled in tandem.

My last full day in Vietnam began with the trimming off of my IV and the strapping of my body, well tucked under fresh sheets and two heavy cotton blankets, onto a stretch-

69

er. I had been under a single sheet in seventy degrees, and now I was going into ninety-five degrees with blankets.

"Why?"

"Because you'll need them in Japan," answered a medic. "It is the middle of November, you know."

I frowned at the logistics, stocking blankets in Nam so hospitals in Japan could use them.

"How about if you just keep them folded up until I need them? Is that all right?" I had to do something about this little problem too. Talking to someone who had left, asking questions of nobody.

There were no good-byes when they rolled me out and down to the van . . . to bake. Of the many people who had worked on me and provided care, I had met no one, Doris Schaffer the sole exception. She had been kind and given me a Coke.

The two personnel who slammed the oven door, deferred by languid conversation, relaxed. After a while they went on leisurely to see if it was okay to head for Tan Sen Nhut Air Base.

Typical rear echelon bastards, I thought. I threw off the blankets as best I could, struggling like a wounded worm. Five minutes, and the oven became a furnace. *If they don't come back in the next five,* I told myself, *I'm gonna have to get out of this truck. Crawl out or die.*

I wiped at the sweat streaming from my face. The five minutes elapsed. I contemplated the action, the crawl. It would take all my energy just to move off the stretcher, and I'd have to reverse myself to open the doors. Could I manage it with my feet? I gimped up, edging myself off, plumbing for the floor. My foot swung in the air, higher than I had figured. Teetering then with the will of one whose life is at stake, I slid down. Down. Pain burst like flames, upward as wounds pulled against their steel sutures. I sank into my crematorium.

"Hey, what are you doing?" The front door opened, then the rear.

"Fuck you, you fucking scumbags."

Inaudible reviling passed as whispers. The three of us helped my broken form back where it belonged. They went to the front, still taking their time, listless in closing the doors, uneager to scrap with the Saigon traffic. They were silent through the first maneuverings and stops, but rolling free on the main thoroughfare, they began their complaints to each other. It seemed unnecessary. They would have traded that same shit too many times before. The gripes were for me—they had to assure me that they had it tough too. Their words slapped me around on my pillow. Held down to listen, I did not learn that the horrors of war had leaked into their lives because of daily communion with the dead and handling the ghoulish near dead. No. It was their NCOs, the Vietnamese, where they had to live, the hospital, Saigon. Grim Reaper that the war was, it was mere embellishment to the interruption of something important that they might otherwise have been doing, that cumulative pain-in-the-ass common of the "Big Green Weenie."

My unloading at the air base twinned relief with more open-ended apprehension. I greeted each new event with hope, yet instinctively sharpened my wary edges for the next trial. Someone retrieved the large manila envelope of X rays and medical reports, my bill of lading. This inert collection of anatomical malfunctions had been delivered, first and second echelon repair exhausted. I hoped that soon someone would sit down with those schematics for one hard think.

The gurney rolled again, stopping, starting for unassessable reasons. Turns, bumps, ramps. Inside we . . . I glided silently along, then jerked this way and that at various intervals. No funhouse frolics here, only power failure. No spiderwebs hanging, no shrieks and moans, no ghosts or skeletons, no 3-D nightmares . . . no nothing. I was cached in a room.

From my position against the left-hand wall I surveyed the empty space to my right. Cool and noiseless; no sounds from the corridor. I guessed ten feet to a wall, another ten to the end. It felt windowless, solid. A faint low hum could be heard, a distant vibration like a refrigerator, somewhere. Was I alone!? I had discerned other patients. They'd arrived about the same time as myself, under separate cover. Was some comatose comrade lying on the far side? His moldering remains? I gave an almost reptilian performance in sensing him.

"Hey!" I called out. "Anyone in here?"

Sudden and dulled, my voice confirmed my desolation in a room smaller than my first estimate. A tiny canker of fear ulcerated my thinking. Was this the way it would be? Transited, freight forwarded, warehoused, toe-ticketed, left? My mind pronged at the sound of somebody out by the doorway.

"Hey."

"What do you want?" he answered.

I didn't know what to say, that I was scrabbling for human contact angered me.

"What the fuck am I supposed to do now?"

"You're not supposed to do anything, why?"

"Am I going to stay here like this? Here in this room?"

"This one's the same as all the others. You don't have to do nothing but relax, you're only going to be here until tomorrow."

The canker bore in like a smoldering droplet of acid with the three monotonous hours that followed. I daydreamed a half-meditative reality that spliced together outtakes from the war. Images kept blurring into the stygian solitude of my room. I twisted in frustration.

"Are you eating solid food yet?" A female voice came like a sunbeam, and the clench of seclusion fell into pieces.

"No," I said truthfully, but the sound of that word in the direction of her solicitous voice was terrible. "I mean, yes! Come on in here. Right, I'm on a solid liquid diet—still pretty hungry too!'' I stammered, too nervous to form a verbal lasso.

"Are you on a liquid diet for any particular reason?"

"Yeah, I got wounded," I replied drolly.

"You know what I mean." She chuckled. "Do you feel up to eating?"

"How about some broth? Hell, I'll take whatever you have."

"Sure," she said, warming, "coming right up. I'll get you a tray."

She and a medic pulled me up and placed a chair under the mattress so I could sit up. Hungrily I wolfed down the soup and decided to finish off the roast beef, mashed potatoes, peas and milk, then promptly threw it all up. My call for help went unanswered, so I wiped my mouth on a sheet and slumped there for a long time, my abdomen aching from the strain of wretching, not knowing what to do with the puke-flooded tray. When he finally arrived, the medic let me know he was ticked off, as it complicated his collecting trays and required a change of sheets.

I was not disturbed for the next five interminable hours. The removal of stimulation was an old torturer's trick. He did not take away my senses, only cleaned up the place. I could hear, but what was there to hear? I could feel, but what was new to discover about my sheets? Smell? Taste?

The entire world had evaporated to thoughts. Unconnected snips hung for tantalizing moments, to be replaced by involuntary ideas that skittered like small rodents looking for a crack. I struggled through periods of restless tension, unable to concentrate on a scramble of loose visions, with occasional lapses into lucid mental order. In these brief interludes I could order up anything, set up thoughts in a neat concatenation, like slats on a picket fence. I had to keep this up, yet the more of it I did, the less capable of it I became. It wore me down.

In bewildering fatigue the irrelevant scraps of my

existence leapt upon each other. Emotions were mugged again in the fray. Mercilessly, sleep became elusive, no escape from forced thought.

For what they called supper, I got broth. I passed it up, seeking a max load of medication. It would be the preferred way of spending the next twelve hours, and it would require a nurse to bring it. I would take the pills slowly, one at a time.

Day brought voices and small clatter. I greeted it like a lost love, and my attention followed the banter as though it were the eloquence of a great debate.

"What?"

"Yeah."

"Huh?"

"I don't know."

Contentment. The disassociation of emotion and thought had abated. Having done my time in solitary, they were readying me for flight to Japan.

They rolled me into some larger room for breakfast. Nearly overcome with my release, I drank in the preparatory putter of the staff like a deprived junkie with a new stash. Four other wounded guys had spent the night in there and were now almost old friends. I tried to join in their general pissing and moaning by describing my hard time spent in the hole, but an overhearing medic reminded us all about an officer's privilege to have his own room. A period of uncomfortable silence followed.

"What happened to you?" I asked of the bed next to me.

"What the fuck do you think? I got shot," he replied with a blend of nasty disconsolation and jumpiness.

"Where did they get you?" I sympathized.

"What does it matter? My fucking gut! Like it could be anywhere—like I got shot, right!"

His words erupted and startled me. To him the wounding seemed worse than the actual wound. To me there were wounds and then there were wounds.

"It's not that bad though, huh? You sound like you're on top of it."

"What the fuck do you know, asshole officer!?"

"Will you leave him alone," asked one of the others.

I looked toward him, not really sure who he was speaking to, but another one settled it.

"Yeah," he jabbed. "You must be a lieutenant, right? So we don't have to take no shit no more."

"I can dig that, man," Gut Wound agreed.

I resumed poking at my tray and did not speak another word for the rest of the time I was there.

The C-141 taxied, cool. My recent equanimity reconnected bright, clear images with the surging power of the engines as catalyst. I was there again, long sleek wings sweeping off the top of a fuselage fat with paratroopers, like the last time I had been in a Starlifter. I stood poised and confident, stick leader, first in line, first to go out the door, the head of a human centipede which in a moment would spew itself into the sky to magically segment into a cloud of olive mushrooms, floating on the wind.

I was back there, looking at the jumpmaster, the skin of his face rippling grotesquely as he presses his head into the hammer blast of air for a preview of the drop zone. I get to stand in the door, to savor anticipation. I'm spreading my legs an unnoticeable fraction farther apart. I flex the knees and see myself seconds in the future, a drab green speck against a firmament of gray and a land of dun. I am hooked up, checked out, ready to jump and ready for war.

By the time the medevac plane gained cruising altitude, my thoughts of earlier days became obscured. The Republic of Vietnam faded. In place of nostalgic memories returned a more recent preoccupation—brute nothingness.

For the next five hours I would be bound to my stretcher, too restless to sleep. There would be five hours of listening only to the continuous high-pitched whine of jet engines, and staring into nothing. When a nurse came around to ask how I was keeping, I grasped my option for survival.

"Not too good," I called out affectedly above the noise, grimacing. "It's . . . getting . . . pretty bad!"

"Okay, I'll get you something," she yelled sympathetically.

Beautiful, it worked; that something would be a shot. Nothing else about this trip was to change for the better . . . but soon it wouldn't matter.

Shortly after the nurse had fixed me up, I lay drifting in the warm waves of Demerol; but aware of something—my blankets being moved off on one side. Unconcerned, I floated farther downstream, suddenly remembering that my bag, a cloth sack with some of my personal belongings in it, had been tucked under the blankets with me.

"Hey! What are you doing?" I shouted suspiciously, moving my left arm to search for it.

"Just straightening out your bed," came a guy's expressionless voice. "Go back to sleep."

Bastard, I thought, trying to take my stuff! Pulling the bag between my legs, I warily checked inside with my hand. Good, it was all still there: wallet, pocket transistor, wristwatch . . . the rest was unimportant. I resumed my peaceful somnolence, my possessions clamped safely between my knees.

After landing at Tachakowa Air Force Base in Japan, I was taken aboard a Huey for a thirty-minute hop to the hospital. As I was wheeled into a building, I tested my latest drone for conversation.

"Where am I?"

"Camp Zama," he mumbled stopping the gurney in what seemed to be a corridor.

"Never heard of the place . . . Anything here besides a hospital?" I asked inquisitively; fruitlessly, as he had already gone back outside.

It was a long hallway, me at one end. Far down at the other I could hear people talking. Large double doors clattered with each departure. All became quiet, a strange reception for what I assumed to be a large hospital.

Telling myself things have *got* to get better, I waited with flagging optimism. I've finished the roughest part, I told myself.

The late afternoon sun warmed me through the doorway windows. Basking for a while, I relaxed, but as it sank away, my mood turned cold, as did the hallway. Time whiled itself God only knows where. Nothing to do, not even cracks in the wall to study. Twisting to my side, I tried to sit up, but benefits weren't worth the price in discomfort. I had a transistor in my ditty bag, but it had been without batteries since leaving Can Giouc. I explored in my ditty bag for some way to amuse myself, my dog tags, a razor, two Purple Hearts . . .

Time dilated and decelerated. As it lagged, a depressive noose began a slow constricting labor on my senses. By breathing deeply with concentration, the squeezing of my senses eased for a time, then started constricting anew. Buried alive with only a few hours of air.

"Hey, somebody!"

My voice bat-winged down the corridor. Trapped and panicky, it fluttered away into the bowels of the hospital. I needed help, but the thought of bellowing again from the basement or wherever I had been put sobered me. I could earn an additional diagnosis and worsen my situation. Although, hell, even a "hummm" or an "ah-huh" from a psychiatrist specializing in id drainage would be better than this. I fumed with peevishness that broke out like physiological rebellion. Sounds. I did hear sounds. Of course I wasn't alone. But why did they just leave me?

I thought again of another unblunted cry, but yelling for no one?

"Ain't much you can do for a guy that bad off."

"Shit man, how do you take care of somebody that just yells at nothing?"

"You can't do nothing for him."

With my good hand I massaged my face. My trust in

people was prostrate. I could not comprehend their conception of me. Did whoever leave me think that I was relaxing, taking a comfortable snooze? My attention shot to the scuffle of someone ambling past.

"Hey you!" I roared. He gave up a tremulous sound in surprise. "Look, pal," I said in the most convincing manner I could summon. "I need help. I want you to get the first nurse you see."

I spoke dryly, with the practiced drama of a steely command. He rushed off and returned with two other dudes, probably the first two he ran into. They attempted a few hesitant half questions.

"Who are you people?" I inquired. They told me and reported that they worked in personnel and were only on their way back to their billets.

"I'm Major Maguire," I said. "I've just gotten in from Vietnam. I'm bleeding internally. It's also coming out of my gut and soaking under me. Get a doctor here or I'll mark your names on the wall in blood before I die and they'll charge you with murder." I figured a little hyperbole would goose them into action.

All three went off, although one hung back for a moment, unsure of what to do. The building fell again into somber pitch. Occasional rattles from double doors far in the distance kept raising my hopes of someone's arrival, but the faint clatter remained personless. I would not let this go on, I'd decided. I would not lie there, a passive medical shipment. Could I try to get up on my own? Maybe if I leaned across the gurney I could get to those doors. The thought of the incident in the van frustrated me.

The sound of another approach echoed. What would I say now to the dudes? I would have to reenact the crucifixion at this point. Expecting some frail excuses, I braced my arm under me and pushed up, a human claymore. My jaw muscles bulged with anticipation of the explosion.

"I will be horsefucked up the ass or see you dead

before I spend one more goddamned-son-of-a-bitchin' second here."

"I'm Dr. Nishimura," came a scant voice. "You sound angry." Without an accent, he spoke tolerantly, as if all his patients were deranged.

Geezus Kerist. "Do you know how long...how motherfucking long I've been rotting in this hallway?"

"No, I'm on call, Major, and came in as soon as I got word—about half an hour ago."

"It's Lieutenant."

He was already shining his small light in my eye and probing my eyelid with his finger.

"Sorry, Doc, but I got here around four or five this afternoon. It must be past midnight!"

"It's not quite eleven. Do you see light?"

"It's still six friggin' hours," I snapped, not wanting to leave a subject that I determined had to be dealt with.

"Do you see light?" he repeated. That identical question asked by Dr. Burgess in Saigon, that trick question.

"Should I?"

"Well, yes, you should."

That same answer cornered me just as it had the first time.

Sure I should see, anybody with at least one eye should. "What I meant was, it's probably understandable that I don't because of all that blood in there, right? My old doctor said it would take up to six months to clear. Feels like it hasn't been hurt at all."

"When we get you up to your room, we can elevate your head and the blood will clear sooner, a week perhaps."

I wanted to pursue the conversation, to render out just one word, of something I could interpret optimistically. But a week seems too short, I thought. For someone with an eye as bad as mine, one that doesn't see any light at all, six months seemed a reasonable amount of time to wait for its return. The connection between blood and sight was beginning to seem less than salutary. My desire to hear the truth stood spindle-legged next to the glomping fear of bad news. That "Yes you should" had struck like a snakebite. Its initial sting, annoying but tolerable, was followed by a slow, rapacious numbing of the neurotoxin, dead but still alive. I berated myself for not asking the one hard question.

Morning dripped consciousness. Shadowy homunculi kicked at the emotional and dozing perplexities of the night before. Escape. Tunnel out of my useless carrion and invade someone; an old idea, but how practical—take on a host, some unsuspecting slack-jawed dope. Hell, I could turn the dude into a smooth machine. I was smarter now, could have cosmetic surgery.

I had a roommate. He turned on the TV. My attention squinted for understanding. A man, a woman talked. The audience laughed slightly. She sang. They both sang. A Japanese Mike Douglas. Perseverating talk followed. My partner must have been as desperate for stimulation as myself. Talk continued at length. Clipped Oriental syllables thrummed along in a new gauntlet of redundancy.

"You get anything out of that?"

"Yeah."

"They're doing something interesting, huh?"

"I understand Japanese."

"You do?"

He grunted something and continued sitting quietly.

"Kind of unusual to speak Japanese, isn't it?"

"No."

I waited a long time for a finish—some illumination.

"I still think it's unusual. I mean how many Americans—"

"I've been here twenty-four years."

"Man, you mean...you've been here since MacArthur arrived...What have you been doing?"

"Worked the NCO clubs."

"And they never sent you anywhere else."

This made no sense at all, but his flat laconic manner had me fended off.

"I haven't had much company lately," I said. "What are you in here for?"

"Gall bladder."

"Did you have an operation?"

He got up, switched off the set, and shuffled around the end of his bed.

"I said, did you have an operation?"

"Yeah," he replied, and went out of the room.

I wondered about whether I'd interrupted his favorite show, and wondered about my bad luck. Several twitches of nerves tugged at my limbs. I paced back and forth inside myself. *I am going to do something about this shit.*

In my restlessness, I'd discovered the call button. I pulled it from its clip and mashed it with the surety of one pressing a detonator. He strode straight through the doorway and wheeled in on my bed to rap me on my shoulder.

"Breakfast, right?" he barked in a gravelly black accent. "Five minutes."

"Who are you?"

"Sergeant First Class White, ward master." He took my left hand with his left and pumped it. "What can I do for you?"

I was disarmed, about to rip him open with a full magazine of invective. "Sarge," I said calmly, "I need some help. I'd like you to get the head nurse on duty. I want to talk to you both."

In a few moments I addressed them both. "Things have been tough for the last two days, a lot tougher than they need to be, and I'm not talking about my wounds. I'm talking about my treatment. For two days I've been left, abandoned. I have a doctor who appeared to have minored in the eyeball. There is no way I'm going to put up with it anymore."

"We're going to take care of you," the nurse said stolidly.

"Right, and you can start by moving my roommate." I motioned with a tip of the head toward his bed. "Get some wounded guy in here, damn it. You must have one, and I don't care how fucked up he is, as long as he can talk." White gave a sturdy squeeze to my upper arm. "The captain 'n' me'll square you away."

For the man in solitary confinement, mealtime must come like a rapture, nourishment subordinate to activity. Even for a little socializing. "Hey, Turnkey. I was just thinking."

Food. The act of eating challenged. My right arm strapped to a board had gotten a new IV; that fool of a left was now in charge. It was all an energizing diversion.

White mustered twins to help, the Barrios brothers. They were eager to just spoon it into me. In waving them off, I suffered, attention cashiered.

Fork-speared slabs of meat went into the mouth whole. Peas skittered in bank-shot evacuation of my tray. Child-like spooning of mixed everything gave way to the hand. No need to tell me what it is, or where. Even obdurate morsels slathered in hospital grease failed to evade the predatory hand. I preferred the feral to the helpless.

After breakfast Sergeant White and the twins wheeled the ol' sarge's bed down the hall, replacing it with one containing a nineteen-year-old spec four from the 173rd. He had caught a blast from behind, and something imping-ing on his sciatic nerve left acute pain. I learned of a third bed in the room when they brought in another spec four from the 25th Division. Although a grunt, he hadn't been wounded, but had contracted some alien liver fluke in the jungle. Well enough, his being ambulatory would be an advantage for me and the kid.

"Baldwin," I called to him. "Do me a favor, will you? How about trucking on down to the PX and get me one of those nine-volt batteries for my radio?" I reached behind my head for my sack, pulling out first the pocket radio, then my wallet.

"Shit! Fuckin' damn!"

"What's the matter?"

I opened the empty wallet and tipped it toward him. "Eighty-one fuckin' bucks."

"You think some dude clipped it?"

"No, not here, there hasn't been any opportunity for it. It happened on the plane from Nam. Bastard waited until I was fuzzed on dope."

"You mean, like a medic?"

I nodded and whacked the folded leather against the sheets that covered my thigh. "Tell White to get the duty officer," I said hotly.

Shortly, the officer arrived and introduced himself as a doctor. He sat down next to my bed and I began to detail the incident of how they'd traded my military script only minutes before boarding the plane, of how the medic had gone for it and of how there were no other possibilities.

"I don't know what I can do for you from here. The air base is a good forty miles away; besides, the plane would have probably gone back to Vietnam by now."

"Yeah, sure. For another haul!" I bristled. "And the more blown away they are, the more the bastard can rake in."

"I'm not familiar with these kinds of matters. I'm only responsible for what goes on in the hospital."

"Kerist, I know I probably can't get my money back, but it's the principle of the thing. It's not a case of somebody pilfering footlockers in the barracks. He's robbing the wounded."

"I understand the way you feel, but I—"

"Look, anyone could sort this thing out. You get the manifests, find out which plane, which crew. From what I could sense, there were only a couple of male medic types. Drag their asses up here. I'll bet I could identify the shitbird's voice."

"I'm not a CID agent."

"That's no reason we can't still get on this thing."

"Are you sure it isn't possible that you could have mislaid it along the way?"

"I told you the whole story! I caught the dude in the

act. After that I tied it with a special knot. It's been that way till now."

"Well, perhaps you lost it before then. It is possible, you know."

I started at his words. The line of inquiry had disappeared down a hole. From here he would ask, *Are you sure you didn't drop it here around your bed.*

Oh yeah, Doc, I forgot. I must have . . . while I was thumbing through it. I guess we can all forget now and again, huh, Doc?

Sure, you need to be more careful now that you can't see.

I promise.

"I'll put this in my report. Something may come of it. The C.O. will get a copy. I can't do more, I'm sorry."

"Right, Doc," I said sarcastically. "Put down that I was dead on my ass drunk last night and I don't know what happened to it." I grimaced at the doctor's departure at the newest prospect—easy pickings for the world's scum. What was some fabulous tale against the quite understandable foibles of blind inattention?

I turned in the direction of Baldwin. "I know what the fuck I'm doing," I said stridently.

He remained quiet.

CHAPTER SIX

I rotated the large Tupperware sphere and inserted a plastic star into its interior through a star-shaped hole. An oval, a half-moon, were hurriedly pressed inside. Petulantly I fed the rhomboidal straggler into the ball. Done.

Why was I cooperating with this?

"Ah! Very good," she said. "Forty-seven seconds. Excellent kinesthetic memory. In just three tries you've nearly cut your time in half. Shall we go again?" That voice: a tentative bird's, but her words stalwart and matriarchal. I dumped out all the pieces and corralled them tightly with my forearms. Part of me said, Let's really burn this time. But because her quirky professionalism hinted of a future of blasting from the blocks to shave hundredths from a second, the other side of me quietly noted that if I could come in at somewhere around the minute mark, she'd figure me maxed-out and quit.

"Do you have one of those wooden peg benches, the ones that you whap down with a mallet then turn them over again?"

"No, I'm afraid we don't have one of those." She took sarcasms like mosquito bites on the hull of a tank.

"You could time me."

Occupational Therapy. My second day and doing fine. I had asked for it, to occupy my time. I had gotten Major Mot, an impassive stub of a quasi-Oriental who looked at O.T. like I looked at the infantry. She'd been up this hill before with the brain-damaged, neuromangled, amps, the blind . . . She'd occupied them all. My condition was new to me, and some exploration of it did stimulate my curiosity. Then I realized that even a slightly motivated patient gave her an intoxicating rush. For a session of treatment I became her egg, and like a great flightless moa, she'd squat on me. I would become her fledgling, cared for like her very own species.

"Christmas'll be here next month, Major Mot. My parents will be surprised when I tell them what kind of stuff I want this year."

"Oh? Do you have something in mind?"

"Sure, Major Mot, get out the toy catalog."

"Tomorrow, we'll relearn how to tie our shoes."

"Right. We gonna strap laces around these slippers or what?" I raised my half-bent legs and displayed the canvas footwear like a supine toad. I wiggled my feet.

"There are some techniques that are quite useful."

"I've only got one pair of civilian shoes. They're boots with zippers up the sides. I'm not the wing-tip type."

"See, you're avoiding the issue. You must face it and not buy zippers."

"Look, I bought them last year. You don't need techniques to tie your shoes anyway. You just tie them. I never needed to see to do that."

"Things are not the same now. It'll take time for you to see this. We'll see what happens tomorrow."

"Why don't you get me an M-16 to tear down? God damn it. I'll do a trigger housing faster than anybody in this hospital."

"We don't have any M-16's in this hospital. We try to stay with items of daily living, like shoes."

We were at it again, me and ol' Motha Mot. Not arguing, just tediously wearing me down. When I gave up altogether, I'd be ready to hatch. In a few moments, though, none of her exercises would matter. My coopera-

tion would earn me an early release into the custody of
Lieutenant Sheila Waldman. Waldman all to myself. At
any moment now my favorite nurse would show up at the
door. Comic relief in some character. Uptown black, street
hip, Puerto Rican mama, downtown Jewish grandmama,
anything. I guessed her purpose, to get me laughing hard
enough to piss down my leg.

The wheelchair jerked from behind and spun away
from the table. "I'll take you back and save them the
trouble of coming for you."

"No, no, it's all right, Major Mot, she . . . they like to
come up for me." I scrabbled for an excuse to retrieve the
only real compensation at all for this therapy.

"We can take a shortcut outside," she trilled.

"It's too cold!" I fretted. This would eliminate even
the chance of running into Waldman. I dramatized my case
by cowling up the collar of my bathrobe, clamping the
lapels across my chest. Feigning a shiver, I jabbed both
hands under my armpits. Even so, we hurdled over the
cracks and ruts of an old sidewalk. The day would not
reach its zenith.

Heedless of my head-down pout, Mot commented on
the weather being actually quite warm. I scrutinized by
smell a sense of unseasonableness, yet found it difficult to
assess an unknown latitude of an unfamiliar land. Crisp
leaves. The sun. My first time out since my arrival . . . rem-
iniscent of late October in Connecticut. The sun. It came
down on me, on my face, in throbbing ripples. I closed my
eyes and relaxed in the jostling chair, then on impulse I
looked up to the source of the heat. There, high in the sky,
slightly to the right, it vibrated the nerves of my cheeks,
undulated on my forehead. Quickly I blinked open my
eyes. Nothing either way; not dark, not light. So strong
was my feeling for it, for its warming, its brightness, by
experience, by expectation—that I couldn't be sure of
either. I remembered, don't look at the sun. I turned away,
the preservation of sight in this twilight between having
seen and not seeing.

I glanced back a couple of times, trying to discern some difference between its brightness to the vacant left and the remaining right eye. A penumbra of vague sensation ringed the eye; an eclipse of dark blood.

I needed to think about something less perplexing, like a silk-screened vision of a Japanese pagoda resting on a distant knoll with delicate enchanted trees surrounding us in the quiet. Japan. A woman in a kimono lingers tentatively on the arch of a dwarf footbridge. She entices with the wisp of a parasol.

"What's it like around here, Major Mot?"

Major Mot as guide described the concrete parking lot and rear freight entrance to the hospital. As we cornered to reenter the hospital buildings, I sensed the presence of something large and close. Reaching out curiously, I touched, then gave it a knuckle rap. "Dipsy-Dumpster."

"Excellent!" she exclaimed. "You must do that more often and develop good sensory integration. You don't want to begin self-stimulatory behaviors."

"Say who?" I half turned toward her.

"Oh, ticks like rubbing your body."

I'd get Waldman to do that for me. I wished.

"Or rocking to and fro."

"Okay, okay. I got it." Keep it up and it would be Mot who would have me pissing my pants. Incontinence as a warm, mellow, tactile thing.

Back inside, we detoured through the ob-gyn clinic. A dozen pregnant women cross-talked to a dozen more. Mot slowly maneuvered through the chain of legs and handbags. Female conversations died away, the dampening making me feel exposed. What were they thinking? Were they putting their husbands in my place? They didn't need to, with their husbands stationed here. As a toddler asked, "What wrong with dat man, Mommy?" I flushed and pretended to look them over.

My ward lay in wait as if holding its breath for my return. A stack of charts dropped with a clap in the nurses station like an anticipatory signal. My ward had a curious airy feel to it, like it was an enormous room. It might have been a gym, I thought, and they've just rolled in beds and arranged lots of partitions to fool blind guys into thinking they're actually in rooms. Sometimes I heard sounds from other rooms that, like audible darts, seemed to sail overhead. I'd asked about my theory and been told, "Wrong." The sensation remained.

As usual my bay was deserted. I'd been moved, to this all-officer ward, the week before. At that juncture Baldwin had gone home to Maine and "The Kid" had cried so much at night they'd given him his own room. I'd been encouraged at the prospect of moving down here but had been lonely ever since. There were other patients, all right, but I was the only combat casualty, the only infantryman.

The bay accommodated twelve beds, which were filled by a heart attack suspect, an engineer with fainting spells of unknown origin, a warrant officer and light colonel—both M.P.s, one clearing for retirement, the other with diabetes. Nearest my bed was a major with a cyst on his rear end and a dentist who had twisted his ankle in a rut outside his dental clinic. Another dude had a kink in his neck from trying to header a volleyball spike. Others were so taciturn in their occasional drifting in or out, I knew nothing of them.

Convalescents to a man. Each morning my spring-loaded tourists wound up and aimed for town. Crinkling with presents, they ambled in late, having closed all the bars between the hospital and Yokohama. All had come from Nam, but, in spite of many apparently cured conditions, none would not be rotated back, not even if it meant no more than a change of dental clinics. Incandescent jealousy sluiced through me, not because they were going home, but because of their freedom. An estranged witness, I heeded their dressing and going out, their coming in and going to bed and their blithe unmindfulness of it all. I clenched teeth when I learned my lame dentist had sauntered up Mount Fuji on one of his photo jaunts. The next morning, in his role as patient, he moaned more convincingly than one of my men whose foot had been ripped off by a mine.

A new roommate, a chopper pilot who'd glided his stalled bird down, down into the ground, became reliably present with his two broken ankles. But with his jaw wired shut, he was a vexing conversationalist. For words his tongue frolicked in its cage, lathered with bubbling spit, and most of the time he just read or napped. As randomly as they came to me, I'd shoot across all the jokes I could remember. In an experimental mood, I slid out of bed and into my wheelchair, which was still where Mot had left it. Rolling across toward the other beds, I probed with my left leg. I bumped his bed and gave it a shove.

"Hey, Hicks. I can eat boo-coo pussy and you can't."

He gave up a muzzled taunt. "Kitty litter is as close as you'll get to that."

"Waldman's first on my list."

Another snuffling retort grunted at me.

"Right there in my rack, Hicks," I boasted. "And to show you what a straight-up pal I am, I won't even draw my curtains."

"You know we can hear everything that you say over the intercom down in the nurses' station."

Waldman at the doorway, her comic Brooklynese saying that it was okay but her presence telling me to knock it off. There might be other nurses in the office listening to my open-ended musing with Sheila as my star. That would be decidedly not okay. She could trade bluish remarks comfortably two to your one, the way she wore her body, like an old flannel shirt, and without apology. That she'd been dealt four queens was described in bawdy detail on the ward. Half the comments were made for her benefit, and she accepted them as chunk change for the lust she generated as naturally as the bobbing of her insouciant breasts.

"Sheila, I *need* your help."

"Not in front of Hicks," she quipped.

"It's with O.T." I swung the wheelchair and began to toe back across, about as effectively as a one-legged turtle.

"You mean sweet Mama MoJo?"

"She's got plans for me, perverted plans."

"Well, you do seem a bit preoccupied with sex. Inscrutable kinkies from Big Mama Mo, huh? I'd go with it."

"Starting tomorrow, she's going to have me making things with my hands. Crafts like little wool hats or potholders."

"Knowing you, that would be a problem."

"Sure, unless she lets me make some cold weather lingerie for you out of goat hair so you'll remember me every time you move. Waldman, you've got to help me get out of that place. There must be something else for me around here."

"You are scheduled for physical therapy tomorrow afternoon, and seeing as you don't even get up until noon—"

"Seconal sunrise."

"We could phase out O.T."

"What am I going to do in P.T. all afternoon? I can hardly move."

"That's the whole idea. You need to begin walking, and you've got a ways to go. When you make some progress, I'll walk you around the hospital for exercise. Mot will never find us."

Through a tiny spot in front of me, I could see paradise. A trembling tachycardia began to take hold.

The vinyl table felt cold. I lay on my back as Carol mauled my body like a massage given in spite. I winced at a few tender spots.

"I'm checking your general condition," she said. I waited for assessment, but instead she laconically hoisted my bad right leg. Keeping it straight, she pushed the foot several times as if testing my hip joint. Then placing one hand behind the knee and another on my ankle, she jacked the foot down like the end of a pump handle. I spasmed in body lock. She pumped again, harder, farther down. My head jolted back and off the table. My mouth stretched wide, gurgling, but her action worked my chest like a bellows delivering an operatic blast that searched the rafters for high octaves. Taking a breath, I wheezed, raucously. Sweat broke from every pore, eyes watered and nose began to run. The busy clinic became silent, everyone numbed by my caterwauling.

"You've broken my leg," I whimpered. The surprise of this incomprehensible act cut as sharply as the pain. She had seemed so kind, a friend of Sheila's even, but put a man in her mitts, and dark shadows in her life found professional expression.

"Are you here to work, or put on some kind of show?"

"Go to hell! That's my leg you just fuckin' ruined."

She took a frustrated breath but spoke calmly. "Your leg is fine. We have to do this, stretch it, otherwise it will fuse and stay this way for good. It's hypertonic. I've barely gotten thirty degrees out of it. I know it hurts now, but with a few more motions it'll be a lot less painful."

"But it's not healed yet. The wire was only taken out two days ago."

"Trust me, Steve. It'll be all right."

I imagined her levering it downward, with the four surgical points that held my knee together giving way; tendon, ligament, and cartilage raggedly exposed. "Sure. Go ahead."

With her prudence and my discomfort, she got nearly ninety degrees.

"Now, push against my hand, palm to palm. Come on, push!"

"I am." My hand sank under hers. "Let's try it again." Her efforts were like trying to propel a dead snake by pushing its tail. A nervous laugh slipped from my insides where a hostile riot fulminated. No girl's stronger than me, except maybe some androgenous Russian shot-putter, I thought. Being bare to the waist, I touched arms, shoulders. Damn, I'd lost a lot. My whole body had atrophied. Shrunk . . . and so much gone so fast.

That evening I soaked in my first bath since being wounded. Closer assessment was equally grim. *Who is this guy? He's all bone against skin.* Everywhere I felt, bones protruded. I clunked in the hard porcelain tub, padded only by water. *Is this me? The same soldier that left the States an iron-hard 168 pounds? You couldn't render a single teaspoon of lard off my butt.*

Hardly dry, I called for a medic to help weigh me.

"A hundred thirty-one pounds!? I haven't seen this weight since . . . I don't know." Back in adolescence. Then I'd wanted to be bigger, a man. Now the feeling was worse. I wanted to be a man again.

"Damn, scrawny as a blind chicken!" I railed at the bemused medic. "I've got to do something fast."

After a restless night, I hit the physical therapy clinic, consumed. I worked every exercise known, every muscle. Repetition after repetition. Set after set.

Carol supervised from a distance, but finally interrupted. "I know you're no stranger to this sort of thing, and I rarely see such motivation, but you're overdoing it."

"If it doesn't hurt, it's not doing you any good."

"You're going to be so dead that you won't be able to come back for a week."

"Shoot, I was sweating over cast iron in a weight room when you were standing on the corner waiting for a school bus."

"I'll bet I'm eight or nine years older than you."

"Like I said."

I rolled the dumbbells off the ends of my fingers, forearms and biceps burning with fatigue. Another shot at the wall pulleys suddenly did seem less attractive.

"You want to kick the chair and walk back with me?"

I nodded. Sheila helped me up, then tucked my arm in hers. A cluster of emotions spurted at the inevitability of walking again, but they were only a small part. Sheila caused the rest.

Under my own power, certain new phenomena intensified. Phantom objects and fuzzy structures loomed and seemed to mentally block my way. I flinched to avoid knocking my head into some low overhanging thing that wasn't even there. A surcharge of adrenaline intensified the wobble in my unsupportive legs. Sheila's arm poured an emollient heat into me. It neared overload. Even the momentary touch of a bra strap, with contractured hand, almost caused sexual apoplexy.

I hesitated and ducked. Sheila joked and sighted it as evidence that I needed Major Mot. I laughed. I wanted to walk down the corridor like it was merely a stroll in the dark, a night uncluttered with interior apparitions. But were these things actually so unreal? I asked myself, Might they be distorted perceptions of barely firing nerve impulses? Although these flickering feints were not new, the intensity of their sensations was.

Ever since the blast, I'd been seeing ghostlike wisps and glints in the darkness, phantom objects. It was as if lost little lumens were struggling through the opaque clog of blood in the back of my eye. Glimmering, they trailed off elusively, into the murky creatures at the bottom of the sea, way down at the deepest places; threadlike things that in perpetual darkness created their own light.

In recent days my mind seemed overactive as that convoluted organ, my brain, tried to make a hole in my skull to look out. For so many years the shades had gone up each morning, the lids opening to the day. Now, caught in something of a cranial geode, it hit the light switch again and again. Frantic. Sheila offered more walks in a variety of environs as therapy. She wanted to do it with me when she was off duty.

On one of our walks we were joined by Carol, the physical therapist, as I shuffled along in a huge corduroy bathrobe. I fought a war, a battle between urbane officer and dottering patient fool. We shunted into an enclosure with a queer sepulchral feel to it.

"Where the hell are we?"

"At the altar of the hospital chapel."

"It's empty."

Carol commenced to marry Sheila and me. I laughed at their bizarre interchange.

"We're gathered here in this holy place . . ."

"Yes, this troth of plight."

"To love, honor, and walk into the rising sun these two kamikaze."

"To have a mink stole, from this day forward."

"In sickness . . ."

"And enema on Valentine's Day . . ."

"I promise I'll be gentle, my love."

"If there be any man who objects . . ."

"The enema freak in 4-D."

"Let him forever hold his piece."

"See, he's supposed to hold you now."

"I now pronounce you pan and fife."

"It's supposed to be pan and pan flute."

"I expect that I get to be the satyr."

"Yes, you may now rub her nuptials."

I do, I thought as she kissed me on the cheek. Some psychorampant thing in me cried out, *Flay me alive and give me more pleasure than this*. She was too high, up at the top of a lofty peak that I could never scale, not with grapnels, not with pitons, not with a well-belayed line. She was a prize that would pay off only at the end of an epic quest. Yet there she stood, a tactile fantasy, complete, my bride.

Cast-iron plates on steel bars, rowing machines and inclined boards. Wall pulleys. I punished my body. It improved my thinking, if an obsession with Waldman was the only thought. Endless crippling workouts were a hard breathing mantra, prayer in foot-pounds. Each day I orbited her, this Rappuchini's daughter, a paean to romantic impotence.

We sat over empty coffee cups in the snack bar, a new level of intimacy. I wondered how much she did like me, and measured it by what she gave me over the other men. That weighed in as some hefty thing, but what could I do with it? It had paid for the coffee.

Sheila broke the silence by pulling something out of her purse.

"I got a letter from my fiancé."

Her last word flashing, I grunted acknowledgment.

"I guess I never really mentioned him to you. He's an ensign in the Navy. On a ship off the coast of Vietnam. I'll read it to you."

I gave a quizzical frown of which she paid no mind. She paraphrased several pages of shipboard activities, quoting some descriptions verbatim. I guessed she wanted me to hear his philosophical heart, although some lines reminded me of Key on the deck of the *Minden* watching Baltimore burn. Suddenly she was into the "I love you darlings" and "I can't waits." She did not paraphrase but read each sentimental word.

" 'And I will from more deeper deprivation of you be in acute need of you—easily the most beautiful woman person I've ever come across. Being away is proof positive. Each moment emphasizes my love for you. Only when I hold you in my arms and hold my lips to yours will life seem right again. I love you, darling.' "

I felt forced to watch her lovemaking to a stranger. What the hell is she doing? I wondered. It's obviously a clear message to come no closer. I was bothered; I had not started anything. I never intended to, just strained mightily against wanting to. Hell, I knew my place. As this shambling dude, I knew that I wouldn't compete well against a genteel Naval Academy poge. My condition, the great leveler. But that goddamned message blared. Steve, before you think of it, don't.

"I hope he's safe," she said.

"I'm sure he is." I smiled ruefully, a lament to the passing of U-boats.

How does she handle the usual half-dozen suitors at the club? I wondered. No problem. After a few drinks they'd hotdog it and earn her rebuff . . . If I were here with just a twisted foot . . . you bet your ass I'd take a serious shot at her. Maybe plow right into a stop sign, but at least I would have earned it.

A soft aural mosaic wafted in of her taking me back to my bed—about half the men in the bay present. I sensed their attention as I took off my bathrobe. I motioned to Sheila and the bed. "Go ahead, hop in. I'll be with you in a minute."

Whoops had filled the room. With some eloquent wink she'd gotten in. Oh, how she could disarm.

Why is everything so different now? The answer yawned like a great maw in front of me. Resignedly I leaned forward and fell in.

Things aren't the same, and a lot more things than just not being able to see. I'm the same, it's everyone else who's changed. They don't see me the same. Women don't see me the same!

It was nearly one A.M. The ward was lifeless, sound in remission. The sick would soon return. Lying there, it seemed as though my skin stretched tight. I was turgid with distended emotion. I felt bad enough to cry. It had been years. *Suppose Hicks hears me?* My face warmed at the thought. *Maybe the latrine. I can sit there, door shut, and blow it out from both ends.* I lay there, not a single salty drop welling, but like an ember kicked free from a fire, cooled gradually and went out.

Although cooled, it was temporary, as sleep is, and was reignited by the day, to renewed interrogation. *Why me? Why did this happen to me?* Seeping into a sourful scorn, I questioned, *Of all the officers in Nam, all the infantry officers even, how many have gotten in a mess like this? Both eyes!? The answer has to be, not many. Plenty*

got shot up, blown away, that's part of the job. But this?
Just look at the odds. The numbers had to be way in my
favor.

And what about my career? The whole thing is
hanging. If it wasn't for my eyes, I could be back in Nam
in six months, right on time for my promotion . . . take over
a company. I'd be a real son of a bitch with a second shot
at it. What about all these guys? They're fuckin' golden.
Why not them instead of me? How about Waldman's
"Ensign Courageous"? My mouth was parched, dry from
induced injustice.

A real beaut of a headache began to crown at my
skull, thumbscrewed from the forehead to the back of
the neck. I dropped back and impacted the offender to the
pillow. Eye bulged with an intense stab inflicted to the
cerebrum. Turning back once more to a threadbare memory of those unsuspecting moments before Skinner tripped
the blast . . . something clicked. . . . *God's revenge. How*
else could something like this have happened? It has to be
God getting back at me. That's the way it's done, leveled
from nowhere. But why me? Have I been that bad?

My tombstone—mind scanned the bloody evacua-
tions, a pictorial that gave serious illumination to the past
few months. The dead and mutilated were a sterile matter;
those vicious moments ended so fast and so suddenly. We
acted out a weird funeral by loading a medevac and having
all our memories of their numbered days whisked away so
mercifully in that chopper. The rest of us standing, fewer,
moved on as benediction. Always the same until it was my
turn to be whisked away into someone else's vague memory. But I was actually somewhere, banished like Cain to
the land of Nod, permanently marked, tantalized by Waldman.
Only God could craft such a punishment for a nameless
deed that I could not recall.

In my heart I wondered about some vagrant evil,
park-benched out of notice. I knew myself to be too
indifferent for that kind of baggage. Maybe "the deed"
was my indifference. I hadn't been to a religious service in

a while, but for soldiers in the field that wasn't too unusual. I hadn't prayed in a long time, not even when I was in the bad shit, not even when it squeezed my rectum tight as a fist. How about the others, the skating dudes? About as close to prayer as they ever got was a punctuational "God damn," and as close to a church, a whorehouse.

My memory revealed nothing, not one event or grimy thought that could account for any of this.

A hairline crack emerged, attracting me to it for closer inspection. It was not the only fissure in my life, not the largest, but its peculiarity matched the overlay to my search. I remembered the battalion chaplain, a casual friend collaring me outside the tactical operations center. He was getting together an ecumenical discussion group and wanted some officers there. He had been unable to find any, so I couldn't say no.

Arriving early at the mess hall, I seated myself in the officers' section and soon realized that I had separated myself from the group. Alone, I was curious about who would show. A dozen or more E.M.s clumped in one or two at a time, none of them mine. I leaned back and smoked with a languorous cup of coffee, a portrait of aloof indifference to the topic, "Being Saved." Several guys got up and told of how it had happened to them, of how at some juncture in their recent past they'd accepted Jesus into their life and of how you needed to do the same if you were ever going to be saved. The way they told it, it was the only way.

An Irish Catholic from New England, I lacked rapport with this part of America. The soul of Bible Belt America suddenly made me feel alien and foreign. The one time I had attended Catholic mass in a Vietnamese church, the familiarity of taking communion with a people that believed in a body of theology that had watered my own roots had been comforting.

A well-known loser from Charlie Company rose for the denouement, and I paraphrased his words mentally for amusement.

"You guys know me as one of the great hotdogs of this battalion. But after I reveal to you my secret, you will no doubt look upon me differently. Yes, I have the Lord right here in my pocket. Jesus with me wherever I go. Hallelujah!"

That ponderous jerk's actually a closet backpacker of Christ himself. Now born again—it was true, he definitely needed a second shot! I ended my mental jaunt to "Sardonica" and kept waiting for the right moment. I wanted to leave but I stayed. There wasn't a right moment. Nearby sat a dude I knew who had brought along a baby monkey. I had him pass it over. I was looking for a little entertainment.

Unfortunately, the monkey preferred to remain fetal at my chest. I'd once seen a chimpanzee smoking a cigar, so to liven the monkey up, I gave it a drag off my Lucky. The frightened creature bolted for the railing that separated me from the group. It fell or jumped, and hung itself from its leash with choking squeaks. I made a grab for it but the rope slipped from my hand and the little fella hit the floor with a thump. Leaping again, it pulled the end of the rope across the table and got a dousing of coffee. The scowling owner quickly retrieved his trembling pet, but the incident was a perfect disturbance to close the meeting.

Walking down the sodden road afterward, I mused with detached cynicism over what I'd heard. From the banality of it, I moved in on God in general. I had decided that He was irrelevant for me, and it was that very moment of exclusion that clawed at me as I lay in Zama.

I had forsaken God. The moment became clear. I had felt good, unburdened, unencumbered. I remembered a couple of dudes from Alpha Company had passed. They had saluted; unnecessarily. They'd given me a friendly hello. I'd considered their recognition, their respect. That hairline crack expanded. I was a leader of men, and proud. Someday, I thought, I'll be a general and I'll do it all on my own. Looking over the barbed-wire entanglements near E Company, I'd asked, What has God got to do with all this? With me? With my advancement? Little. I was born fine the first time, and I've saved myself enough times to know how to do it again. I'll do whatever has to be done myself.

I had forsaken God. Me! Sleezeballs would be forgiven for not knowing any better. I did. Without provocation I had gratuitously done it.

Sitting up on the edge of my hospital bed I searched with my toes irritably for the discarded slippers. The nostalgia of that scene of a few months earlier drew from me a desire to experience again that deliberate audacious self-confidence, to stand there again on that same road. I found one slipper, and what I'd exhumed from my conscience gave way to the reality of fragility and dependence.

The feeling grew like worms inside me; spreading and multiplying, they gorged themselves on my fiber, and I fell back and lay like decayed, oozing fruit.

"Look, Father," I directed querulously at the priest who had dutifully answered my request. "What I want to know is about my being punished like this. I think I know why, but I'm not sure."

"What do you mean by punished?" He had at first seemed reluctant to leave the ice-breaking chitchat, but now his focused tone backed me up.

"Well, I thought it was obvious."

"All right, then, punished for what?"

Father de Ligne and I sat facing each other in the hospital chapel's rear; a cube as muffled as a soundproof chamber used to test hearing, carpets and curtains swallowing up everything the ward regurgitated.

Father de Ligne sounded detached. I wondered if he was interested at all. Chrissake, I thought, lounging my posture to take off the pressure. I'll have to ask again. After all, priests are supposed to have the goddamned answers to this kind of question.

"Aren't I being punished for rejecting God? Isn't that why I got screwed up?"

De Ligne's chair squeaked. "I'd like to begin by disagreeing with you."

"How can you? It's so obvious. Here I am, and the rest of them are out there clean, having a blast."

"Not all the rest. You have been seriously injured, but its meaning is entirely your own. God did not punish you like this, other men did. They did it in a war, for whatever reasons it is being fought."

"I left the gooks behind about a month and a half ago. They didn't lay on me the trial I've been going through." Provoked by his even response, I wondered if he wasn't part of the punishment; a package deal with a priest fatigued by too many morose, mangled men, all looking for some way out. "Tell me what I've got to do," I said impatiently.

"Steve, I understand the trauma that you've undergone and are still going through. It's this new vulnerability that has brought you here . . ."

"Yeah, but I want . . . whatever it will take . . . to . . ." I wanted to say to get fixed up, but felt ridiculous at the thought. He was hardly going to orchestrate a miracle. "I don't know, everything is fouled up. I suppose I just want God to do something for me . . . make something happen. Even if it isn't the way things were."

"And what does God want from you?"

"I haven't the foggiest."

"Let's take your reasoning, then. If you are being punished, then He is involved in your life."

"Right, like this?" I grumbled. Deflected from my preoccupation, I regretted coming . . . yet his steady patience placated me.

"You won't know what . . . or how . . . until you ask," he went on. "You can of course refuse and ignore God as in your past, or you could accept and listen."

"Damn. If I have to stay like this, how could it be worthwhile enough to accept?" I shot back, my passion barely contained.

"That's up to you. You're going through an anguishing

time. It can rid your soul of a lot of unimportant matters. Tragedy can allow you to get face to face with God."

"Sure. He blows up mines in front of you to get your attention."

"You know what I mean. You can turn against Him if you wish. I've seen many who have. But then they've got nothing left, no capacity for love, only despair and depression. They tend to become passive and less able to effect change in their lives. They're more blaming, and generate their own objects of blame. But there is an opportunity here. You can choose to trust in what is ultimately good. Right?"

"I guess so. I can't escape, but it's hard to see that I have any choices. I just wish I could trust in anything, but I feel like I've been left behind in some incredibly black jungle where there's no chance at all of getting out. I'm sort of a shadow with bones, no longer of any consequence because I'm not the real thing, only its shadow."

"Trust has to do with trusting yourself. That should come natural for you—although it's been severely shaken. Agreed?"

"I suppose."

"The other part of trusting is, of course, God, being open to His help. You'll never get it any other way. If you're not receptive to possibilities, you'll never see them."

I couldn't respond through the turbulence of things I couldn't put into words. Back lying in bed, things had seemed so clearly worked out. I was frustrated. I sat forward and hunched up on the armrests. I wanted to go.

De Ligne changed the subject. "What about your physical condition, your eyes in particular—any prognosis?"

"I don't know, Father," I said dejectedly. "In a way, that's all part of the jungle. I thought I would be able to see when some blood cleared from my eye. A lot of it has and nothing has changed. I expected that at least by now they could see in better and determine what's the problem. I don't even know that much."

"Yes," he whispered sympathetically. I did not need the prompt to go on, not on this subject.

"My eye doctor has only seen me three times since I arrived, maybe fifteen minutes in all. One time Lieutenant Waldman and I—you know her?"

"I've seen her at mass and a few other times. She's quite a character."

Staccato images interrupted my thoughts. Me and Waldman getting married in the nearby chapel. Then, me, my pajamas suddenly done in by a Navy uniform. The treacherous bitch.

"I'm in love," I said.

"Considering her, I can understand it."

I looked at him with a hesitant smile, a near invitation to career off into a thing on how we both understood what was never to be and of how unrequited desires were and of how painful fantasies could be . . . and of how I could play Waldman brinkmanship with anyone in the hospital. Instead, "Sheila and I went up to see Dr. Nishimura together. She had gotten an appointment because she kept seeing yellow spots. I got into his office with her and made him take a hard look, with more than just his pocket light."

That incident, my sitting in his exam chair, lay like a lone white cue ball in the middle of a billiard table.

"What did he tell you?"

"He said it was a 'bad eye,' said it, I mean like it was *really* damaged. He really wanted me to see his light. I told him sometimes I see weird stuff but I couldn't truthfully say that I saw the light. It all seemed to hang on that one thing."

"Did he say that nothing could be done?"

"Not actually. I think doctors seem to hesitate on that sort of thing. They don't like to tell you that your problem is bigger than they are. It's easier for them to let you lie around, and out of your not getting better let you put two and two together . . . You know, Father, I'm not the kind of guy who comes to pessimism easily."

"I hope not, Steve, it's the antithesis of what I've

been talking about, but you realize the opposite isn't necessarily a generalized optimism. You're going to have to be selective with what you can be optimistic about."

"I'm being shipped back to Walter Reed next week." I nodded in tacit agreement. "Possibly doctors there will have more to offer than Nishimura. I realize, though, I felt that way when I left Nam for here. I thought I would get my sight back here. Even so . . . I'm not as afraid of the uncertainty as I was."

I lit my second cigarette and hovered the burning match over an ashtray. For one introspective moment I considered the black flame, its fast-growing heat at the end of a cardboard stump. I opened my thumb and forefinger and its very existence became nothing.

CHAPTER SEVEN

"My name's Dan Bunnel," gagged a voice, garbled as if something was wadded in his mouth.

"I'm Bob Johnstone," spoke another from near the bathroom door. "Who were you with?"

"Around here, he's known as 'Mad Dog,'" interjected Bunnel.

I smiled, then answered, "Ninth Division."

"Good, this room is for infantry only." Johnstone followed, inquiring of me rather than my unit, "Airborne?"

"Of course. Airborne Ranger."

"Outstanding!" He thumped the board at the end of my bed. "There's a sign on the door outside. Says 'Beware—Rangers!' That makes all three of us in this room now."

Automatically, I leaned forward, putting out my hand to shake with him, but received something in it that stopped my heart. My jaw slacked, mouth gaped. A hand grenade! Its potential realized in stirred memory, the footage spun furiously through the sprockets of my head.

I hefted its weight, on the verge of it dropping from my loose, inert fingers. I could *"see"* it, lever kicking free, and that iron O.D. egg expanding outward slowly into splintered bits, like the last thing I ever saw. The stark, blood-drained expression on my face hit the others. The were liking their unexpected success.

Mad Dog retrieved his frag. "I knew you couldn't see

and wouldn't be expecting it. It's empty. Got a couple of them from a friend up at Meade."

Still stunned by its surprisingly extraordinary effect, I asked to have it back. He obliged and dropped it in my lap. Casually I tossed it from one hand to the other, a rational relationship with the object reestablished. "I love thcsc babies," I affirmed, my feelings of buried nostalgia for its detonating spectacle returning.

"Did one of them get you?" Mad Dog asked quietly.

"Not sure, it was covered over . . . maybe something a little larger—booby trap. One of my point men tripped it. Fucked up three of us. What about you?"

"I was ARVN Airborne. Got a 105-round command-detonated on me," he replied.

"Did you get hurt bad?"

"Yeah, well, I was at first. A lot of shrapnel got me. I've had a lot of plastic surgery on my face. Left knee's bad, but I'll be able to go back to duty in a couple of months."

I turned toward Bunnel.

"I was up in the Michelin Rubber Plantation. Sniper got me in the head, behind the ear. The bullet came out the front and took half my jaw and a dozen teeth with it. Just had my last bone graft."

"Now what?" I asked.

"A lot of heavy dentistry. And God knows how long it'll be before I see duty again. I've been here at Walter Reed over ten months already."

Through my two roommates I was reunited with the rcal Army, its infantry, the war, a break I'd grieved over for weeks. My resentment had heated over transit from Japan to Walter Reed Army Medical Center in Washington, D.C. Alone, again deprived of all stimulation, I'd demanded from myself every reserve I had. That kind of merciless infliction over, I reassured myself, toasting myself mentally for landing back with soldiers, my own environment—I swilled a sentimental gulp from a Styrofoam cup filled with scotch and ice, compliments of Bunnel's night table and water jug.

"Lieutenant Maguire?" inquired a man at the door.

I turned and spun my legs over toward his side of the bed in assent.

"I'm from the hospital's Veteran's Administration Office." An attaché case flicked open and documents rustled across the length of my bed, the man's mouth locked on full automatic. He began enumerating the retirement pensions, medical, educational benefits, and training due me. I sat immobilized, my comprehension stalled back at pension benefits. He paused and flurried through a few quintiplicates, darting over the array rodentlike. He solicited my signature. "Just this," he encouraged fastidiously, "and we'll have everything in order when you're released to us from the Army at the end of your boarding out."

Realigning the paperwork with a few taps on the lid of his case, he repeated his request.

I thought vengefully, You sonavabitch. I'm here for doctors to work on me, and all they can produce is a civilian bureaucrat to fix up a file on me to have me expedite my own discharge. "I'm not signing because I'm not leaving the Army."

He sputtered in astonishment, unprepared for my refusal to sign. He was unable to comprehend that any client of his, savaged by the war, would ever balk at a discharge. None ever had!

"Just print my name across the top there," I appeased, "and hold them for a while."

"It says here you are eligible to go to a Rehabilitation Center," he coaxed, "and the sooner the better."

"Eligible!?" I steamed, "How the fuck did I earn that?"

"The centers are structured to train disabled veterans in various skills. We do have you down as Loss of Sight."

"Like I said, just hang on to those papers. I won't be signing them today."

I rubbed my empty cup coolly, reacting to the one

thing that meant anything to me, the one thing I had left—my status as a wounded soldier.

There was in me a nettlelike hope that my eye examination would be a solid turn around, the onset of treatment. I expected several eminent eye surgeons, at least one a living legend, to bend over me, inspired to formulate opinions and establish procedures for the kind of sophisticated surgery my case would demand.

A ten-minute checkup by an unconversant doctor was what I got.

"Left . . . now right," he instructed. "Up, hmmm, down. Fine. Can you see the light?"

That question again! "Well, I'm not sure." I squinted.

"Is the light on now?" he tested.

"No." But I had heard the click of the switch. He had turned the light off.

"Now?"

"Umm, yes."

"Now?" he asked again.

"I don't think so."

"Now?" he asked, and I heard the snap yet again.

"Yes," I said, but he slid away the apparatus. Had I guessed wrong? Reversed the switching? Anxiously I thought of how I could keep him engaged. I was afraid I'd done it again, induced that yawn in my eye doctor, failed the light test. He scratched a note next to me, the final summary for my file.

They all ask me if I can see, I thought. That means they can't tell. If it looked really bad, they wouldn't bother to ask. It must look good enough to be possible. Everyone says it looks normal. What if I tell him that I can see, barely? Then will he start breaking out the tools?

"I think I can see something, sometimes. I can see your sleeve." I reached out and touched a crisp, starched area of his medical coat. "It's all white, isn't it?" His attention veered from his writing.

"Do you see it now?" he asked. I moved my hand a foot or so to my right and felt it again.

"Now?" he said quickly. I stretched my hand to a certain sensing of its presence but grabbed at nothing.

"I think it works better out the corner of my eye, like peripherally." I turned my head and concentrated on spotting a movement to my side. It was an old target-detection trick. I wondered if by hard effort I could will some thin slit in the darkness, a razor crack of telltale light at the bottom of a faraway door. *Something*.

"Sometimes I see flashes when I go outside, or even when I enter a room that might be well-lighted."

The doctor said nothing but continued to write.

Was I just "seeing" the rustle of his stiff sleeve just that distance from his voice?

"Aren't you going to do anything for me?"

"Of course, we're preparing you for transfer to a V.A. facility. You'll receive a full range of rehabilitation services there."

"You mean, you're not going to do *anything* for my eye? I can't see anything anymore!"

"I don't believe there is anything that can be done."

"Wait a minute. First it was the blood, then it cleared so you can look at what's wrong and try to do something. At least tell me what the problem is."

He said nothing. Had he moved somewhere else in the room?

"The fact that I can't see any light seems to be a bad sign. Am I right?"

"Yes."

I pursed my lips tightly. The heavy chrome ball had rolled clean, straight down without touching a single flipper. The last ball.

Almost from relief from so long a tangle of half inferences, I examined my new medical knowledge—that ophthalmologists treated eyeballs only when they met the first requirement: they have to be seeing at least something. It was simple. Shine the light, ask the question, ship me out.

An entire morning elapsed while I waited for the stunted eye exam. Mad Dog had checked out for Christmas leave. Bunnel was plunging clothes into his suitcase, hurrying to do the same. Lying spiritlessly on my bed, my hands propped behind my head and legs crossed at the ankles, I prepared myself mentally how I'd spend the three days left until my parents came to drive me home to Connecticut. There were no more scheduled appointments. Meals would be brought to my room. Solitary again... crap... at least there was a TV.

"Coming to that Mad Dog party tonight?" Bunnel asked from inside our walk-in closet.

"He hadn't mentioned it to me."

"Just came up this morning," he called, now from the bathroom.

"Anybody else be there is PJs? It's all I've got."

Bunnel came out and stood, silent, as if the news had been somehow unusual.

"Damn," he whispered discerningly, and began rummaging through both his suitcase and the closet. "Don't worry, you're thinner than me but about the same height. Here, sport jacket, pair of trow, shirt... Want a tie? You can get shoes over at the PX... Sergeant Carroll'll take you. My wife's here. She couldn't find a parking space so I've gotta go. We live out in Chevy Chase. I'll get someone to pick you up around eight. Need anything else?"

"More ammo, couple of claymores... and a Det kit."

"Mad Dog's probably got plenty of that stuff."

"Ranger Maguire." The door kicked open as a wheelchair scraped through. "Andy Wilson here. You're not gonna go dressed in that, unless you want one of them student nurses to prepare you for some procedure."

"Be pleasant change from what I've been getting. Anyway, it's only around seven o'clock."

"Quarter till eight, pal," he corrected.

I suppose I did know it was late, half expecting to be

left behind anyway. "Are you going in that wheelchair?" I asked flatly.

"No. I just got out of traction and had my colostomy closed. It's still easier to move around the ward in this. I've got braces for walking."

"Oh, I guess there actually are some people that get work done on them here, then."

"I wouldn't recommend a colostomy," he retorted, ignoring my unfriendly tone. "Get moving."

The door swung shut and I threw a mock salute, arm halting in midair. Why am I being so sour? I asked myself. Another Airborne Ranger promises to rescue me from this hole and . . . damn eye doctor's still pissing me off . . . How the hell will I handle this party?

Wilson was back in a minute and plunked down a couple of cans.

"Where'd you get cold beer?"

"Refrigerator."

"Right."

"It comes through some deal with the pharmacy. Everyone's allowed two cans a day. I'm next door in the orthopedic ward, and most of the patients are old retired guys who don't drink their share. That leaves about as much as you want for those who do. If we run out, we use your ward's."

"Thanks." I held up the can in a studied hesitancy, my first beer since preparing for that last mission.

"Your eyepatch looks fucked up."

My hand jerked up instinctively to this new disguise for my plastic orb.

"Make it come down diagonally, so you don't rope off your eyebrows. I think Moishe Dayan has his all the way under his ear."

I slung the black patch as he suggested, tentatively.

"You got to be shitting me, like this?"

"Yeah, he probably does it to keep it from blowing off in the desert. It's okay to be blind, but you can't go around looking fucked up."

I adjusted the patch and managed a half smile. I liked him.

Mad Dog's place was a few miles away in a downtown Washington high rise. His apartment was packed with noise and music. Wilson noted that the whole of the Officers' Club had come straight there from Happy Hour. As we edged and squeezed our way through the crowd of nurses, doctors, medical staff, and wounded officers, I wondered which person he intended for me to meet in the jabbering swell. Andy became diverted by a girl he knew, and I inched my way around without his assistance, occasionally zoning in on clutches of conversation, deciding that people lip read more than they think they do. Direction didn't seem important, and I sidewayed through voids in the conversations. It was easier than I expected. Rooms seemed not only defined by their walls, but by the fleshy yammering bulk stirring in them. I intuited an azimuth on the kitchen as much by opportunity as by dead reckoning.

"I know you," a female voice closed in. I looked toward her, only half sure that I was the "you."

"You were just at Zama. I'm a nurse there. I used to see you all the time with Sheila Waldman."

I nodded and motioned my glass. "Any scotch in here?"

"There's bunches of stuff in here, I don't know . . . Barton's Reserve, I.W. Harper, J and B . . ."

"That."

"You sure have improved," she said. "In fact, you look great."

I hunched my arms back in the too big shoulders of the sport jacket and noticed the sleeves were slightly too short.

"I never see the patients get better. They just go off and get replaced by new ones coming in from Nam."

"What are you doing here?"

"Escort duty. I get it about every other month."

"I was supposed to have one, but at the last minute she didn't show, and it meant I had to be strapped to a stretcher all the way back. They'd just as soon send me back in a coffin."

"Too bad Sheila didn't get that job. I think she's getting married."

"It'll be bigamy."

"Hey, Ranger," growled Andy. "I've been keeping an eye on you across the room, but you got away from me when I lost you."

"I got me a new escort."

Andy prodded us both out of the kitchen to describe an extensive display of some two hundred Army patches, many of which dated back to World War II. These were flanked by primitive wall-mounted crossbows, made by Montagnard tribesmen and bannered under a four-foot high replica of the 101 Airborne insignia, Mad Dog's unit on his first tour of Nam. Andy deliberated on the older of the Airborne regiments. The Zama nurse listed next to me, a certain breast burrowing into my upper arm. I leaned back to max out the sensation but she suddenly decided she needed to go look for her shoes.

The crowd was thinning, segmenting into medicals and us, our group dominated by Mad Dog. My opinion of him had formed, the most gung-ho soldier I'd ever met, a kind of renegade as an Annapolis grad. We believed him to be its only representative among Airborne Rangers. He had so many things going on in his mind and his life that he seemed impossible to know. He attacked the world in which he lived like it had been ransacked, with him in a pivotal race to put it back in order; this should go here, that there. Everything had its place, and righting things held no essential difficulties.

"What's the situation with your eye?" he barked suddenly, zooming in on me. "Did the doctors have anything for you this morning?"

"No, from what I can tell, things are piss poor."

"You mean they're not going to do anything for

you?'' he said with alarm, as if it were medical inactivity that was keeping me from seeing.

"I'd like to stay at Walter Reed awhile longer. I'll get promoted in a few months, but only if I'm still here. I'd like some of my other problems to be worked on in the meantime, but that's a no go. They won't even discuss the matter. They want me booted into this blind rehabilitation jug-fuck right away.''

"You shouldn't have to get out,'' Andy snapped with the kind of perspicacity that comes with just the right measure of alcohol. "You could teach at Fort Benning. Building Four wouldn't be hard to get around in.''

I could easily see myself in front of a class of a hundred or more, lecturing on ''The Platoon and Company in the Offense,'' but not so easily out in the choked corridors, bumping among the officers and candidates who'd be eyeballing a tangible product of our profession. I anticipated the raw embarrassment of a fellow officer's aversion. How could I live as a constant reminder of what those men needed to forget?

"Sure, Andy, I'd tell 'em, 'I did not heed the words of my instructor and look what happened to me.' '' I raised my voice in the strident tone of an infantry instructor. '' 'While watching things explode close up—' ''

"Convalescent leave,'' Mad Dog interrupted, saying it like it was some code word for what I wanted.

I frowned, expectant of explanation from this military guru who seemed to have more contacts in the Pentagon than the average one-star.

"Sure, you go home for a month, do what you want, then come back long enough to sign out for another month. Petrovitch over there has been doing it for two years. Granted, he's had a few operations and his legs aren't healing fast, but they're not packing him off to the V.A. to do it.''

"In a couple of days my parents are coming down. I'll be getting thirty days for Christmas.''

"That's automatic. You'll have to work on excuses to extend it."

"Thinking up an excuse good enough to cause my eye doctor to reevaluate would be like peace-talking the NVA into giving up." Saying that, I decided that during the next month I'd try.

We stood in the middle of the living room like pilings at neap tide, the empty glasses and potato chips left behind like seaweed, the quiet detritus of a good time. I didn't actually want to go home, away from these particular guys.

The nurse from Zama apprehended my elbow to ask for a ride back to the hospital. That she'd come to me seemed unaccountable, but shortly we sat in the backseat of Andy's "soulboat," '65 Ford knee-to-knee close, trading heat on the subfreezing vinyl. Dormant juices flowed in me and ran like sap in the spring. She was fetchingly drunk, at the point of a mellow wobble. I was glad as her head tipped to my shoulder and the side of my face was half buried in her hair. Waving Andy past her guest house, she insisted on walking me back to my ward. We didn't speak until just inside my room I said thanks. Suddenly she massaged her fingers into my shoulders, my neck. Enclosing her arms with me in them, she kissed forcefully, like we were old lovers who'd been away from each other for a long time, or new lovers who were about to part for a long time. Short and a little on the heavy side, her breasts were so large I was drawn and pushed away at the same time. She held tight for a long time, then kissed me again, an ease-giving kiss. With a soft good-bye tagged on, she left.

"Norma . . . Nora?" My cigarette and whiskey voice husked in confidence with my toilet, "I'd like to meet that pair again."

My dad came back rankled, bristling. "What a jerk. He's got the personality of something that died. He just sat there, he didn't move anything but his mouth."

"Maybe he's just bummed out because he can't do much for me."

"Forget the clown, Steve, we're going to see someone in New York, someone with a reputation for results. I've got it all set up. All the rich people go to him. You pay for what you get. With these Army guys, it's like socialized medicine, they get pay no matter what happens. They're all the same. One time during the war, I went to sick call with an ingrown hair up my nose. This doctor makes me an inpatient; next thing you know, he's got me varnishing hardwood floors inside the closets. From what I can see, things haven't changed much."

My father's approach was not a sign of middle-class indelicacy, but of the kind of appraisal built into a man who's supervised a factory's quality control; my lifetime in lengths of wire and cable. From habit men were categorized like the big reels he's overseen. They were satisfactory or they were unsatisfactory, passed or rejected, shipped or scrapped. Maybe a life with machines could incapacitate discourse . . . men either got the job done or they were clowns.

My fifteen-year-old brother, Gary, loafed on my bed, fiddling with the controls that elevated first the head then the foot. The mattress bucked and contorted as he tested it out. I leaned against the bed appreciating the effect of my civilian clothes, purchased the day before with Andy's help. My brother and I had been alone after our parents had been summoned for a private audience with the doctor to discuss me, the child-man. Gary admitted to relief that I looked better than what my parents had prepared him for.

After the conference, my mother seemed in a half trance, a reaction to be grateful for. I had wearied of blindness as a topic, as an entity. Just now I was weary of the whole subject. I longed to shove it aside and pretend I'd come home from the war unchanged.

"I had a hell of a time trying to get that jerk to tell us what's wrong. I had to ask him four times. Finally he took out a picture of a cut-away eye like you made in school one time. All he pointed out was there's a couple of small pieces of shrapnel behind it. I still don't know what's wrong. I got him livened up, though, when I told him you wanted to stay in the Army.''

''Damn, Dad. He'll chalk me up as brain-damaged. Probably thinks that I want to even if I can't see.''

''No, I said to him *if* your eye got better. He did say yes, and still kept trying to tell us about this board he's putting together to get you out. I don't think he has any intention of doing anything for your eye.''

It wasn't new information, but hearing it again in different words, with the defined clarity of my father, erupted like an allergic inflammation inside me, angry weals that no one could see. My brother, in control of distraction, whirled my bed upward as high as it would go. So high, I was sure a patient would need a running start to get in. The motor strained. Gary reversed it. Then it went so low that a patient could crawl in.

My father clapped his hand to my shoulder. ''There's got to be one doctor in this world who can do *something* for us.''

CHAPTER EIGHT

In one respect my Christmas at home was not unlike any other. The cast was nearly the same: parents, brother, a younger sister who'd added a husband. It was a small family; even its extension was—an aunt, an uncle, one cousin, and a pair of late seventies grandparents. Distance and death had subtracted the few others who were or had been.

They'd come as they would on any Christmas, to say the same things, eat the same food . . . and in a case or two, to open the same gifts. The event's only alteration was me. As if suspended in sparkling Lucite, I was watched, free only to be blind. My sensibilities seemed insulated from their genuine grief. Drink helped, or rather I used it to reduce real emotion and postpone tiring thought. Its analgesic effect coated me like a thin veneer, but sufficient for me to ignore the Lilliputian arrows of overheard chatter. "Eeh love, do you 'ave to feed him?" my immigrant grandmother had asked my mother sorrowfully. I had frowned momentarily from nearby as I tested for just the right amount of vermouth in a martini and considered the pathetic blind men she would have seen in her day.

I tried, feebly and clumsily, to convey that the trauma was not continuous, the fury of the tragedy not sustained; the thing being done, being blinded, distinct from blindness.

119

It was like attempting to communicate with someone on a train traveling rapidly abreast your own in the opposite direction. While windows machine-gun past, they are seen with expressions frozen in a millisecond; but it is only a melting image that is held in the moment. Their recognition of me blinked away that day, and the succession of days pulled after it.

Friends, or rather friends of my parents, checked in like polite intruders to comfort them. Subdued, they too watched the act of what it was like for me to be blind. It was troublesome that many were holding out for the return of my sight, praying for it . . . and saying that my only impediment was time. Trapped by their insistence that miracles do happen, I wondered about disturbing their faith . . . sooner my left eye grow back. I kept away from long odds like that, preferring instead to nurture a sure thing.

A slow auguring of events emptied me of the last nodules of hope. I had gone to the superspecialist in New York, but hadn't seen him. Passage to the "Big Man" had to be approved by another ophthalmologist, but my eye had failed its exam. The "Big Man" was obviously like me, liking the sure thing, operating on only those his protégés could guarantee. I had hoped that he'd built his reputation on going after those eyeballs that all the rest had written off. My father was present, and the doctor, speaking only to him, was tactful and equivocal, except for his tone. When he stated, "That eye has been very severely damaged," he sounded so grave that it was as if a crazed gang on the subway had just single-mindedly gone after the eye with ice picks. The eye might look normal, I thought, but it had to be some kind of an abuse of optimism to pray for it.

Afterward I moped along toward the subway with my family as dejected as a penniless man, a man begotten of hopelessness. I supposed that like me, somewhere in the life of any derelict there would have been a definite point where he'd stopped trying—that point where he realized effort never made any difference. I felt like the unemployable at the employment window. How many more times did I need to sit in an examining chair and say no to *do you see the light?*

In the eye doctor's waiting area, my brother, Gary, had read me the postered walls. In retrospect their urgings to prevent loss of sight, to take care of your eyes, were more revealing. I needed to have captioned them, "God help you if you don't."

In the droning hive of Grand Central Station we came to a standstill to spiritlessly chart our next move. Alongside an emptied train . . . Gary saw it first, there next to me, a G.I. on his way home from Nam.

I reached toward the coffin container that was on a baggage wagon and touched the taunt-lashed Stars and Stripes that covered it. I became agitated by a swarm of unknowns. Where was it going? To his home here in the city? Is this the way they send you back? I imagined him belonging to a pregnant wife, already in enough grief with the news, and now she'll find this on her doorstep.

Isn't anyone in charge of it? I could easily conceive of some antiwar types taking off with it. They'd concoct some weird theater of exquisite desecration "to hasten an end to the war."

I patted the coffin, and the hollow echo reverberated in me as a kind of communion with him. Inches from me I finally had someone who understood. You won't have to live this thing out, pal, I thought in friendship. Look at me, facing fifty years, like this.

Blindness evoked curiosity, not morbid, but paradoxical in that it attracted and repelled at the same time. "What was it like?" they all wondered. Blind, blinded! They introspected, then nervously distanced themselves by talking around me. If the condition wasn't actually pathetic enough, I could help sharpen the image with a little carelessness. Once, in front of a full living room, I left my chair to go to the kitchen. With a casual misjudging of direction, I drove my forehead into the nearest doorjamb.

The embarrassment was stronger than the smarting, but I sensed in the room a concert of defensive pity.

A few bumps and knocks could have been only a quirk of behavior, an aspect of not being able to see properly. But no, I was blind, I had become the condition of blindness. Sure, I was sitting just a few feet away, but as remote as the far reaches of space. One can step outside and point up; there at the end of the finger, ultimately the end of the universe; pointing right at it yet, nothing further exists.

Still, there was the war. "What was it really like?" they had all asked. I answered easily, an armchair encyclopedia of the infantry. Their reaction was unexpected. I defended the war simply, outlining my experiences in it. I had no idea that I was so out of sync with the television's version of my war. I had been preempted and discredited before I opened my mouth. Network journalists and commentators had their own ideas and had already described my reality of fighting enemy soldiers as, at best, a delusion. I thought the communists were the enemy. When I came home the U.S. Army was . . . me?! In combat we'd fought the North Vietnamese Army, a very respectable foe, which now had killed tens of thousands of us. Reporters had been telling my visitors that they had been unarmed rice farmers and their women and children. It made no sense to me at all.

My sometime girlfriend had been the first to attempt reeducation. She was a college student in Boston, and a few months before, I'd written her from Nam, describing some of the details of life in the bush and the war around me. Her reply had been startling, an abrupt departure from her usual welcomed and easygoing letters. I read her attack painfully as she disclosed the "real truth" about what I was doing. I could tell from the details of her own activities that just being on campus seemed like it could put you closer to the truth these days. At that point she was preparing for the upcoming moratorium against the war. As I sat on a paddy dike, her lavender paper with flowers in the margin glaring up at me in the squinting sun, it seemed there on campus the gift of revelation beamed straight into her noggin.

I had been disarmed by her sudden shrill tone and had anxiously sent a peace offering, suggesting that she did have a point or two. In fact she had no idea what the war was about. It perplexed me that she wasn't listening to me, but I hadn't wanted to lose her as a friend. At the end of her letter she'd quoted Wilfred Owen. I quoted Robert Browning in my reply. The argument still pendulumed between us, softened by the genuine sadness she felt for me; yet I scrutinized her for a sense of vindication. If the war could perpetrate such acts on someone close to her, the issue was inarguable. Where had my notions gotten me? Between my feelings about the war and hers on what had happened to me, we saw increasingly less of each other.

Gradually I understood what was going on in their minds. The old arrogant attitudes of Airborne Ranger, Infantry, of "I can do it better," wormed about like overcompensation for my loss, my war, a rationalization for tragic futility; all pathetic caricatures swaggering around in combat helmets and flack vests, surrounded by civilians.

Still, the retelling of particular instances in the war could pour from me self-indulgently as I relived the events, the action in my mind immune to subtlety and discretion. I caught myself disgorging a scene on one occasion where an NVA trooper had burst, crawling lizardlike from a bunker, a blur of escaping, disappearing motion. Graphically I detailed to this woman, a friend of my mother, how I in that instant, caught between magazines, had screamed for a few of my men to "Get him!" Running quickly ahead with M-16's, they had begun ripping bursts of automatic fire into him at close range. Incredibly, the dude, clutching his weapon, had only slowed a bit and pressed on like a head-wrung chicken, already dead but deceiving us with determination. I had wanted the grotesquerie ended but could only repeat my command more shrilly. The weapons erupted again and again. Still additional holes drew in bullets while throwing off huge chunks of flesh on his opposite side. Nearly obliterated, the man and his crawl of flight stopped.

Stopped also was my audience, perceiving that I was blinded, and wrong on the war, and half cracked. Not surprisingly, this war did all these things, they'd been told.

Visits began to thin as late January's sleet and snows continued into the slush of early February. Mercifully, I was left nearly alone. Between college and the Army I'd been away for most of six years. My hometown and I had never been close, so I hadn't been missed, homecoming existing within the walls of my parents' house. I bunked in the guest room, the passage of time having disposed of my bedroom and boyhood things. The changes outside and around me seemed almost as great as those within. Old friends had followed distant jobs and careers, a few had just vanished, and for others, marriage had replaced former shared interests.

Though it was not entirely voluntary, the problem of inactivity was partially solved by sleep. Free from regular barbituates and hospital routine, my body forgot its diurnal rhythms. Night was day, day was night. I'd go twenty-four hours awake, then be plunged into sixteen hours sleep. For days I was awake only at night, and lived a troglodyte existence.

Before leaving Vietnam I'd sent ahead the soldier's basic exit pack, the assortment of expensive stereo gear. It had preceded my return and my father set it up in the basement. I'd tinker with tapes and records, absorbed inside headphones, illuminated by the faint glow of a red power-on switch. Ever since 1956, when I bought my first rock record—Chuck Berry's *School Days*—rock music had mimicked my emotions like nothing else. Over the years, I steadily watched it refine from primitive vitality to intricate self-searching, and it was then that I discovered progressive rock on FM. For me it dwarfed the moonlanding of a few months earlier in excitement. WHCN in Hartford projected it through a collection of articulate hippies who seemed to be lovingly playing their own private collections. A waterbed spot every hour or so covered the extent of their advertising.

Through days and nights I was sustained by rock like some neurological food, through its atavistic rhythms and exaggerated drama of heart-pained love. The raptures of the idyllic and the torments of the unrequited became real. In nothingness, the one thing is everything, the reality. Rock music swashed through my senses as love for a woman, but competed with the war in a kind of fade-in, fade-out sequencing. She teased me with pumping desire, then I let her slip away among scenes of the Mekong.

Action, paddies, men and choppers, had been so densely packed that they swelled, forcing me from her arms. The scenes were relived, then changed . . . What if the gooks had come from that direction? From behind? What if we had taken that trail instead? Should I have been meaner? Hadn't my compassion spared more than a few commie bastards? God! Why did I ever follow Skinner and Voss? It was all insidiously inverted, a nightmare from which I was trying to awake into my dream and back in Nam where I belonged, or in her arms, Waldman's.

One evening a friend screeched into our driveway. We had for a time worked together in a factory. He'd been in Nam the year before, and for this I had some affinity toward him. I had wanted to phone him for weeks but had resisted. Anyway, here he was.

"Hey, old man. Lookin' pretty good. Ready to do a little drinking? Wait till you see my new car. 'Yaz sir, here come duh judge!' I like the eyepatch. You look like the guy in those shirt ads." He was effusive and bantered continuously, but I felt sarcastic and asked where he'd been for the past five weeks. He ignored the question, although I knew for a fact that his mother had been hounding him to come over. I grinned with forbearance;

lame as these days were, I'd better take my social life when it came.

Later as we sat in a bar, I was amazed to see how little we had in common. It was as if great bags of our former selves had been litter-bugged out the window of his GTO on the way to town. We plumbed each other awkwardly for news, and feigned interest. The topics became more local, dwindling to no more than the bar and our table.

"Another pitcher?"

He was self-conscious, but a couple of pitchers were an adequate antidote.

"Hey, you should see the chick behind you, what a set of jugs!" He drew out the words lasciviously, then gulped. "You—You don't mind me . . . I mean, you're not being able to . . . you know, see and all."

"Nah, I don't have eyes in the back of my head anyway," I assuaged his feelings and laughed it off. Ultimately the common denominator was found, the war.

"Yeah, in the Fourth Division we really saw the shit. My unit especially." He seemed compelled to tell me how hard it had been in order to make me feel better—less pregnant. It seemed he told me every worn-out story I'd ever heard, laced with the technical errors of fourth-hand tales, so exaggerated that each airmobile was like a landing at Tarawa, every night spent on Pork Chop Hill. Any offerings of my own were pygmified, so I granted indulgent nods and yeahs for his punctuation.

When he brought me home, the war still raged, his M-16 white hot and near to melting, bodies piling to the moon.

"Yeah, C.O. was crazy, really fucked up, you know," he said, the prelude to another story. "Would have to take over for him all the time, run the whole show!" Buck Sergeant Al, the company RTO.

"I turned down my promotion to E-6," he went on randomly. "All those medals too, couldn't use them, you know."

Drunk and weary and sad, I produced an SKS rifle

which I had captured early in my tour. "I'll never have any use for it," I sighed forlornly. "You take it hunting in Maine. Here, keep it." The sudden gift charged the moment, but my feelings of the night were understood.

"I came over, Steve, because we're friends, because I really wanted to . . . not because you're blind." He added more distractedly, "We could go out again sometime." Toying with the bolt, he drew it back and released it, the crisp mean sound of the metal in the quiet scored the obligation.

Calculated details of a distressed fiancée and troubled home life, my counterfeit but elegantly sentimental forgeries, had been worth sixty days extended leave. Most days I remained at home, not wanting to at all, but completely immobile on my own outside it. Mainly I spent the time waiting. It seemed stone mad staying at home, sequestered in a chamber, making myself believe I was in the Army. I wanted to go back to Reed, to return to the several friends I'd made just before Christmas. The hospital was the only remnant of the Army left to me, but if I went, I'd expedite my departure all the sooner.

The dilemma grew. Toward the leave's end, I called the doctor, requesting more time, hoping I could stall things until some congressional contacts tied me officially to Walter Reed until my preset promotion to captain. Word came through the local congressional office, which phoned with the verdict: "Not even the President can make a medical decision. We assure you the V.A. will take care of everything you need." Word was also that my eye doctor, contemptuous of and irritated by congressional meddling, issued a fiat on extensions: "Not a day more."

I upped my TV's volume to mask the tattoo of bleak wintry raindrops on my windowpanes. Another cigarette would probably be a good choice, a good way to exhibit scrupulous melancholia.

A day or two after being turned down by the doctor, my mother was hanging up a jacket in the hall closet when she called, "What are you going to do with all this stuff? There's not enough room in here for it."

I went over to see what she was talking about and found eight or nine starched fatigue shirts that I'd left behind when I'd gone to Vietnam.

"Oh yeah, my shirts . . ." I said in nostalgic absent-mindedness, as if I'd been searching for them for a while and given up. I felt the embroidered black and gold tabs on the shoulders "Ranger, Ranger, Ranger," and below them the blue and white patches with raised bayonet, "Follow Me."

"Ranger. Yep, 'Only the brave and the bold' get to wear the black and gold." I grinned as I rhymed this part of a cadence.

"Yes. If it wasn't for that Ranger stuff—" she blurted, suddenly overcome. I stood between her and the open closet as if ready to defend something that couldn't speak for itself.

"What are you talking about?" I snapped.

She turned to and fro in frustration, wanting to lay blame somewhere for what had happened.

"Blame God, maybe the NVA, but *not* my being a Ranger, not me. That's me, Ma, me! What did you want anyway? I know, stay in school like your friend Natalie's son. He's a dentist now. She can be proud of him, right? Meanwhile there's guys getting torn to bits."

"It's not wrong for a mother to want that. At least she has a son in one piece. It's the war that's wrong."

"Wrong! I'll tell you what's wrong. Your college classmates all comfortable and smug seeing you off with a 'so long chump, I'll be staying here in the student union with my beer.' I know what you're thinking, Ma, like them. 'How could I be so dumb—go off and throw myself into a mangler when I didn't have to.' That's it, isn't it?"

She sniffled, a wet-eyed cry; but I had neither the ability or the desire to comfort her. That mothers didn't want their sons blinded didn't need a thought, but not wanting the thing to happen was different from not wanting the thing after it had. I could remove the thing only by removing myself.

"I'll hang them up in the cellar," I said, turning away and scooping the bundle under my arm. Feelings ran raw in my mouth, as bitter as a loose droplet of Novocain from a dentist's needle. I thought of old friends still in school, unscathed, with pompous pronouncements on the war, and thought of what it was like to parachute at night into a mountainside in northwest Georgia, of how sleet could be borne in on frozen fog to coat you with a carapace of ice, of bug-eyed hunger, of hallucinating fatigue, and of the Rangers I had shared it with. No. She didn't understand, few would. Men were fighting and dying in Vietnam, and I needed to be there. Who around here could understand that?

Later that night my father cornered me in the kitchen. From long experience the approach told me that he'd been in council with my mother and was ready for a "discussion."

"Your mother and I want to know what you're going to do when you get out."

"I've got to get my face fixed and my gut maybe operated on."

"We meant what you're going to do when you get out of the Army and the V.A."

"I don't know. This guy at Walter Reed said I've got a bunch of educational benefits."

"Will you be living here with us?"

What had begun as an innocuous question suddenly revealed itself as something else.

"We wanted to know," added my mother from the doorway.

I didn't know what to say. Did they want the truth? I hadn't thought about things like that at all, just drank Guinness all night and dreamed of fucking Waldman and fantasized about getting surprised by gooks. But that question was a statement of a future modeled after a retarded child come to adulthood, forever unable to care for himself, and so cared for by his aging parents. The image disturbed me; a buried insult from parents who wouldn't trust me not to become a "burden." Thoughts cascaded too quickly for me to attach words—of my house being only a place where I used to live, and my own parents merely people I used to know.

"I'm going back to the hospital," I said.

CHAPTER NINE

"I figure I've got a week and a half before they have me out of here." I aimed toward Mad Dog in one of his quick stops at our room in the midst of his frenetic travels. "They're done with all their evaluations, only the typing's left... Then I'll be out. I've got nothing against the Veteran's Administration. I'll go eventually, but it's right now that's the problem. I'm not ready to be tossed out there. I need a little time—time with other grunts, guys like Andy Wilson—time to work out what the hell I'm going to do. But I've run out of options."

"Steve, you never exhaust all your options, only the ones you think you've got." He faced me directly, in a studied assessment of my plight. His thinking always zigzagged like a man running in an open mortar attack.

"I could get my friend at the Pentagon, General Maxon, to help—talk to the Surgeon General, three-star to three-star. I'm pretty sure that would work, but if it didn't, we'd kill chances to use other options. Their backs are already up over that congressional thing you were into. We'll save Maxon in case all else fails."

"Like what else?"

"Like, listen to me. First, go and get yourself a good close haircut, shorten up those sideburns. Spit-shine a pair

131

of shoes and get on a fresh set of dress greens with all your medals.''

I gave a puzzled frown.

''Then march yourself up to the eye clinic and ask for Lieutenant Colonel Balen. He's not one of those doctors who got captain's bars handed to them the day they walked into the Army. He was a grunt in Korea. Worked his way up until the Army sent him to medical school. He'd understand earned promotion and won't see it as some unimportant matter.''

''You think that will do it?''

''Not quite; but you see, this guy, although he's an ophthalmologist, is actually a closet plastic surgeon. The thing is—he loves operating. He'll do it on anybody.''

''Is he any good? Sounds like he's just practicing on people.''

''He sure as hell is, but he's not bad. The first time I met up with him, I was just walking down the hall when he yanked me by the shoulder, hauled me to the side and asked if I wanted my right ear fixed. It was shredded then and part was missing. Anyway, he did a good job, but it didn't quite match my good ear. So I had another operation where he went at that ear so they'd both be the same. Perfect. You've got to talk him into doing plastic surgery on your left eyelid and removing that scar.''

That afternoon a nurse walked up to the eye clinic with me. In uniform talking easily with a girl at my side, I did not feel like a patient.

''I'd like to see Dr. Balen as soon as possible,'' I directed with conscious authority to the receptionist. ''Tell him it's Lieutenant Maguire.'' I had no appointment, and Dr. Balen had never heard of me, but I hoped he would see me out of curiosity.

''Do you have an appointment?'' the receptionist asked reflexively.

''I don't need one,'' I impressioned in flat Bogart. Assuming I had some prior arrangement, she acquiesced. I sat down with my friend.

"Maguire!" a harsh voice squalled, interrupting our exchange. "Good God, what are you doing here like this?!" my own resident eye doctor from the ward added reproachfully. "In uniform?!" He said it as if I had been sitting there in full battle gear.

"I'm going to see Dr. Balen," I blurted.

"About your eye?" His inflection rose. My being out of pajamas indicated a patient out of control, a masquerade, the scheme that it was.

"No, no, no," I said dismissively, as if it were not even close. "You see I've—"

"He left," whispered my companion, "you ought to be more careful. I told you there's only one way with him—his way. He's pissed."

"I made a mistake telling him who I'm here to see. He's probably gone looking for Balen now."

"Wherever he went, he was in a hurry."

Although the eye clinic covered three floors, Dr. Balen found me before my ward doctor's return and accompanied me into an equipment-filled examining room.

"What do you want?" he asked, both discreet and curious.

"I get my promotion to captain in three months. I want to postpone my retirement that long. It looks like my ward doctor is going to ship me to the V.A. in a matter of days. Besides, I've got ulterior motives." I stripped my eyepatch off smartly. "I need some plastic surgery on my eyelid so it'll close better, and I understand you're the man to do it; and if it's done here, it can stretch things out and I'll get my promotion."

He drew close. It was more than he could pass up. He pushed and prodded the lid repeatedly from several angles. He left and returned towing in a colonel who did a bit of poking of his own. After a short conference, Dr. Balen announced, "Okay, I'll do the operation in six weeks. In the meantime we will have to get you off the ward to Forest Glen, the hospital annex. I'll sit on your records until after your promotion." He nudged the tissue between my cheek and nose into one last pinch. "I'll see you the week before this operation."

A consolation. Since being wounded there'd been none. I would receive what I had earned. I wanted that promotion because it was mine. Now a fugitive's breather in an unrelenting chase made it look like I was going in the right direction. Mad Dog would be dryly entertained.

Returning to my room, I walked past without noticing, of course, the clothes and suitcases of a new arrival laid out on the first bed, and stepped into the bathroom to perform a less than cerebral act. Senses failed to detect the presence. He sat casted to the seat—two legs, silent without even a single constipated grunt. I turned at the sink, flipped open the zip and thrust for the final step.

"Hey!" bellowed a protest. I jerked back as if I had plugged myself into an electric socket, bladder valves banging shut in paroxysmal spasm. It was as if the toilet itself spoke, booming from its outraged porcelain mouth.

"What the hell you think you're doing?" he added, sounding like I had taken unfair advantage of his position rather than the near violation itself.

"You son of a bitch, you bastard, you let me do that. You know I can't see," I swore in simulated anger, my face contorted in the effort to look as savage as possible. My reaction gave me the advantage, and he stood up sputtering, coins dropping from his pockets onto the floor. I strode from the room with the bearing of a field marshal.

I stood, hesitating in the hallway, smothering an impulse to visit Andy's ward. My ward was different from his. There were few wounded—mostly old retired officers recovering from minor operations, not really sick men, but men who took their conditions seriously and mostly remained in bed. I wanted the company of my own kind, but weighed that against the tedium of bumping into his bustling ward's wheelchairs, metal tray carts and gurneys. Without a long white cane, traveling was tricky. My solution was to straighten a coat hanger and convert it into a probe. It was a poor idea. Too flexible, it whipped back and forth like a rapier, slicing the air. One or two old fellows, not realizing I was blind, complained that I had a screw loose.

Toilet jockey would need a little time to compose himself . . . so I started toward my ward's dayroom, tracing my hand along the wall. Halfway down, one ear cocked for the office sounds, I felt my way around a large canvas hamper full of dirty sheets. But a step farther I smashed my bad knee into a displaced lounge chair's hard wooden arm, jolting a teetering ashtray onto the floor.

"Shit," I hissed through clenched teeth at the stab of pain and sound of broken glass.

Sergeant Carroll pressed from his desk, gliding to the doorway on his swivel chair. "Hey, sorry about that, sir," he said understandingly. "We pulled that chair out to make way for some scaffolding. They've gotta fix the lights. Need anything?"

"I need to know who the fuck is in my room."

"I know I promised you privacy down there, but there's no more empty beds on the ward. He's only here for tests."

"You got any beer?"

"Later this afternoon . . . forgot to order it. You're the only one on this ward drinking it right now."

I nodded and added an inaudible "Double shit!" Stepping across into the dayroom I began filling myself a cup of coffee. "Anyone in here?" I spoke into the quiet. No reply. Good, I wanted to be alone. Dropping into a large, overstuffed couch, I sank back and put my feet on a table cluttered with magazines and newspapers. My right leg still smarted. I began to reminisce fondly about the time I had parachuted from a chopper in a strong wind. Missing the small drop zone, I had been blown into some trees, hitting knee first against a large branch. Injuries like that set the jaw; like this, they lowered the head.

Agreeably, soothingly, my mind roamed to that earlier

period. Humping the hills of Georgia again, I daydreamed of my old job, Ranger instructor. There were certain places in those remote, sun-blazened woods that I always liked, places that were just right. Hiking along pack-weighted, I'd suddenly find my surroundings exquisite by lay and line. I picked favorites. One place in particular was perfect. By a cooling stream with trees forming a terrariumlike pouch and concealed by lush, closeknit vines—I felt I belonged there, and often maneuvered my students into camping at the spot. Nearby was a road, unmarked on the map—more a logging trail or fire lane where I could rendezvous with a jeep to collect extra rations on the sly, my students having been left below to grunt with all theirs from the start.

Once, I hiked up to that road with a lieutenant from another patrol. Tired of waiting for the jeep, we lay down in the stone-nuggeted sand, marking the rendezous with our bodies and going to sleep. I awoke to a screech to find a hard rubber tire snug against my skull. Expecting us to scramble aside, its driver had pretended to run us over . . . and nearly had. A hundred thousand acres stretched through Stewart, Quitman, and Jasper counties; a miniature country to play in, with an imaginary enemy waiting to be fought with classroom tactics and pretend bullets. It was a long way from the muck and gore of the Mekong Delta . . . sure, and a long time in events, the whole of a year since I'd seen the toasted brown of that Georgia landscape.

My knee twinged again, too long in the same position.

"Hey!" exclaimed an old voice. "You're missing the game." He clicked on the tube and the play-by-play of basketball erupted into the room. "Baltimore and . . . can't tell," he said, turning up the volume. "Damn Bullets games are always too snowy in here. Yeah! Here we go," he said, continuing his own personal psych-up.

"Wow. This guy is still around," I groaned to myself. He seemed to be suffering from an inability to talk of anything but sports. Suffering hell, he was in raptures over anything involving a ball! I left him in a dialogue with the TV commentator.

In the hallway, I veered right to avoid the lounge chair and stepped into dazzling pain as some skewer thing connected with my eyebrow and drove downward squashing the eyeball. I staggered back roaring a corps of four-letter words.

"What happened?" The head nurse skidded in my direction. "Oh, dear, you've hit that scaffolding." I reached up and felt the end of a two-by-six and the end of a bolt that I'd found with my eye.

"Are you all right?" came a couple of anxious voices. "Did you get hurt on one of these boards?"

In the welter of injury and their attention, I felt it was time for some drama.

"If there was even a chance that I might see again, this ward has just ended it." I spun around and strode unmindfully down the center of the corridor to my room, where I got my coat hanger to slash my way out of the ward and into Andy's Snake Pit.

Once, I had been secure in my ability to navigate at night in the wild better than anyone, barely needing a compass, as lethal and confident as a slithering bushmaster, so acute was my sense of nature. Disparagingly, I thought, all that has little to offer me. Alone in the woods now, I'd be as devitalized as a very old dog arthritic and sightless, with predatory instincts diminished, shuffling huntless through the motions.

Andy was in the pit playing chess with Dave Stretton, a captain from the 173rd Airborne, who was in bed with two painful mine-mutilated legs, both casted past the knee.

I negotiated my way to them and interrupted. "Andy, look at my eye, will you?"

"You still taking shrapnel or what? Your eyebrow's bleeding."

"I just bashed it. Ran into that scaffolding down on

my ward. My eye feels okay. Guess I just squished it some. You got any beer?"

"Yeah, just a sec," he replied, going across the room. "Look, why don't you get one of those long white jobs. I've seen them up at rehab. It'll keep you from busting into things. Save your ass. That coat hanger is a joke."

"Get two of them and put them on your head," cracked Stretton. "You could go as a roach."

"One rung above you. But look, those things are hard to get . . . It means mobility training."

"And you couldn't use some of that," Andy retorted.

"I've already tried it. And mobility means Alvin."

"So? You went out with him before, why didn't you get one then?"

"Because he's a fucking jerk!"

Alvin had appeared at my door with a soft tapping. "Lieutenant Maguire?" he asked in affected castrato.

"Yes, ma'am, what can I do for you?"

"I am Lieutenant Alvin Erskine, your mobility instructor," he delivered icily. It was an honest mistake, but one that he didn't forgive, and one worsened by my manner during instructions. The feelings became mutual. I had ideas on what the Army was about, and they did not include Alvin's kind. I was bad at controlling this prejudice.

Within an hour I'd mastered the technique of traveling with a long cane, but Alvin made me prod and scent around almost every obstacle he could find along the sides of the corridors. I wanted to walk in the clear middle, but for an entire day I submitted. Whenever the condescending bastard returned me to my room, he outlined the course of training planned from the next day on. I was anxious to get outdoors. He'd have me inside for at least another month of the same tedium, as if he had trained in the same school as Major Mot. I had plans of my own, like keeping the cane and canceling any more training. Alvin was smarter than that.

"I'll take that, please." His feathery voice had just the hint of something concealed, something mean, like the delicate edge of a straight razor. The cane was snatched from my relaxed grip before I could counter.

"What are you doing?! I *need* that thing around here! Can't even go down the hall without it."

"No, you're not ready yet. We don't give out canes until patients are ready."

I grabbed for the cane or whatever piece of him I could get, snarling, "Give me that, you mother..." But he was already gone.

Mad Dog Johnstone was in the hospital for a few days and was on the telephone. He clunked down the receiver and pounced to my side of the bedroom.

"You want me to get him back here?"

I knew a nod was all it would take, but said no, believing that there were probably more tactful ways to get a cane.

The following morning I got a phone call from the rehab office. "Lieutenant Erskine would be happy to continue mobility training with you, but you seem to have an attitude problem that is an obstacle to your progress. I've made a referral to the Psychiatry Department so you can get the kind of help you need."

"Look, you tell Erskine if he comes down here on my ward, he's going to get hurt...and as for you, sweetheart, you can grab one of those canes and go rotate on it."

Shortly after I hung up, Sergeant Carroll came in saying, "There's a woman major up in rehab who's burned over your insulting her."

"Major?" I inhaled. "Tell her... I've already left the ward...and that goes for every time she's looking for me."

*   *   *

"So where do you go from here? You're in a bind, then," commented Andy.

"Maybe I'll get one at some civilian place. Some kind of medical supply shop or something."

"Right, so go ahead," he sighed, patience thinning half at the chessboard and half at my man-made dilemma.

"Your knight's trapped," murmured Stretton. Andy grunted.

I slipped away unacknowledged.

CHAPTER TEN

Weeks passed. One morning during grand rounds, Dr. Balin split off from the pack of eye doctors and slipped into my room.

"We're going to have to hide you at Forest Glen, the hospital's annex, for a while," he informed me in quiet undertone. His secrecy stressed the fragility of my situation. "You're too conspicuous around here. Questions are being asked about you."

I nodded. Although the Chief of Ophthalmology knew I was still around, he wasn't knowledgeable about our scheme, the surgical contrivance and stall. My ward doctor had been outranked; but doctors have a protocol of their own, rank being only a minor factor. It was wiser to withdraw from this hill rather than risk any further affront to him. I recalled how adamantly he defended his authority after my return from convalescent leave. "I repeat, I don't care what you want. I'm the doctor responsible, and I say it's in your best interest to go to the V.A." He beat his palm on the end of my bed with his hand for emphasis, adding, his voice skirling, "And I don't care about congressmen or senators, you're going!" I had sawed cross-grained into a nail.

His logic ruled. Recently I'd met a sergeant who had misplaced both eyes, a leg at the knee, and half a foot on a trail not far from Chu Lai. With the identical orthopedic

problems, he would have stayed at Walter Reed until his
prosthetic limbs were as good as they could get. The
blindness thing overruled. He was transferred to the V.A.
Blind Rehab Center in Chicago with paddy mud still under
his fingernails. He'd be shunted off on an orthopedic ward
with old dudes, a blind rehab day student. Prosthetics took
a long time, and the doctors would have asked what a
blind person would do in the meantime. My ward doctor
had asked the same questions about me, about what I
would do while my other problems were being tended to.
Dr. Balen's urges didn't seem pretext enough to delay my
rehabilitation.

The specter of my plans eroding filled me with
apprehension. A stillborn promotion on the eve of a
discharge . . . better they throw me out tomorrow morning
than that! I thought. Why was I in with the eye service
anyway? I didn't seem to warrant any treatment from
them. My primary diagnosis got me these guys, but did it
always have to be this way? What if I got hit by a car
tomorrow? Broke both legs? They'd diagnose me as blind
and put me on an eye ward? I had to preempt them with
something bigger, something physical, something just like
I had.

For a long time I had been experiencing a painful
burning sensation in my sternum, a kind of acid indiges-
tion royale. I burped continuously, and the antacids that I
gulped only teased the plumbing. "Okay boys, the Ph is
dropping again, open the gate valves wide on the HCL."
Sometimes it got so bad I could imagine swallowing
Drāno as an antacid. My exasperated doctor had said,
"You'll go to the V.A. for that."

I sought a consult with Andy, a resident expert in the
area. The beneficiary of massive surgical reworking of his
insides, his scars railroaded across his midsection to a
bellybutton roundhouse now relocated a few inches off
center; hash marks of a particular kind of military service
and medical education.

"When I got hit," he told me, "they put everything

back in, but obviously in a hurry. I started coming apart in Okinawa and they had to go back in . . . then again, after I got here. There are some doctors, you know, just sit there and wait for the patient to tell them what's wrong with just the right details. If the patient can't do that, it's his own problem, and it is a problem. That's why Gomez is the guy you've got to see. He's the only one who really listened to my symptoms—asked the right questions and eventually solved the problem.''

I called Dr. Gomez's clinic from my ward and booked an outpatient visit, adding that by coincidence I could be found on Ward Two. Dr. Raphael Gomez, Lieutenant Colonel, Deputy Chief of the Gastroenterology Service, surprised me that day with a knock at my door. He fit Andy's description, with the convivial charm of a South American banker, asking sundry questions as if wanting to know me thoroughly before taking me on. I told him everything.

"I still want to see you in the clinic tomorrow. I think I know what the problem is, but I want a closer look. I have some tests that I need to arrange for."

"My eye doctor's not going to like this," I reminded.

"I can assure you, my friend, it would be different if *he* had what you have. I can resolve these problems by making you the property of internal medicine. I think we must hold you until we make you better."

When he had gone, I caved in on my pillow, enormously satisfied. Not bad. I wouldn't be leaving Walter Reed. Not for a while. Sitting up on the edge of my bed with a triumphant flourish, I lit a smoke and mulled over my newest prospects. Like Andy, I'd have a gastroscopy. It was his least favorite test, during which a fat tube is force-fed down a rebellious throat into the stomach, causing a patient to gag and heave with each millimeter. Then air is pumped in so the physician can look around. "It's like swallowing a garden hose, nozzle and all, just to get a drink," Andy had said.

I flipped on the TV, still preoccupied with my central

anatomy. To stop this continuous burning in my chest there would have to be a few tortures traded along the way.

While listening for the program to declare itself, I felt a curious heat at my back, a rustling sound. The wooden match. I'd flicked it a couple of times but . . . I scrambled for the trash can next to the night table, near the curtains. Lined with plastic and half filled with used tissues and styrofoam cups, its flames greedily lunged upward to embrace. They singed my face.

Attempting to drag it into the tub, its hot metal burned my fingers. I hurtled over the bed closest to mine and, snatching another trash basket, I sprinted, thinking only of water. Was the fire spreading? Water sputtered from the wide open tub taps in gurgling plops. Seconds elongated.

Choking in the acrid fumes, I flung myself back into the room and dumped the water. More smoke; belching a new signal. If the nurses smelled it, they'd hit the fire alarm and start evacuating patients. They'd fire-ax my ass.

I fell, panic-kicked to the door to seal off the whole thing. It was a tight fit and could be locked. I thumbed the bolt, spun back to haul open the window, then hung glassy-eyed out over the sill, hoping the breeze and ventilating system would clear the noxious haze.

Whump! "Hey, what's the idea? I almost broke my nose!" Terri, a WAC orderly.

"You can't come in," I whispered to the doorjamb.

"But why?" Patients don't barricade themselves in their rooms.

"It's locked."

"I've got to change the sheets."

"Can you . . . do the others first?"

"Hey, sir, you got a girl in there with you?" she squeaked.

"Do me a favor, Terri, and cover for me."

"Sure," she said with a knowing inflection, the kind of understanding that comes from personal experience.

*   *   *

My door knob wriggled and the door thumped again.
"Come on, Terri, you can't be done already."

"What?" Andy's voice barked. I retreated from my
perch at the window and unlatched the bolt.

"Man, you've got to do something about your smoking. You must be desperate to want to get out of here and
on to pulmonary ward. What are you smoking anyway?
Rubber hoses?"

"I had a fire in my waste can. I should have stuffed
the other can into that one, but I wasn't thinking and went
for water instead. It got going in the meantime. Damn
smoke was a pisser."

"I really can't see any now, but it smells bad. Maybe
if you left the door open it'd diffuse a little more. Bed
curtain got a bit blackened. Here, if I slide it around to the
other side nobody'll notice, but I'll get you another one
from my ward later on."

"You smell smoke, sir?" the ward NCO called from
the corridor. "Seems to be mostly down toward this end."

"Um, we think it's coming from out there." I motioned
to the open window. "Maybe some workmen are burning
leaves or something."

"I don't think so. It smells like plastic."

"I saw them when I came in," Andy said. "They put
the leaves in plastic bags first, then burned them—weird
dudes."

"Hey, Sarge," I diverted. "You're not going to stick
another one of those geezers in here, are you? Ol' rocket-
rear last week sat on the toilet for three days. Didn't want
the TV on, hated rock and roll comin' out of my
radio . . . complained about how hungry he was and wouldn't
eat the food."

"They thought he had cancer."

"Yeah, 'mucho sick' until they told him the tests
were negative. His wife pulled up the car outside and he
packed and hurtled out that door like it was a bank heist."

"It's all right anytime we've got under twenty on the
ward—any more than that, I've gotta move them in here."

After the sergeant left, Andy and I loitered in the hallway.

"Andy, how do I get to the Gastroenterology Clinic? What's it near?"

"It's way up the other end. I can take you."

"My appointment isn't until tomorrow. Besides, I want to try it alone."

"I noticed you got that white cane. Did you make it up with that major?"

"One of the nurses talked to her for me and we worked together around the hospital for a couple of days, but I got her ticked at me again when I asked if she was married—if she'd ever been. I got this lecture on how she was a professional and I shouldn't be into her business. Bit at me like a seeing-eye dog gone rabid, then dumped my ass and threatened to serve up that queer dude to finish me off. So I quit. Got to keep my cane, though."

"Dr. Gomez, eleven o'clock, Maguire."

"Oh, he'll be with you in a little while," answered the receptionist. "Take a seat in the waiting area."

Now the tricky part: Which chair isn't already occupied? First find the chairs. I cautioned a couple of oblique strokes rightward. Luck. The cane clogged between the legs of two hard plastic chairs. I plopped into one of them and stretched out.

"How did you know that was a chair!" gasped a twittery female from directly across.

"Well, I . . ." Intuition? An acute sense for the sound of aluminum impacting plastic? A suspicion of chairs in chairs' logical places? "Radar cane."

"My goodness! You know, I saw you come in here and I thought there's a poor pitiful man who can't see, but look how wonderful he's doing. And aren't these new inventions all so marvelous?"

"Yes, ma'am."

"How does it work?"

It lay on the floor, an unlikely high-tech item, already

scarred and slightly bent from sticking it in spokes to quick-stop someone's wheelchair and from confusing elevator doors.

"Space age electronics," I said. I had heard that something like that was actually being developed.

"Landing on the moon has done so much for us all."

"Yes, ma'am."

"But how can you tell what's a chair with it?"

"Impulses."

"Oh, I see, different ones for different things!"

"Yes, ma'am," I said, now sounding like Joe Friday.

"Hey, finally caught up with you." Andy halt-legged into the clinic and eased down next to me.

"He's telling me about his radar cane," informed the woman.

"Yeah, it's a beauty," he said, picking it up then giving it a couple of introspective whaps on the floor. "Rug."

"Gimme that," I groused. "You can see."

"I had my eyes closed."

I bopped it off the floor a couple of times myself. "It's not a rug, pal, it's a carpet. It's high-caliber training that makes the difference." I aimed the cane like a divining rod. "It's wall-to-wall in the whole clinic." I swung it wide, "Wall," then back and nicked her foot. "Shoe."

"My goodness, then you were trained to do this?"

"Yes, ma'am."

"Do you think they'll do an operation?" Andy asked.

"Sure, it's the only way they can get those extra organs out."

"Oh, my," the woman said. "You have extra ones?"

"Yes, ma'am."

"I had some," Andy reflected, "a supernumerary hippocampus located in the anterior spleen. Donated it." He patted his side. "I've got three more appendix left, they say multiple appendices—used to have a fat gut, couldn't lose weight—till they found a lot of extras. Born with 'em. I've been donating to those who had to have theirs taken out.''

"I thought you didn't need them."

"It's when they go bad that you need them," I said. "Think of how good you feel when they're good. You don't even notice they're there."

Andy cut in, "It feels good to help other people."

"My husband, the colonel, wanted to donate, but he was too old. I think mine are getting too old now too. I don't think I have any extra things inside me."

"No, ma'am, you'd know if you did."

"It's very rare," Andy added. "In fact, my friend there and I are the only ones."

After my appointment, Dr. Gomez accompanied me back to the waiting room and saw his old patient.

"How's that stomach of yours doing?"

"Gastric juices flowing well," answered Andy, "but I don't know about this drainage system you installed down into my shoe."

"No problem, come back tomorrow and we'll cut a hole in the arch. Nobody will ever notice a drop or two of excess stomach acid."

We walked into the corridor with the doctor's hand on each shoulder. "It's an interesting problem you have, Steve, especially for a guy your age. I'm looking forward to doing something for you."

"He means to you." Andy rapped me in the shoulder. "While I was sitting there, I saw them wheel in the big number nine gastroscopy hose. They got it waiting for you. They used it to check for cracks in the Chesapeake Bay Bridge Tunnel."

"Don't listen to him, my man. I'll give you enough Demerol—you'll practically be enjoying yourself."

On the next level, near an elevator, Andy halted abruptly. "Here!" He wrenched my arm and twisted me around floppily. "Sit down!" he ordered.

"What the—"

"Wheelchair!" He accelerated the thing into the elevator and pushed the button.

"Good one, almost brand new," he whispered. The door rumbled shut. "When we see a chair like this outside a clinic unattended, the best thing to do is get somebody in it who's in PJs then zip down to the pit."

"You've too many down there already. I'm always busting into them."

"Nah, man, not good ones like this." He jerked the front of the chair and me purposefully in a hard zigzag. "Front end's secure and won't wobble at high speeds, the vinyl's not all chewed up, and the big rear wheels run smooth as a racing bike. Had one once that wasn't aligned right, and had to fight all the time to keep it from pulling left. Stretton will want it right away... to add to his collection."

I laughed but held in reserve the possibility that this could be just the preliminary to a put-on with me as the mark.

Captain Dave Stretton lay propped up in his bed watching a talk show on television.

"What happened, Steve?" he roused. "What's with the chair?"

"Nothing," Andy answered for me, and wheeled around the side of Dave's bed. "We just picked this baby up outside hematology. That one you're using has had it!" Andy began to shift the elevated leg rests to the new one. "Look at this old thing," he went on, going over its faults like a car dealer taking in a trade. The axle made a mournful grinding sound as he shoved it out of the way.

"You know, Andy," Dave twisted downward and reached into the bottom of his bedside cabinet, "couldn't have been timed better." Fumbling through, he went on absorbedly. "Betsy and I got engaged this morning. We're celebrating tonight at the Blue Room of the Shoreham, Tony Bennett's there, you know, the whole thing." Straightening back up, he whacked the top of the table with a can and snorted victoriously, "Brasso. It's all that chair needs. The true military touch and tonight everything will be right.'' Dave swung both his casted legs to the side of his bed, braced himself in a well-practiced manner, and slid to the floor, saying, ''When I get done with this chrome, you'll need sunglasses to look in my direction.''

''That's not really what I had in mind for it,'' said Andy solemnly. ''That's a racing chair, not a nightclub, dinner, and dance chair. *Tora, Tora, Tora* is on tonight, so afterward we're all going to blast down the ramps from the movie theater all the way back to the pit. I'd put money on that chair with almost anyone in it. You and Betsy gonna miss some scorching action. Too bad, those corridors will someday be more legendary than the 'Brickyard.' You interested?'' He turned to me. ''Just imagine the smell of gasoline and burning rubber on asphalt.''

''The movie, yeah, the race? Not after what happened to Dave and me on the way back from the barber shop.'' I began describing how I had mounted the back of Dave's old chair dogsled style, balancing clumsily in canvas slippers on two-inch nubs of metal that stuck out from the base of its frame.

Although my weight made the chair slightly unstable and back heavy, we didn't do a back flip because Dave's plaster-entombed legs projected straight forward on the precarious counterbalance of a support board. The ramp's downward tilt helped, and we glided down the first segment at a moderate clip. Dave steered, alternately applying friction to the hand rims. We bumped shakily onto the flat landing of a cross corridor and pitched to the next grade, accelerating.

This ''Henry J.'' of a wheelchair groaned from some visceral point in its underpinnings. Its rasping turned into a burr as both the chair and ourselves began to vibrate, then shimmy violently. We careened forward still faster, too fast for Dave to steer, too fast to stop without a pair of heavy leather gloves. With nearly a hundred feet of downward incline in front of us, we would have to stop, or like some human demolition ball we'd drive into the tiled wall at the end and regrout every crevice with our gore.

With squint-eyed prudence I hunkered hard on the rear handles and skidded one slipper lightly on the speeding floor. Shhhhh. I increased the pressure on my slipper, but too much and I'd be pulled off to go tumbling down this concrete hill in Dave's doomed wake. Perched on a single quavering foot, I retrieved the other to regain balance. There had been no effect. We were humming.

With seconds left Dave yelled profanely and forced his forearm and bathrobe sleeve hard into the wheel. We veered right and sideswiped the wall, the chrome rim grinding into the paint and plaster with a tortured screech. Its rim smacked a doorjamb and slammed us around clockwise into a spin. With a great heave the chair keeled over, sprawling us on the floor. Office staff rushed from their rooms with help in trade for explanation; but Dave and I reticently loaded the heavy casts back, righted the chair, and calmly shoved off.

At the end of my story, Dave was still rubbing the chrome with pillowcase and polish. He looked up and lamented, "From now on, I'll have to leave that sport to guys who're already amputees."

"Well, Andy," I added, "you know I can lay rubber and do wheelies here in the pit, but that's not the same as making those dead-man turns."

Tora, Tora, Tora was our kind of movie, a war movie seen by men who make war; it correlated with us. We responded, not to the movie, but to the rending spectacle—intrinsically attracting; immense destruction of ships, planes, and men in a molten inferno of steel and lead, battling to the ultimate; it was a solvent for our dolorous inactivity and a primer for what was to follow.

Nine members of Ward One Formula one'd their wheelchairs, bogging the corridor outside the movie theater with bathrobed drivers and restless spokes. Ahead lay hundreds of yards of ramped, switchback hallway, hairpins mixed with right angles, which ultimately ended with the checkered flag at the Snake Pit.

I held Andy's ex-chair, "Soc et Tuam," as he unlocked his straight leg brace, forcing it into an uncomfortable ninety-degree bend. Davetelis pulled "Iron Butterball" alongside, one of his legs a white battering ram casted to the hip. Amputees in "The Silver Wraith," "Sidewinder," "Don Garlit's Dream Machine," et al, advantaged, were in the front rank. Without excess weight, and unconcerned about reinjury, they would disappear in an elbow-pumping blur.

Cory Coggins, a chaplain who had lost one leg just below the knee to a booby trap, was such an amputee—reckless, hunkering forward, and aiming to win. With one of the better chairs, emblazoned "God Squad" on the back, he glided smoothly around Andy and Davetelis and into the pole position. Everyone else then pushed and pried for a better spot in the front rank. They were beginning to choke off Andy at the wall, so I yelled "Go!" and everybody bolted.

Half a dozen of us referees traveled behind on foot. I didn't need a lot of description of what was going on. Coggins had wheeled into an instant lead, and all the way down I could hear familiar voices in echoed curses as wheelchairs bumper-carred into each other and the walls.

Coggins moved to the inside and was comfortably ahead, but reaching the first bend, which doubled back and down to the next level, he got into trouble. Tearing ahead and needing a drag chute, he braked the left wheel as best he could and leaned his weight to the inside for that extra margin, but it wasn't enough. The chair spun out, flinging him wildly. The rest of the guys caught up and deftly shot through in a file between Coggins' smoking wreckage and the wall. Hooting and laughter faded as the rest of them rounded the corner and scorched down the next leg.

Coggins quickly popped up and, pogo-sticking on one foot, righted his chair and was back shifting through the gears, but not quite so freely as before. As he made the next landing, instead of following the pack he hung a left. It was possible to get to the ward that way—but considerably longer. Except for one thing . . . We walkers shouted taunts and laughed after the cheating chaplain as he disappeared behind the sliding elevator door. I thought the racing commotion had dissipated completely into the distant stretches of hallway, but around the next turn we found them halted and face-to-face with the chief and assistant chief of Orthopedics. Taking turns, the two colonels flayed the racers. "I *cannot* believe," one ranted, "that you men, officers, would risk serious injury for such an incomprehensible cause!"

Nothing new, I thought as we slid past inconspicuously, ears eager for details of the ass chewing.

"Donneley," he addressed specifically, "you are a field grade officer with an above-the-knee amputation, not a nursery schooler in a pedal car. Davetelis, you just have to breathe wrong and you'll lose both those legs. And Holiday! My God, man, one good twist of that neck and you'll be so paralyzed you won't be able to do anything but blink your eyes!"

We all straggled back to the pit nearly together, silent and sullen. Coggins, stretched out on his bed watching the tube, taunted, "Hey, hey, hey, if it isn't the Grand Prix aces themselves. There's a good movie on, *The Twelve Stooges Meet Richard Petty at the Walter Reed 500*. Whao! What's the matter?" he asked innocently.

The next morning the chief lectured all the patients and accompanying doctors from the orthopedic service on the seriousness of reinjury. He paced the floor and orated about neurovascular compromise with bone involvement, of wincing proportion being a sure-bet amputation.

"Captain Stretton," Colonel Bevan remarked as he strode toward the double doors, "I didn't see you last night."

"No, sir, I was out."

"How about you, Coggins? Were you up at the theater?"

"Yes, sir."

"Well, then," Bevan turned to face the rest, "if you *all* would follow the chaplain's example, our jobs would be made a whole lot easier."

The white-coated gaggle of doctors left in the same clump they'd arrived, and with their departure there was a collective grumble. For men who were used to flying choppers, gunships, and commanding troops in combat, wheelchair races were a scant risk, one that never even rated consideration. But now what? Lay around resignedly, entirely devoted to watching and waiting for shattered bodies to heal?

CHAPTER ELEVEN

"Two bucks, Maguire," demanded Dave Stretton, as I clinked my way into a card table in the center of the Snake Pit. Dave whapped his hand, palm up, across my knuckles. "You owe."

"What for?"

From opposite ends of the room, bedside TVs dueled obtrusively with the exaggeration of late morning game shows. Wilson and Cassidy sat beside Stretton staring; at a huge board game, they said, that re-created the Normandy invasion. Stretton hadn't answered. Pure absorption in battle. Lately, to say anything interrupted some move or turn. The recent introduction of war gaming annoyed me. It extended the stultifying lingua of card playing and was rapidly turning me into a social invisible.

I scowled. "You said two bucks, but not why."

"Pit party... M&M's promotion party. Everybody's got to chip in for the booze."

"Why not have it at the Officers' Club?"

"Man, you are a dumb-ass sometimes. M's a pit member, right? It's got to be here, so the traction guys can come. Hey, you can't do that, Andy! I've bottlenecked all the British troops with those two Panzer divisions."

On Friday evening seventy or more people crammed their way in to be assaulted with tape-decked rock and popping corks. With the exception of two men in traction and four more whose beds were wheeled in, everyone dressed as if invited to some ambassadorial cocktail party.

As guest of honor, M&M, now Captain Marion Mayo, had concocted one of his "Soul Specialties." He began by pouring fruit juice into an enormous punch bowl, originally a giant stainless steel caldron from the mess hall. Next he added various bottles of wine and champagne. This was followed by blasts of gin, double-handed kickers of vodka, and great glugging snootfuls of rum. Finally, he launched a gallon-sized lump of orange sherbet into this pernicious lagoon. Mayo, presiding over a stumpy legion of styrofoam cups, dipped his own through the thick froth, coaxing, cajoling, and finally begging others to join him.

A number of stuffed snakes, mostly presents from girls, decorated the pit. On top of Andy's locker sat a large wicker basket, its lid askew. A brace of baby cobras poked their hooded heads and peeped with tiny button eyes at their carnival-prize cousins. The newest and longest, a giant purple one, pythoned its way across the upper frames of three beds.

This traditional event for officers differed from those I'd known because it would be at least half female. My contacts with women at the O Club had made me less hesitant, less deterred by their assumed squeamishness of me and more preoccupied with getting opportunities to socialize.

Women had always been capable of breaking my concentration—the nicer, the more distracting. I believed myself to be significantly more tantalized than the average guy. Just like in Nam, where I was convinced mosquitoes targeted me alone and left others biteless. Other men seemed to be casual about women and seemed to marry only after being chased down from behind. I noticed them in all directions, but I let the Army take away all that. For the past few years it had galvanized me to the micronecessities of its technology. I had wanted to be a man among men, and the Army cooperated. What had I built for myself but a life of wincing fatigue in the merciless elements among other strain-uglied men? This had easily taken that mason jar of libido and shoved it way back in the root cellar of never.

The reexposure to women had me wondering if I were on the way to becoming some kind of hermaphrodite, a womanless Adam, a man with only a vague yearning for something that did not yet exist. Waldman had gone down to the cellar. She hadn't only brought it back, she'd put it on the stove.

Walter Reed offered a kaleidoscope of females at every turn, and turn I did, with the hesitant indecision of playing pin the tail on the donkey at the end of a wharf.

I tried to fix my problem into military terms and saw a need to refocus, to switch from random targets of opportunity to a more certain point objective.

I steeled myself for this foray, the mere acceptance of the problem determining the goal. Although this foray was measured in pure desire, there it lay out in front of me, like a trek across some fog-shrouded tundra.

I wondered if a couple of favorites who sirened from the vague rocks of my imagination were even at the party. The whole Snake Pit swilled to the pulsating sound of Sly Stone, bodies juking in the negligible space, and the air full of simultaneous jabbering; it re-created like a composite photo fit of every party experience of my past. Such occasions called for that zoom lens to detect a wooing eye, the signal of a smile, or that free spot next to the girl I wanted to meet. Instead, Captain Andy Wilson activated himself as confidant and forward observer.

"Don't you know," he boasted with the same effervescence as the bubbling champagne he was pouring into several cups, "I'm one of the best beaver spotters around? You looking for anyone in particular?"

"Carla, Audrey, or even Monica . . ." I listed.

". . . Well, Monica's next to McCann, sitting on his bed. Carla checked into the women's ward this afternoon.

Someone said they thought she had hepatitis. Audrey is sort of close, sitting in somebody's wheelchair..."

"So now you can watch a great beaver handler at his work!" I raised my cup in a flippant toast.

Like most girls at the party, she was a RAIN, a student of the Walter Reed Army Institute of Nursing. Audrey was soft-spoken and difficult to hear over the rapacious beat and thickening volume of voices competing to be heard. She held my hand and we shared the growing intoxication of the room.

"Turn off the music. Quiet. Come on! Shut that thing off," Butch House, the ward doctor for orthopedics, shouted. "Cassidy doesn't have any pants on!" Chris had just had skin grafts on both legs, and his sheet had been draped over a tubular frame so nothing touched raw flesh. Several guys in conversation nearby leaned to look.

"Whooah. Look at the size of..."

"It's all swollen..."

"...and nasty-looking!"

"Can anything be done, Doc?" the mocking continued.

"Oh yeah," House slurred loudly. "It's out of my hands, though... seen it many times. He needs a nurse."

"Jealous bastards," smirked Cassidy. "Why don't you drop your trow for a real laugh?"

House began unbuckling his belt.

"Airborne," someone yelled.

"Airborne?!" the former Green Beret doctor asked, leaving the belt dangling. "How many of you all are Airborne?"

Nearly all the patients echoed back their affirmation, "Airborne!"

House collared into position, two chairs at the end of a pair of parallel beds, and stood, legs spread to jumpmaster a load of troops from an aircraft.

"Stand up," he bellowed, the first of his preparatory commands, as if to be heard above the mythical engines. "Hook up." Andy, myself, and the others followed the farcical orders and checked out our invisible equipment.

Sliding along pretend static lines, we shuffled in two files, mounted the chairs, and tumbled to the floor with both precision and ersatz parachute-landing falls.

Jim McCann, a first lieutenant from the First Cav., lay in traction in the doorway, the last bed to be wheeled in. He was psyched up and drunk. With his one good arm he pulled on the bar hanging from his bed frame and brought himself nearly erect, his casted leg still attached to the ropes and pulleys. He had taken four rounds from an AK-47, and his left side was shattered from shoulder to knee.

"You're going to screw yourself up, Jim," warned one of the girls.

"Let him jump," growled Doc House.

McCann winced and dropped back to the mattress.

"Pussy!" someone razzed.

"Right, and in a few months I'll be back in Nam fucking with ol' Chuck, and you'll still be here sitting on a bed pan . . . and loving it."

"Plan on getting your old job back?" I asked. "Pop-up silhouette for gook target practice?"

"Shut up or I'll dump my urinal on you."

"Sure . . . just as long as it ain't filled with M&M's punch."

Nearing midnight, the party withered, and with it the desultory flack that had been traded all evening. The tile floor, usually buffed to a high squeaky shine, was sticky with mashed food and drink, crushed cups and cellophane wrappers.

"Okay, the punch bowl's dry. Who's going downtown with me?" quizzed Dominic Sambucci, attempting to rouse us heavy-lidded stragglers. "I know this place over on Wisconsin Avenue. Used to go there when I was at the Pentagon. It's where a lot of the Redskins hang out."

Eight patients, myself, and Audrey loaded into two cars and roared off on our way to a small inconspicuous bar on Wisconsin Avenue. Noisy conversation ceased as we clambered through the entrance. The entire top of Sambucci's head was bandaged except for one eye and a hole where his nose should have been. There were two amputees on crutches, two with leg casts, one in a wheelchair, and Andy with his leg in a brace and one arm casted. I poked gently along with my white cane and slid with Audrey onto a long vinyl bench that ran the length of one wall.

"Just your basic bar; nothin' special," Andy whispered from my other side. "Tables, chairs, cigarette machine by the door, jukebox in the corner, red carpet, dim lights . . . the bar's small, only about five stools . . . back wall's interesting, though—it's buried in pictures of football players. Hundreds of them." He got up, eagerly stumbling over the both of us to close-inspect the display.

"What happened, your school bus trip over?" asked a gruff voice, calmly, as if it had been a real possibility.

"Come on, Philly D., you remember me. Sambucci. I used to come here two years ago. Dominic."

"Hey, yeah pisan," he said, and added with a snort. "I didn't recognize you wid a turban pulled down like that."

"I got it in Vietnam. It's supposed to be a custom fit."

"Whose globe and anchor on the mirror?" one of us asked. "You a gyreen?"

"Yeah. I got hit in Iwo, was in the hospital almost two months . . . still got ten percent disability."

"Get some wounds," came the rebuke. "I got more time than that in a nurse's bed."

"I never got no treatment like that. You must be officers. My name's Phil DiCenzo. I own this place. You can call me Philly, 'cause that's where I'm from." He leaned on the table as if to consider each of us more closely, but he had obviously been sampling his own stock and needed a little extra balance.

"Walter Reed guys, huh?" he graveled reflectively, as if he just then understood.

The waitress tabled a forest of tall beer glasses, all directed from heavy voices along the bar.

I slid my hand in a small arc and found the base of a glass.

"Hey, you blind?" he asked.

"Yeah." I raised the brimming beer to my mouth and glanced up.

"You hear about the blind skunk?"

I shook my head.

"It fell in love with a fart."

I broke into a smile. He tousled my hair and turned back to the bar.

"That wasn't very nice," Audrey breathed faintly.

I laughed. "Your sympathies lie with the skunk or the fart?"

"I heard some of the Redskins come in here." I was distracted by Andy's bellowing above the crowd. "They're all pictures of the Redskins, guys going way back..."

"Whaddaya expect in a place called the Goal Post in the middle of Washington?"

"I come from Conneat, Ohio. It just seems strange. I've been a Browns fan my whole life. Sam said some of the Redskins come in here." There was a pause, and finally Andy asked, "When...? I mean, which ones?" He seemed uncomfortable in the man's unusual presence.

"Hey, Sonny, c'mere. I got some friends of mine I want you to meet." He summoned the great Number 9 over to our table and pressed Jurgensen into felt-penning his signature across a stack of eight-by-ten glossies of himself out in the field, helmetless as on football cards, arm poised, a quarterback set to pass.

"Let them have anything they want," Philly D. ordered sonorously to a demure waitress, "and why don't you start by getting 'em some pizzas from next door." Jurgensen sat down with us, and we were in just the right mood to badger him with questions like how many field goals he'd kicked and passes he'd caught in the last season.

"How come that sign over the door says 'Cover charge fifteen dollars, drinks ten, beer five'?" Andy asked Sonny.

"Philly D. points that out to strangers he doesn't like, people he's prejudiced against—anyone in sneakers, or Bermuda shorts . . . Anybody else he doesn't like the look of."

From the outside, the Goal Post said its name from a plain sign that looked as though it had been bought on the cheap. A brawny drugstore and a corpulent pizza parlor shouldered it from either side and gave the whole facade a woebegone look. And there it struggled, in the front rank of Wisconsin Avenue, somehow attracting an animated clientele to the fanciful inside. It quick-stepped the entire O Club of the hospital, cashiering the nightly allegiance to move downtown and join Philly in his clubhouse. Andy and I became charter members, tenured in a week as our Bob-and-Ray-like patter found new ears every night. A creative repartée was actually a defensive necessity.

For some years a blind disc jockey who had recently moved on had been a regular. He left Philly with a reservoir of blind gags. He developed a dog-fox eye for that moment my guard went down in the hub of conversation and a week since his last try. Drink mutants. I'd absentmindedly haul up my beer, and three dozen swizzle sticks would hackle my nose like I'd sniffed for the rear of a sea urchin. Ice cubes floated like curious debris. A swap for water produced a sensation of beer that had sat out for a week. Milk assaulted me in the guises of paint, tomato juice like chilled guano, and prune juice like afterbirth from a crankcase. The surprise would almost stop my breathing.

For me Philly typically hand semaphored the bartender for his specialty of the moment and he usually made a few beers at the Goal Post unpredictable for everyone else as well. One evening patrons found an ornery billy goat installed in the men's room. A special Sunday opening for a wine tasting meant making the wine. A great oak tub was cartwheeled in and two waitresses in bikinis romped purple-legged in a hundredweight of grapes. In one attempt to take the Mickey out of him, a couple of his friends varoomed motorcycles in through the rear door. He waved his hand impassively at the roaring bikes. "There's no room in here for that. Get them tables and chairs out of here." Patrons dutifully carried on their drinking on the sidewalk while the carbon-hazed air vented off.

One lazy spring afternoon Andy and I sequestered ourselves in the far corner of the bar to talk. Philly's sister, Angela, straightened up the other end, occasionally impressing Charlie Pride into yet another encore with quarters from the till. We'd spent the week partying with some visiting nurses, and the experience needed some dissecting.

"You're not going to like this, Steve. You need to hear it, though. I was talking to her just before they left, and asked her how she was liking you. She blurted out about being nervous, and I asked her what she meant. Like the 'creeps' she said. She said it was real 'spooky' that you couldn't see her, and she wished she hadn't gotten stuck with you."

"What?! Why the hell was she so nice to me, then—like the whole weekend?"

"That's what I asked her. She just said she thought you were cool at first, but that was before she realized you couldn't see, and by then you were the only extra guy."

"Stuck with me, huh!" I gritted menacingly, readying to kill the messenger.

"I talked to her about that, but I didn't want to get into a whole thing about how girls lead guys on by being nice—and how everybody just wants to have a good time."

"Look, do you think anybody wants to hear that they're giving people the spooks, with something they can't do anything about?"

"You can make changes if you can learn which ones do and which ones don't. Besides, I don't think any of the others were spooked. In fact, I think she was genuinely entertained by you until she found out."

"So I need to work out some ways of hiding it . . . like for a long time."

"Come on, anyone can get it wrong on a broad," Andy chided.

"Like that? If I could see—say I was standing at bat, facing Hoyt Wilhelm, I'd strike out, sure. And how about the same with me not being able to see? I'd be swinging while the catcher threw the ball back. Anyone can get it wrong with a chick. I'm going to get it way wrong . . . I'm always asking myself, 'Isn't this the way things are going to be?' "

"I can't answer that any more than you can." Andy sighed and rapped his lighter lightly on the table.

"How many others are doing the same with me? Hell, this blind shit gives *me* the creeps. It's like skulking around in the world. How about Audrey?"

"No," he said thoughtfully. "I'd get word through her friends. Some of them hang out in the pit. She seems genuine enough to work on."

"I will, but I'm worried about what it's going to be like when I leave the hospital. It'll be a bitch trying to meet girls. Here, it's all under one roof and I get help."

"Things will change. You already get around much better than when I first met you. Pretty soon you'll be going to that V.A. rehabilitation thing."

"Yeah, sure. That's when I learn to be real good at being blind. You know that Cobra pilot, John Todd? He's just back from blind rehab in Chicago. He said it's good for learning mobility, but as far as companionship goes, there's nothing there but a bunch of indigent old dudes who went blind from diabetes and the like. There were some Nam E.M.s who couldn't get past what the Army had done to them. Where I'm going might be different, but it won't be like Ward One . . . Can anything be useful and irrelevant at the same time? It's the part that will come after all that I really dread. It's not just the problem of making it with chicks, it's life itself. Sometimes I'm not sure if you can really make a distinction. It gets to me when I think about living blind out there."

"You are 'out there.' Where are we right now?"

"I'm not alone, Andy. I'm not *out,* out there."

"Oh, out out."

I called Angie for a refill and began telling Andy about the only blind people I'd ever thought about; I'd never actually known a single one. Every afternoon on my way home from high school, I would see a man of indeterminate age making his way down the street. He had skin like smooth putty, the cheeks strangely bloated, fleshy and mirthless. His dark-ringed eyes looked shriveled and gruesomely vacant, and he would zigzag along, head lowered, clutching his cane with both hands. As far as I or anyone else knew, all he ever did was tap his way to a run-down corner drugstore and maunder with its near-fossilized owner as the sole customer at the decrepit soda fountain; but when the owner died, the blind fellow was never seen again.

The other instance of blindness remembered was even less savory. While at the Citadel in Charleston, I used to regularly notice a crippled black man on King Street. A blind, almost frightful creature, he would collapse into unused doorways, his crutches and braces scattered and body heaped atop rubberized legs. Then, for whatever time, he'd gaze, both eyes rolled back at the footsteps of passersby; as if he didn't care whether he got a measly coin or not, the metal cup sat awobble, plaintive but empty. Now I was one of them.

Andy stirred and lit up another smoke. "Look man, you're going to be retired. Money is not going to be a problem." He pulled in a long breath. "Not like *that* anyway," he added, annoyed.

"Well, pride alone will keep me from being that kind of casualty. But look, I've only got three options on my future. One . . . I could kill myself. Two, I can play hero.

Three . . . I can do what I'm doing right now, nothing, taking on days one at a time."

"Yeah, big strong Ranger!" he taunted. "And after all you've been through already." He'd riveted on the first option as if it was my preferred choice.

"Suicide's always an option for anyone whose life's become intolerable."

"Oh sure. In-fuckin'-tolerable, like some college shitbird whose exams got too heavy. Belt around the neck and up onto the pipes. You don't know what your prospects are yet."

"Hey, I was only speaking philosophically. Things would have to be a lot worse before I'd consider it."

"Shee-it!" He was bursting. "Why not go down to Georgetown and get some acid, you could see inside your head all the time and none of this would matter."

"Don't be ridiculous, you know what I mean. Of course I'm not going to do that . . . or give up, but sometimes I have the feeling everything could slide . . . despite my efforts. What abilities have I got? Only ones that are good in the Army, and I'm not in command anymore."

"You're still in command of yourself."

"I've been relieved," I replied scornfully, not actually disagreeing, but not wanting to hear him tell me so.

"It's a challenge."

"Yeah, like option number two. It reminds me of John Wayne. Remember the movie where he was this Navy pilot who gets racked up and is left a quadriplegic? Bypasses his severed spinal cord on sheer willpower. Goes on to be a hero in the war. Go up to the neuro ward and sing to them 'You Gotta Have Heart'!"

Andy remained quiet. I gulped at my Michelob, ice cold, and with the air conditioner's help, tensed uneasily in the chill.

"It ain't real," I said finally.

"It's a useful analogy."

"No. It isn't. It's not even like guys with both legs gone. We've both seen them, guys fucked up bad at first, but in a few months they walk out on artificial legs and drive away."

"Some do. Some choose to stay in their wheelchairs," Andy added harshly.

"The point is, for me there's no choice, no prosthetics. No artificial eyes to look through. Nothin'!"

"Great soldier!" Andy bawled, pleased to be returning to his favorite theme. "You run out of ammo? You go for the bayonet . . . or hand-to-hand, right? You adapt. Remember . . . flexible posture, mobile, hostile, agile."

I smiled at his Fort Benning-ese. "So what am I gonna do, take the bayonet at tomorrow?"

"Modify," he corrected. "Prod your attitude with it and take on a week a time. It's not so bad, Maguire. We're having a lot of good times . . . Hell, with one or two exceptions, you really are doing better than I am with the broads. That's for sure."

"They're only crushes," I scoffed with a playful wave of my cigarette. "Besides, you'd do a lot better if they didn't have to be blond, blue-eyed, and five-foot-two."

We both lounged back simultaneously, the seriousness broken. I sensed that there had been enough of my vaguely focused groping even for Andy's indulgent ear. Philly appeared, bearing his way into the bar, and began bellowing for his sister.

Suddenly Andy leaned around and called out to him. "I've got an idea and you're going to help. Date of the Century." It came out like he'd just thought of it that instant, yet he sounded like an announcer introducing a new matchmaking program.

Philly grunted something unintelligible and sat down next to us.

"We want to take a couple of chicks and do it up big, you know, really make an impression. You have connections and know where to go in D.C."

"All right!" Philly exhaled broadly, like a great Godfather tolerantly relenting to bestow his approval of some trivial request from his underlings.

We sat, regarding him, hopeful of a beneficent pronouncement. Finally Andy, the architect, felt obliged to speak, to redefine his idea. But Philly interrupted him by standing.

"Call me tomorrow, fellas," he dispensed summarily. "I'll have everything set up for you." He tapped the table with a heavy finger twice and went into the back room.

"Okay, hot shot," I said to Andy. "I've got someone to take, but where's your half?"

I laughed, at the way Philly had said what he'd said like a cold, truculent order. It reminded me of once in Nam when I told my operations officer that my unit couldn't ford a river since the tide had risen too fast. "I'll meet you on the other side, out," had been his curt, radioed reply.

"Audrey's got a friend that's pretty fine," Andy offered.

"Right, Lynn is brunette and at least five-eight."

"I'll survive." He nodded wistfully, "I'll survive . . . anything for a friend in need."

"Need. My little helper. Next you'll be wanting to hold it for me when I take a leak."

"Knock it off. You want a chick, right? So you take her out and do it better than any of the other dickheads around, that's all. Besides, I'm curious to see how it comes out."

"Oh, get bent," I concluded. "I liked the idea from the start anyway. But since you're such a good observer of such things, I promise not to let you down. Shall I do her right in the backseat for you?"

CHAPTER TWELVE

Smoking idly, two colluding figures, we stood beside an empty couch, waiting. Although expensively dressed, we looked out of place, like dandified thugs, Scar Face and Black Patch, imposing ourselves on the ambient softness of the women's dormitory.

Andy, tall and blond, appraised each female passing us in the confined lobby. Some skimmed their eyes over us in return, a few friends added hello. Finally a pair of brunettes, lacking any of the casualness of the others, discharged themselves from the elevator. They paused to speak to each other as if allowing the inspection by us to carry on at a distance. Andy described them to me in brief, smothered sounds while the women sauntered toward us with studied carriage, aiming to entice.

The women were similar in appearance, although one was a finely proportioned scaled-down version of the other, in spite of the absence of the heavy roscoes up front. Dark-hued makeup racooned their eyes; faces all camouflaged for a sortie into the nocturnal capital. They fixed small confident smiles, telling ones, but not with the formality of a first meeting, just enough to show that although they had danced with us before, drunk . . . kissed, this was a premeditated date.

Andy was disarmed, his gaze embarrassingly flypapered to the displayed and accentuated gifts on the one called Lynn, dominating and demanding respect, as if dangerous. I, with a Zapata mustache that lent me a stern quality, probably looked unappreciative of Audrey, my undersized date.

The silver-gray Eldorado bulged low to the curb, moored like a new warship at its berth. A Goal Post friend and cronie of Philly owned a Cadillac dealership. They had Cinderellaed Andy's demolition-red, oil-burning '65 Galaxie into an opulent classic.

"Is this your car, Andy?" Lynn asked, listing slightly to follow its lines.

"No, Steve's."

I tried to develop a look of ownership at Andy's departure from our prearranged script. On our way over, it had been his.

"My brother's had it while I'm in here," I said. "I don't need it much right now, aah . . . he'll be taking it back."

"Not soon, I hope," Audrey commented as we drew ourselves across its supple leather.

"I'm afraid it'll be very soon," I answered while subtly my arm went around her back for a closer look. A soft clinging fabric caressed my hand, inviting me to do more with it, I supposed, than she had intended when putting it on. The girl and the big backseat rejoined memories: the first car I'd ever owned, a '60 DeSoto Adventurer, and the last girl I'd loved. I had left her in New Hampshire just before coming into the Army. The love had been spent, emotions gutted, and I'd dumped her. Like an old car that had betrayed once too often and with too much already sunk into it, she was sent off in a fit of rage like the car that was sent crashing down an embankment. The scene of abandonment snarled in weeds and undergrowth, suffused into a flash of rust and broken glass. Later it was as if ugly sandstone had been worn away, leaving only glistening crystals. I had stashed her face in my memory, like the plates lifted from that car . . . and it wasn't difficult to relive the purr of that engine when it was good and the warmth in that New Hampshire snow. Audrey could be transposed with that crystalline memory. The similarities made it easy, her cool sophistication, her body, her being there. I could nearly see her.

Andy's driving was palpably cautious. It was the first time I had been through Rock Creek Park with him without doubling the speed limit, tires not crying in unrelieved agony on every successive bend and curve.

The Place Where Louie Dwells, our destination, was another con, with our versatile Caddie dealer meeting us in the restaurant's entrance. Earlier, when we picked up his car, he agreed to act as our inside man, pay the meal in advance—then wait. We introduced him as the owner.

"What a couple of beautiful young ladies." He troweled it on heavy. "For their presence alone, gentlemen, everything must be on the house." Turning, he gave an instruction to his friend, the maitre d', and left.

Our new host stepped forward with a regal, "Good evening, Captain Wilson, Captain Maguire," promoting me early. "Nice to see you again." Then, with decorous courtesy, he seated us in the genteel plushness of a room of our own.

Audrey, favorably impressed, asked about our being here before.

"Oh, we've had lunch here with one of Steve's big shot government friends," Andy volunteered swiftly.

"And who was that?"

"Spiro Agnew."

I bit my tongue and disciplined my expression. He was enjoying this too much. Another question and he'd have the other occasions penciled in—cocktails with the Supreme Court, trysts with Tricia Nixon . . .

"What's he really like?" she asked me.

"You'll have to meet him, then judge for yourself."

Turning my attention to choice of food, I thought of what could be eaten with finesse, neatly. A vision of myself skirmishing with a platter of prime rib, cutlery flashing and juice and fat moiling over the edges would only lead to Audrey offering to cut it for me, hardly the élan and éclat for a man of consequence. I settled for a sort of Chesapeake affair, denuded crab and mollusks lounging in a sauce with supine seduction.

The champagne and wine, like liquid subversives, infiltrated our moods, toppling the last remnants of formality. The girls, like a pair of younger sisters, were slipping beyond our tightly intended impression when another iced bottle arrived. "More champagne, gentlemen, compliments of Mr. J. Edward Bambery."

"Who is that?" Audrey repeated her line.

"A White House lawyer," I said, and mused, "Maybe he's in another room and saw us." At some distance I could hear a faint tinkle of glass and voices. Andy and I smiled at each other blandly, sharing the same thought—good ol' Eddie, bartender at the Goal Post. During the meal the four of us traded hospital gossip, Andy and myself recounting some of the elaborate pranks that had become a ward pastime.

Finally, Lynn asked us, "You guys seem to have known each other for a long time, you're such great friends. How did you meet?"

"Africa," Andy answered, his mouth taking in another gobbet of something that muffled.

"Really?"

"Yeah, we both were working with the famous French naturalist, François Tessier, on a project."

"What kind of project?" Audrey tugged in my direction.

"Giraffes," I said, feeling for a match. A waiter's arm telescoped in and I felt the warm blossom of heat hanging for the draw.

"Giraffes?"

"Yeah, we used to have to trap them . . . I mean with tranquilizers and ropes, so Dr. Tessier could run his tests."

"Sure," Andy dove back in, "blood samples and...you know, stuff you shouldn't have to talk about at the table."

"But why were you interested in giraffes?"

"Oh, *we* weren't, it was just the old man and his wife. I think they're awkward to handle, but not bad when broiled over an open fire."

"Ugh, but why did you leave and come in the Army?"

"We were deported from Tanzania," I weaved, expelling smoke with an air of confidence in a thin stream from the corner of my mouth.

"On weapons charges..." Andy cut in again.

"Well, not really like that. It was over a few hunting rifles. I tried to get them into the country and avoid excise taxes. The professor used his connections to get us off. We sold our other stuff to pay off bribes, then headed home."

"We had to trek the length of the Nile; all the way back to Cairo."

"You walked a couple thousand miles?" Audrey asked skeptically, and I could see I needed to get him into the bathroom for a little chat.

"We were more like modern day Stanleys. We hitched all sorts of transport—barges, old trucks, a train or two. In fact, we actually flew the rest of the way from Khartoum. It wasn't all that big a deal."

"Oh, come on, Steve, what about that scrape with lions ... and what about the Geluba warriors in the northern frontier of Kenya?"

"How did you two end up in Vietnam after all that?" Lynn asked.

"War is man's last real adventure," Andy pronounced.

"You know..." Audrey spoke with a sudden edge to her voice. "I've been thinking about that kind of attitude for a long time. I've been an Army brat my whole life, and it's really what you say, Andy. Sometimes I think men bring war into this world just to entertain themselves."

"Getting blown away is not my idea of entertainment."

"But up to that point! You mentioned the motivation that got you there. You—"

The waiters delivering food brought a merciful interruption.

"Andy . . . before we get started, I think I need a quick pit stop."

Audrey burrowed against my shoulder on the way to our next stop, Rosecroft Raceway, nurturing in me a smug sense of accomplishment. Behind I could hear the low throb of the exhaust envelop and infuse into darkened pavements. She was escalating and my prospects firming.

At the track we were brought to the owner's box, escorted there at the mention of a name, to govern the finish line. Andy and I lolled in our seats with the laconic weightiness routine for men of substance, as if to say to our alluring choices, "But for us, you could be down where the only excitement is raking the turds." Andy continued the act in a tone that said it mattered, pensively frisking the statistics aloud as if meshing them into a system. Like old rail hangers, old friends, we behaved like addicts of hoof and harness, amid crumpled racing forms and torn tickets, firm between today's disappointments and tomorrow's sure thing.

I hadn't been as attentive to Audrey as I'd wanted during the evening, having been impressed so often as straight man to Andy's stories.

"Here you go." I whisked a clump of raw cash from my pocket and released half into her lap.

"All this money?" Audrey questioned, slightly baffled, as though I had made a mistake and would take it back.

"It's to bet with."

"But—" she began, straightening the bills, as if reading them would help yield clues.

"Keep it," I said distractedly, "we'll never get caught."

"You mean you—"

"Shhh." I put my finger up to my lips slyly and winked. "There's plenty more."

"Oh, come off it," she drawled, her soft Oklahoma accent more evident and transmitting a tremor of excitement. She leaned, looking down past Andy for support from Lynn, but saw that her friend had a fistful of her own.

As the horses drew up, we made our selections, Andy and I sticking to the "tried and true"; the girls following more intuitive lines.

"Number six looks friendly. I'll bet he loves to run."

"Junior Boy—we had a dog once whose name was Junior. He was real fast . . . suppose it didn't matter. Got hit by a car."

"Oregon Wanderer. That's me, all right, Portland born and bred."

"Yeah, but that isn't horse country like Oklahoma."

Andy and I slowly became mute as betting windows wrested our cash like vacuum cleaners, and the girls' stakes, although not haystacks, had steadily improved.

"Gee," Audrey said with honeyed consolation, "you've lost almost everything."

"No, no," I insisted, "you've got to put a lot in first . . . invest, so you can get a big load in the end."

"You better take some of mine."

I fought it off, saying I had plenty more in my wallet, then relented, took some and passed it to Andy for the next race.

"Okay," Andy finally pronounced flamboyantly, as if a change in attitude would bring them in. "You've heard of Riverboat Wilson, Minnesota Fats Wilson, Vegas Wilson. Right? Right. You're looking at Belmont Wilson; so take it from me, the next one is number four, Medical Jug."

True, it was sort of a hospital thing. That was us all right. So we laid on a packet at twelve-to-one. A winner.

"Look at that, Duke Wilson." Andy slapped the card. "Need I say more?" It was the last race; and although he was in at better than thirty-to-one, we had no choice. Butch House, the Airborne doctor, had pinned this nickname on Wilson when he punched out some deskbound

Navy officer up at the club. It hadn't stuck; but our recalling the event baited the moment, and we went in heavy for the ol' Duke.

Duke rocketed to a clear lead from the start, torching the turf and dropping the pack like expended boosters. At the half he was four lengths ahead . . . sparks flew from his hooves as he used the centrifugal force of the track to sling himself faster.

We jumped wildly, jubilation breaking into Andy's Eddie Arcaro calling of the race, as our Pegasus unchained stretched his advantage.

". . . the greatest horse in history."

"Ten lengths ahead."

"Boy, are we smart."

"We've got the double."

"We can eat at Louie's again!"

A furlong to go and the Duke's legs churned, his nostrils twin volcanoes. A direct descendent from the mares of Diomedes; out by twelve lengths, a trotting fool. Then, like the power suddenly cut on a recording of some robust oratorio, the voices in the grandstand ground down, a chorus doloroso. Andy and the girls collapsed into their seats as if simultaneously blackjacked from behind.

"What happened? No way could we lose!"

"The fucking wheel fell off."

A rippled cheer finished the race. Echoing barks, like distorted gunfire, sounded nonsense names in their order.

"That has got to be a fix," Andy kept saying. "It was like he pulled a cotter pin on the thing right in the stretch," and I imagined the Duke standing out there, stagger-footed in the dust, still hooked to his broken rickshaw, pathetic, the blinders making him look old and tired from pulling a junk wagon twenty years; the loser jockey hopping from his seat, an elfin clown, impudent in his silken harlequin colors, squint-eyed with his I-only-drive-'em expression.

* * *

Some drinks and late night dancing over in Silver Spring, Maryland, were anticlimactic. The point of the date seemed blunted, bent over from a renegade thought...

My feelings were not keeping pace with Audrey's, not reciprocating, and I had expected that they would. I'd set the conditions for romance to proceed, and my objective was being achieved. I leafed through my recalcitrant emotions, finding that Audrey Anne Shaw, as a particular individual, didn't seem to matter. She could just as soon be any beautiful girl who was not too bothered by a guy who couldn't see. But... there seemed a kind of anemic spirit, a lack of liveliness about her, which likened her to that New Hampshire disappointment. Then why did I want her? Did I just need a female, any female? The question irritated. Hell, I was finicky about girls, always had been; turned down more available tail than I'd ever taken... Then why not?

Audrey and I danced, spliced in a slow flush of blues pumped into us by huge nearby amplifiers. With her head snuggled under mine, her embrace was irresistible, her body demanding reconsideration and death to my treacherous thoughts. Maybe I had been a bit premature; there certainly was nothing wrong with her. She was just another woman in that I hardly knew her, but she was willing and not just present flesh ensnared. Maybe... a spark was there but the tinder was a little damp... Besides, she had been my idea from the start... and now she liked me.

That was the game, and if I didn't play it, someone else sure as hell would; she was pretty, intelligent, and twenty-two.

Through the following week we saw each other frequently, although in truncated spurts: chance meetings in busy corridors, lunch or supper at a crowded table in the mess hall, or a brisk drink at the club before she went off to study. Her schedule was taut, with free time pinched between class work and hospital duties; mine was a lazy meandering between Snake Pit and Goal Post.

One evening Audrey suggested we take a stroll in the

hospital rose garden, a well-tended island of floral privacy, rimmed by the hard, practical asphalt and the brick buildings of the medical center grounds. We talked amiably, then lounged on a concrete bench which was cast to simulate sculpture. It was secluded by a lattice-worked arch of pink primroses; no doubt an agreeable backdrop to many a hospital courtship.

Resting my cheek against her hair, my hand coasted from her shoulder to her waist. She molded herself against me and we kissed. Then, looking up, she reclined and said, coaxing, "I have nice hips, here." She invited a stroke with a pelvic nudge under my hand, the bone itself erotic, in a kind of knowing way.

"Your hips are very nice, Audrey, and so is everything else." My hand moved in an approving caress. We resumed the kissing that started before, with more urgency, as if we both had some set goal in mind. My own arousal wambled about like a ferret in a canvas sack.

"Steve, you know I'd be willing to do more with you than I might with others—because of you not being able to see—because of you being blind."

A perplexed curiosity addled my concentration. *What the hell is she talking about? Is she gonna serve it up?* "We could walk down to the Georgian Inn."

"No," she said. "Let's just kiss some more."

I nuzzled up to her. "We could get Andy's car and drive." She did not answer, and I began a foray under her dress, but she pressed my hand.

"No, don't."

You said more, damn it, I mused on a tack to her breasts, but in my mind that would be going backward and I'd already passed her limit. *But she said because I'm blind I'll get more than others. What others? Does she think I don't know about her and that married doctor, spending his whole TDY weekends with her at the Georgian then flying back to his family when he finished his course?* I wanted to tell her I knew and understood exactly what she'd meant. *All the others get zip. Blind guys apparently*

*get to make out for a while, and doctors get fucking
cervical exams.*

I leaned back to detach and cool out and think of a
way to keep this slide from becoming a plummet. "You
said something more. I don't handle relative quantities in
this area very well."

She shifted her weight to her other hip, the mock seat
contentious. "I don't think I should have said what I did.
I'm sorry. Maybe we could walk around some more. We
could go back to the O Club."

"We started at the O Club, Audrey. Is that all you
really want for us?"

"I just haven't decided yet. I don't think you understand me."

A slow paralysis set in as if some anticupid had
blowgunned curare-tipped darts into us from among the
roses. A quiet, heavy humidity sank with the darkness, like
its accomplice, into the garden. I sensed the verdant clusters
of flowers and shrubs as if they were dog-eared leaves of
banana. My nose had never been very smart, more quanti-
tative than discriminatory. "Hot," I said. "Reminds me of
Nam down here." It was hot, the hottest day of the year so
far, and it did remind me of Vietnam after having been
yanked out and dropped into midwinter in D.C.

"Vietnam!" she huffed frustratedly. "It's all you
guys ever talk about."

"I wish I was back there right now." Thinking of it
seemed strangely preferable to entwining ourselves, briar
and rose, on this concrete bier.

"But why? Hasn't enough happened to you? Besides,
I get tired of listening to you guys, especially up at the
club. The war is insane . . . and all of you talk like it was
some kind of game."

"Yeah, to kill a few more communists."

"Well, why?"

"Because I care about the place, and it would be
better off without them."

"But why do you have to *kill* them? You care about the place by killing them?"

"Only way I know to stop 'em." I slid my white cane into a vee formed by my shoes and jabbed just beyond at a crack in the sidewalk.

"But it's their country."

"No, it ain't. It depends on who 'they' are."

"You mean to tell me that Vietnam doesn't belong to the Vietnamese? You should get someone to read you the papers so you would know what this war's all about."

What a snide, moody bitch, I thought. I felt like smacking her into the bushes and walking off, the little dove. But this little dove was Army, born with the dust of Fort Sill in her nostrils—her father now a retired colonel. In six weeks she'd be bumped from student nurse to first lieutenant herself. She was congenitally Army.

"Vietnam is a divided country, and not the only one in this world. It's a political reality. Would we accept an invasion of South Korea or West Germany by their other halves? Not without the shit going bang, but according to you, we've got to let them do it in Vietnam."

"But the people want the communists."

"No, they don't. They just aren't strong enough to stop them without help. Military disadvantage doesn't mean lack of will . . . except to you and everyone like you, and *that's* what's fuckin' wrong." I stood up angrily, anxious to break off the conversation, one that I hadn't wanted, least of all with Audrey, but one I felt so passionately about that I couldn't have left it alone.

Her tone turned icy, and my inability to find my way back alone compounded my anger. I'd betrayed her by what I believed. It was like pricking a pin into a bladder swollen with invective. She hissed just beyond hearing.

"So we have to stop them by dropping napalm on children, women, old people. It's insane." The words jumped from her as if escaping the fiery vision, then fell silent, satisfied that an evoking of the horror could stand as a logical last word.

"The communists have gotten more mileage from that kind of garbage than they could have from a few extra divisions. You're in the U.S. Army and they virtually got you working their side. I'm not going to waste my time with you. Take me back to the hospital . . . now!''

CHAPTER THIRTEEN

Sleep, a necessary flexing for the evening's endurance, was my escape into a seeing world, particularly the afternoon snooze. I loved it, being pilloried in my skull and entertained by a mad projectionist. Dreams were only random cullings from the flotsam of life's snapshot album. They scudded through my head like kinetic portfolios, and in this mix of mundane outtakes and extravagant Dadaesque imagery was Vietnam. In voluminous vermilion robes the Viet Cong stalked me while I hung snarled in a web of trip wires, with my ever faithful Car-15 cowardly detaching its barrel and my bullets turning into Play-Doh.

"Phone call, sir!" Sergeant Carroll's voice bludgeoned the Technicolor palette. He jacked the line into the wall and wheeled a table next to the bed, as whorls of sleep spun in the tweedy monochrome dark.

"Are you coming down tonight?" Philly's voice graveled in my ear.

"Sure," I answered, curious that he was calling to ask about something I did every night.

"What time?"

"About seven-thirty or eight, probably go up to the O Club first."

"Seven-thirty, huh?" he said, contemplating something.

"Yeah, thereabouts. What's this all about . . . Redskins pick their man to match me in one-man push-ups?"

"We'll get to that some other time . . . Listen, you make it exactly quarter to eight."

"Yeah, sure, but—"

"I've got a little something for you, and I want you to be here."

"Like what?"

"A little surprise . . ." His words slewed from the receiver. The phone and the sounds of the bar in the background tinged his voice with more than its usual indelicacy.

"Philly D. just called me on the phone," I said, standing next to Andy's bed.

"Yeah, so?"

"Well, he doesn't just call me every night to know if I'm coming down."

"I'm supposed to know?" he mumbled, turning another page of whatever he was reading.

"Come on, you bastard," I badgered. "You know more than that. He said he's got a little surprise for me."

"Whoa, maybe I do . . ." He clunked down a book and dropped his feet over the edge of the bed. "Last night I was coming back to our table from the bathroom and Philly met me and asked, 'How's things?' so I said, 'Just fine . . . could use a couple of girls, though.' He thought a bit, then told me, 'It's kind of late but maybe we can still call in a couple.' I was only joking, so I said it was you that wanted one. He got all concerned—about you breaking up with Audrey . . . Guess he's sort of . . . done what he said he would."

"That's what I thought," I fumed. "Steve's just broken up with a girl. He's blind. He's probably taking it harder. Solution—get him a shot of poontang—send him upstairs with a bottle and a whore. I gave Philly more credit than that. I could fix myself up anytime downtown."

"Maybe it ain't a hooker."

"Suure, it's his daughter, maybe."

"You could save your complaining till after you've

met the broad. Remember that one named Nikki who used to be around down there? A body like that . . . could even *be* her.''

I conceded with a nod, as I wasn't opposed to a turn with some overdeveloped Nikki. But the attitude behind my scheming friends chaffed. ''It's fucking embarrassing,'' I retorted, ''because they think it's what I need, and this is the only way I could get it . . . I mean, what with even 'Date of the Century' producing a clean zilch. A whore's as easy as the money in your pocket. If things were that bad, I could take care of it myself, privately. Trouble is, if I make up some excuse, Philly will probably write me off as a fag, or somethin' even worse. That's the way he is about this stuff. I can hear him now telling everybody in the place, 'What? Is there sumpthin the mattah wit you?!' '' I bore in with a whisper so no one in the pit could hear: ''Look, Andy, would anyone else around here get tail bought for them? What's . . . umm, the salient factor?''

''I think he likes you more than anybody else around.''

''You scumbag, you got me into this, not him.''

''All right, all right,'' he relented, ''I'll get you out of it. But what do I say when he tells me 'real men don't walk away from pussy hot and steaming'?''

''Maybe I better check it out first, huh?''

''Shit, yeah, I would!'' he expelled, and flopped back on his bed, retrieving his book.

''Good thing I can't see, though.''

''How's that?'' he grunted with burrowing indifference.

''Didn't I hear once, you're not supposed to look gift whores in the mouth?''

An inhospitable back street skulked behind the Goal Post like a kind of slit trench where squatting establishments along Wisconsin Avenue pushed out their tailings of bulging barrels and plastic bags as if collection was forever imminent. Four of us ambled across from Andy's car, scuffing over the soggy cardboard of flattened cartons. Underfoot, a note of crunching glass, and I heard Philly at the rear door. Without comment the others continued through the kitchen, leaving me to follow Philly up the stairs toward the second-floor apartment where he took drunk friends, relieved of their keys, to sleep it off.

"Is she any good?" I asked, feeling puerile as he led me.

"Are you?"

She met us at the landing, and Philly took some pleasure in a syrupy introduction. Vivian's voice rasped of time and times, and I knew. Philly's footsteps tramped the stairs in retreat.

She took my arm and tried to shunt me through the door, but I motioned her to go ahead of me. I hesitated with a studied loiter, superciliously suave.

"Something wrong?" she asked.

"No, it's okay. I know my way around here myself. I've been here a few times before."

"Oh, is that right?" She spoke as if it hadn't synched with something she'd been told.

"Yeah, sometimes we come up here to watch a game on TV." I found the easy chair and relaxed into it, propping a boot on the edge of a coffee table. She remained standing and I gazed upward to regard her. Okay, possibly Philly had been a little stingy. Didn't buy me an expensive whore, just a whore; Vivian wouldn't be posing for a centerfold in her off time. Probably didn't match up to the one named Nikki, whom I believed could wrestle my ambivalence to the ground without much trouble. Ol' Viv would have to know why she was here—not the money bit, but the errand of mercy.

Saying nothing, she pulled off a tab from a can of beer and handed it to me.

"What did Philly tell you about me?" I prodded.

"Oh, don't worry about any of that. Philly D. and I are old friends and we do each other favors every so often."

"That's why I'm here. What are friends for, eh?" I

pulled out a fresh pack of Luckys from my pocket and dawdled over the cellophane wrapper.

"Why don't you just make yourself comfortable?"

The signal. The preliminaries were over, the acquaintances made, and any fuss cleavered off. It was the El Dorado abbreviated to its spark plugs.

I began undressing, stripping to an audience that was invisible in the darkness beyond the footlights. I felt a sense of absurd foolishness. Was she joining me? Would the whole gang leap from behind the furniture yelling "Surprise!" in the ultimate practical joke? Done. But was she? I took a controlled breath, color heating my face, and moved toward her last words. A bed against the wall. There, naked, sitting, her coarse-skinned body complied with famished hands in search of a carnal morsel. It had been a long time, and engines surged, boilers stoked hot in deprivation's wake. My mind drifted to women of dreams and daydreams.

She lay, and I moved with her, feeling short-changed, as if opening a purchase and finding parts missing, half the bits gone. No treat in her eye, and no possibility in mine. No image of her open-mouthed hunger in my entering her. To prolong the act, I'd had a few drinks at the O Club because I knew the price of deprivation, but this blind thing leveled my appetite for her too much. Other uglier thoughts erupted from nowhere—of Vivian as a person, of her as a hole in the mattress. I needed help, firmer thoughts of mutual pleasure to force visions of old memories of love and near love, of the essence of Waldman even.

Lying rumpled in the bedding in the pulse-decelerated aftermath, I soured. Hookers were always this way; they lay like a stubbed-out butt in an ashtray, facing one with extreme nicotine withdrawal. They taunted for a relighting, for that physical need, for easy satiation . . . and of no one watching. Then, silenced by those remaining few stale-sweet drags, they foul at the burnt filter taste, excuses for having done it, gone.

In a moment she bounded with a sigh. Dialing the

phone, she exchanged monosyllables with a baby-sitter. When she hung up, I pressed my curiosity.

"One's seven, the other's nine—girls."

"Do you work anywhere during the day?" I asked, detouring to connect with something in her life.

"A boutique in Bethesda."

She dumped my clothes in a heap next to me and handed me my still cold can of beer.

Just a hardworking mom, I thought with a glug, getting that grub on the table. These are hard times for us all.

"I've gotta go," she said, edgy, her tone professing her need to be done with me.

"Right."

It was always this way, the barb, first covered by the soft flesh of ardor . . . then the hook, the gaff. My gynetropic tentacles had reached out, but this ego fix had been overcut. I thought of Philly, the giver. I had panhandled for sex. This time it had been arms, legs, a naked bottom and breasts thrown into the tin cup; a grant from the Goal Post Foundation. Hell, we were pals, me and him, we *did* things for each other.

Outside, I thought of Vivian while she made for her car. She tossed an over-the-shoulder good-bye, and I caught myself smirking after her footsteps. Just another medical thing, a house call for a hematoma, the fluid drawn. I dawdled by the outside door remembering vague ribbons of my last sexual meeting, a pocket of civility amid pockmarked walls and knobby stairs folding back on a room where her legs were spread. I thought too of the jungle fire and smoke. I reentered the bar through the kitchen, relieved that none of my friends had seen Vivian. My instinct that she was only passable remained. The warrior returns and flashes the symbolic signal—the smile— to his fellow tribesmen huddled in council with a local brew; the ritual completed to their amused approval, of raptures . . . of witness to El Dorado.

Hearing Philly talking from his usual quarter, the only

stool at the bar's end, I left my friends at their table and
rooted a place for myself at the rail. I idled, expecting his
reaction to what had happened above. A feral snort was all
I got. Eddie, the bartender, served up another draught and
introduced me to a minor sportscaster who did the late
weekend sports wrap-up on a local TV station. I lifted my
beer and sloshed it. Philly was ready. "Careful there, pal;
you're messin' up my bar."

After my first careful mouthfuls, Eddie had shiftily
rebrimmed my glass. I leveled a caustic frown in their
direction, mock reproach for their latest.

"Well, hi! My name is Myrna," she said in a thick
rural accent from about as far south as one could go. I
wondered if this pink cotton candy had blandished the
introduction at me or someone near me. She sidled cozy-
close and I knew.

"Ah'd love to dance," she scouted when I gave my
name. "There's plenty'a room for us two."

Barely, I thought, taking hold of her on the small
space near the jukebox. Myrna was big. She hadn't the
spongy starch-fat bloating of some overweight girls, but a
thick rind hanging like a neoprine jacket, firm as the thirty
or so extra pounds the defensive tackles up at the bar
might carry.

Dancing alternately close and apart, she buffeted me
with an enormous front end. It made me feel small, as if
volleyed between them. I had always been susceptible to
large breasts; and although their proportion to the size of
their owner was important, Myrna's couldn't diminish
them. Their scale was immense.

A respite at the bar and Myrna talked of herself as if
gossiping about someone else.

"When Ah first came to Washington, Ah was goin'
to work as a high-class call girl, and make a lot of
money... But," she added wistfully, "Ah sort of put on a
bunch of weight."

"How long did you ... work at ..."

"None, 'cause Ah got me this real nice job hairdressing." She took my hand and placed it against the side of her head. It billboarded the whole industry. As if fashioned by some medieval armorer as head protection, tiny ringlets were lacquered hard and linked like chain mail. Then cascading out and down, it sent out runners and spawned springs and coils to her shoulders. In the snaky fusion on top, a black mamba could get lost.

"It's great!" I said with a mixture of awe and incredulity. It was like viewing the latest creation from Christo.

While Myrna went to get Eddie's attention for a reload of her Tequila Sunrise, Andy jabbed from behind, buzzing, "Man, you got to be out of your mind."

"Still a damn sight better than that weirdo you scraped up in here a while back, Isolda . . . or whatever."

"You mean Chloe."

"Right."

"Well, how was I to know she was a bull-dyke leather freak?"

"According to Eddie that was one of her high points."

"Come on, I was drunk," he pleaded, "and right now, you ain't."

"Andy, I happen to know for a fact that she's not that bad." I winked at him. "Andy, this here is Myrna from Hereford, Texas. Remember Hereford?"

"Yes, sirrrr," he eased out slowly, as if rummaging through the past. "Summer of sixty-six. You and me heading for El Paso . . . stopped into the Esso station and asked the guys in there what kind of action there was in Hereford . . . Crazy Myrna was all they said."

"Well, gaa-aa-lee, why that skunk, that must have been Jeff Tuttle. Ah went with him some. Can't believe you met him."

"Met him? Hell, we hung around with him for three days."

"Dark hair, kind of tall?" I risked.

"No . . . short really."

"Oh yeah, the short one was Jeff; the other guy was the tall one."

"Sure, his brother Johnny. Ah never liked him."

"Me neither—got a mean look in his eye."

"Ooooh," she breathed, "you don't know the half of it . . . but God, I still can't believe you were looking for me in Hereford once. Just an itty-bitty world, ain't it? When you say that was?"

Andy and I yo-yoed the inanity from pool hall to motel in her hometown, Myrna fitting in the particulars and who's who, tickled when she heard them back.

A deep ruckus tumbled from the other end of the room, jamming our conversation. Andy was laughing. One of our friends, Rick Johnson, a chopper pilot, had unstrapped his artificial leg at the knee and stood it up on the bar. Eddie had drawn the empty section full of beer and offered it to Dyron Talbot, a Redskin newcomer. He hefted the foamy-topped prosthesis and poured it all into his 270-pound frame.

"I'll be danged," he exhaled with just the slightest nuance of a burp, "heard of fellers drinking like they had a hollow leg, but didn't know you could drink right out of the thing."

"Ooooh," Myrna voweled, adding, "it's got a shoe and a sock on it, just like it was a real foot."

"A mere affectation," I drolled.

"Somebody should tell him it's out of fashion," Andy said, "now with the wooden peg coming back in." Then, as if to tell me he'd had enough, he gave me a "See ya," and drifted off to join the raucous voices at the other end.

"You know," Myrna squinched my arm for emphasis and pushed one mountainous mammary into me like a nudge from the nose of a horse, "you and Ah will just have to get together . . ."

"Our gametes," I thought out loud.

"What's that?"

"Oh nothing, just means getting together . . . they say it in Europe a lot."

"Oh . . . well, Ah can't take you out to my place, not anyway until Ah gets rid of Delbert. He's my *old* boyfriend come up from Hereford lookin' for me. His friend and him are sitting over in the corner near where you were before. He's real dumb."

I made the connection, having met the sleepy Delbert and his doltish sidekick earlier. Although Myrna mightn't have the mental power to ignite a lightning bug, Delbert had actually demonstrated brain death.

I felt obliged to ask when he was leaving.

"After tonight, honey," she cooed suggestively, "just as soon as Ah can get him to."

It all sounded silly, like talking to Huckleberry Hound as a real person; and there was something about her that did mimic a Saturday morning cartoon. I contrasted her with Vivian, and in comparison the whore seemed as easy as jimmying a bank vault with a toothpick.

"As soon as Ah can get him gone, you and me can have some good ol' fun. Ah think that's just what you need."

CHAPTER FOURTEEN

"Gentlemen, it is important that you bring the flap as far upward to the nasal canthus as possible, but suture interiorally of the punctum. Here. So that when the scar shrinks it will take up some of the tension."

A piece of chalk tapped on his drawing of my canthus. The voice next to me drawled in soothing anatomicalese about my vacant left eye, or as he referred to it, my "enucliated O.L." His Latin sounded so countrified I kept expecting him to fall into a kind of Andy Griffith thing, maybe calling it "the durndest case of gouge-eye" he'd ever seen.

I perched dunce-style, mute on a swivel stool in front of a brace of ophthalmologists—Dr. Balin's canthus ligament case.

"This morning," the renowned visiting specialist went on, "I was browsing through that bookshelf over there, and lo and behold..." He riffled the pages of a book. "... I found a text I wrote in 1947. In the photo here, you see a man wounded in the Second World War with exactly the same problem, even on the same side."

I perked up to model the eyelid, and the old man carefully poked a hump of skin under my eye. "This procedure that I outlined today was used successfully as far back as that. On the next page I included the after photo, taken a couple of months later."

Some doctors came up for closer looks and nudges. It seemed a relevant curiosity to crease up the scar and massage the chewed-up bony rim below the eye and along the side of my nose. They were searching for something; but their curiosity never ran over to the other eye, even though I carried a trickle of hope that out of the combined brains of a dozen eye specialists one of them would say, "Hey! Guys, has anyone ever thought of doing so-and-so's xyz procedure on his right eye?"

I glanced back and forth as they spoke, as if watching them watch me, teasing them to notice the eye; but they were impervious, as if keeping to some stubborn protocol. This was the only time they'd ever spent with me, and it was on an eye that was gone.

I lay rigid, as if trussed, palleted on an operating table that felt like no more than a plank covered with thin foam rubber. Mindfully naked, naked in fact, I shivered in the chill; a sheet shrouded me from head to foot. A single hole exposed my nose and the scarred objective. My thoughts, fuzzed by a couple of shots earlier on, tried to focus on the background. I could hear Dr. Balin and another surgeon bantering and popping on squeaky gloves.

Abruptly they descended on my cheek like the plummet of a razor-taloned kestrel. "This is Novocain, so you won't feel anything." Balin said it as if to himself, handling each injection like a stapler.

Under the sheet I grimaced. What a career, I thought, qualifying for promotion by having my face resewn.

The scalpel sliced heedlessly while they conversed like mechanics looking over faulty parts for possibilities of a makeshift solution. Tinkering, they changed tools and periodically wiped up leakage.

"You know," Balin said to the other doctor, "I'm not following the procedure outlined in the seminar at all."

I waited for Why not?

"Missed that one," his partner replied instead. "Was out at Belvoir."

Maybe Balin wasn't following the seminar procedures because he'd changed his mind after finding things different. How bad is it? I wondered, and wanted to ask him, but speech meant movement, a slip . . . trouble was, he seemed so flat about it, so undisappointed.

"He didn't say what to do when the tissues all adhered to the bone like this. I can't slide anything around. You see here, the ligaments will only go halfway."

"The only thing you can really do is slice a wedge out and suture it up. Pull it up as far as you can and hope it doesn't sink too much."

Shit.

Two days later Balin and his colleague found me in my room for a bandage lift, a viewing. They both gave tender nudges to the spot. "Just like I told you," he told the other, "there wasn't enough ligament to join together. It's given way prematurely, sunk back again."

"Yeah, I almost forgot." Balin poked his head back in. "You have to move out to Forest Glen. Today. See me in two days in my office. No argument."

Moving was an all right deal. A week before, Andy and four others had practical-joked themselves out to the Glen. An orthopedic surgeon had wrecked his knee playing tennis, and for lack of a private room had assigned himself to the pit. All orthopedic patients, he believed, should shut up and turn out the lights whenever the doctor ordered. While he showered, a box of water balloons found its way onto the bank of lights high over his bed. A string tacked to the door recruited an unwitting nurse to dump the load on him in the dark. The Chief of Orthopedic's sympathies showed when he used the "excessive number of empty beer cans for a hospital ward" as pretext to bunk Andy and the rest four miles away from hospital grounds.

I'd wandered around Ward One a few times since, curious of its strange belly-up transformation. Even though officers wounded in Vietnam still occupied half of the beds, the chemistry had been neutralized and they all lay like tranquilized introverts—reading, writing letters, and watching television.

From asking questions, I'd discovered a new lieutenant who'd joined my old battalion after I'd been hit. I pounced on him for news; but he allowed me only a few offhand yeahs and no's, which loosened some irritation. "What's the matter?" I pressed, "I'm only trying to find out what happened to everybody."

"Look, man," he said, "I'm out of it now. It's over and I'm not one of the rompin' stompin' types that used to be here who keep talking about it like they're still in it or going back or something. I don't need it because it just isn't important anymore. How could it be—it's there, I'm here, and that's just about right. It just doesn't matter to me."

"Doesn't matter? Only a broken hand like you got could give you that kind of luxury. I'm stuck with caring. Sorry for taking up so much of your day."

"Son of a bitch," I muttered as I caned my way out of the pit. "I gotta get out of this hospital."

Andy and I excavated six months accumulation from my closet and tossed it bedward. The original toothbrush and ditty bag had swelled into a massive embankment of civilian clothes, a cabinet full of booze, a tape deck, and a trove of Army equipment left by Mad Dog—steel helmet, bayonet, half a case of C-rations, tiger-stripe fatigues, jungle boots, and black beret. We bundled the entire legacy inside a parachute canopy that had hung from the lights in the pit like an expanse of O.D. sky.

The unwieldy silken heap loaded into the nowhere space of Andy's new MGB about as easily as a dead gorilla; and we tore off, lurching in the traffic with tangled suspension lines whipping in the breeze.

"You've got to sign in with the first sergeant in the orderly room," Andy instructed, leading me into one of the buildings.

"Just like the real Army, huh?"

"Well, they call him a top, but he's really only a staff sergeant. There's just him and a clerk. I don't know what for. There's not much going on out here. I suppose they just mind the keys and shit like that."

While Andy showed me exactly where to put my signature, an impudent voice nearby sneered, "Now that you're out here, you'd better get yourself a haircut." I stroked the short stubble at the back of my head. Andy hadn't told me this place was run like a trainee barracks.

"Would you mind identifying yourself, please?"

"Specialist Thompson, company clerk."

"Specialist Thompson, company jerk," I mused out loud. "Well, well. Son, for the rest of your life, you have my permission to speak to me only when spoken to. You got that, Mr. Chairborne?" I chewed on him with a nose-to-nose malevolence well practiced at the Citadel.

From behind the desk a sergeant spluttered, "Hey, you can't talk to him like that."

I cut him off. "Until they make you a major, Sarge, you can sit there with your trap shut as well. Go back to sleep, Sarge, nobody'll notice in your case." I put my hand on Andy's shoulder and nodded in the direction of the door.

As we moved across a patch of grass between the buildings, Andy whistled. "You got a hornet in your shorts or what? Don't you think you went a little heavy on those guys?"

"Fuckin' rear-echelon bastards," I growled. "They're everywhere . . . REMF-ing clerks and jerks. They were seventy-five percent of everyone in Nam. Here in the States I'll bet it's ninety percent."

"Ninety-nine at Walter Reed."

"Draft dodgers dressed up in Army uniforms. You know, the ones who've been to Nam are the worst, spouting 'I fought in Nam.' They just put their year in and that's *all*."

"Ha, a few months of humping the bush, slung with

an M-60 and a couple hundred rounds of ammo, would melt the twerp right out of 'em."

"Right, but until they do that, I'm not taking their crap just because some other officers do."

Several paces inside the building we stopped to pick up bedding. As the sheets and pillowcases were plopped on the counter in front of me, a woman spoke sharply: "You better be getting those sideburns cut off, mister."

I looked at Andy, then back across the counter. "Me?"

"Yes, you. And before tomorrow will be fine."

I took a deep breath. "And who the hell are you?"

"I am Major Thompson," came the imperious reply. I laughed. It had to be a joke . . . the orderly room had called over ahead of us. I took her for an old WAC NCO; there was a branch for WAC at the Glen. A major in charge of sheets?

"Hey," I snickered, leaning toward her. "You must be related to that shitbird across the way. There are husbands and wives in the Army, but mother and son?" I laughed.

"Very funny, Mister Wise Guy. How would you like to try an Article Fifteen . . . for disrespect to a field grade officer?"

Andy hit my arm. "She *is* a major!"

Fuck it, I thought. "Make it a court-martial, Major, and remember to come loaded for bear."

I scooped up the sheets and went out. Andy laughed. "One of these days your big mouth is going to be trouble. They don't know you're blind. We've got civvies on, so they don't know you're an officer. She really is a major— Medical Service Corp insignia. I don't know what she's doing down here."

"Be my guest, Andy, screw her right in her linen closet."

"Come on. Hamilton has already been threatened by the C.O. with an Article Fifteen."

"C.O.? There's a C.O.?"

"Hell, yeah. We're actually assigned to a medical holding company. The C.O.'s another Medical Service Corp major. Him, the real first sergeant, and a couple of clerks have an office back up at the hospital."

"You know the saying, for these people I've got nothing but hard dick and bubble gum, and right now I'm fresh out of bubble gum."

As we finished arranging all my belongings at the officers' billet, Spec. 4 Thompson entered. "Lieutenant Maguire, the hospital called. You have to move back to Ward Two."

"What the— Why?"

"They said if there was a fire, you might not get out."

"Gimme a break, the door's right there, a whole ten feet from my bed."

"Maybe they figured you couldn't see good in the smoke," Andy quipped.

"Yeah, that could be tough, especially at night." Behind me I felt the clerk grinning for the wrong reasons. "Thompson, I'll bet you waited until you figured I had my stuff put away before coming over here with that message. People like you get a deep sense of justice out of inconveniencing officers."

"Be sure to return the bedding . . . sirrrr," he retorted in a snotty tone.

I didn't bother to reply. Wearily I began pulling things out of the locker and piling them back on the bed.

My same old room. It dampened me, like thinking that I'd won the lottery and finding that I'd read the numbers wrong. For months I'd gone in and out, a hundred times; but this time it seemed different, edged in funeral crepe with black hues of wallpaper unrolling to cover insipid green walls, memoriam to the Glen's stillborned possibilities. My mood did up the beds in black cotton, resculpted the TV in shiny obsidian and painted everything velvet jet. Thoughts mutated, another image, a picture in a magazine of a pad completely done up in black and white. Compelling. What would it be like to actually live in such a place? I wondered. With a chick from Chad, we might spend most of our time hunting for each other. But this?

"That's it," Andy grunted, heaving some more stuff onto my bed, as bored with it as I was. I looked up from my interior decorating of a nursery for Rosemary's baby.

"I'm going down to the pit for a while—get me a beer and maybe a game of chess."

"Yeah, yeah, see ya." I could tell he sensed my foul spirits. "I'll just stay in my cell until chow. Thank's for the exercise period."

"Anytime, con."

"Cell? Hell," I muttered to myself. "How about two miles down a coal seam, at the snub end of a tunnel . . . and with my helmet light out. I was embarked on a life as a Morlock. Listlessly I began putting a few of my things away. A sound, a piece of a word, wheezed up from the direction of the end of the bed.

"Huh?" I asked, not really sure of what I'd heard. "Something wrong?" I neared up to his moans, which he projected downward, half into his pillow. He seemed to be wallowing in sedation. A nurse sidled up from behind. I asked, "Is he trying to tell me something or what?"

"I don't know. You all right, Colonel?"

He gave up a sharp grunt this time. It seemed to be the sound of a very old man.

"We're taking him for a mylogram. He's done something to his back, could be a pinched nerve." A pair of orderlies wheeled in a gurney, cautiously flopped the heavy body aboard and took him off for tests.

My private cell—my public-private cell. Like doing life in a county jail, I stayed while cellmates came and went. Tests mostly. Geezers mostly. One, sometimes two, then a run of them, as if Walter Reed had a minor surgery ad special in the Retired Officer's Association magazine.

Pointed exchanges had broken with a few irascibles who'd expected me to orderly their needs. Others became twenty-four again with me. They opened their time capsule for me, France 1918, second lieutenants in shit so deep, Verdun, Belleau Wood . . . that I felt like a soldier dilettante.

At times there had been real pain in the room. Some of my ephemeral companions had died. I had not seen the precise moment of death; near the end they had been taken upstairs, where the last of the juice drained from the batteries, the process of cancer—its tumors, their growth, the shriveling of victims. It was neither a roommate's death nor death's inescapability that left a sludge of foreboding. Most of those dying were around my age.

"How come so many young guys are getting cancer?" I asked the doctor of a friend.

"There aren't so many," he answered, "but you're in a hospital. What do you expect?"

I didn't know the statistics, but it was difficult to watch a roommate be devoured by something like Hodgkin's disease, or something else that until then had only been a name. What had they done that I hadn't . . . or hadn't yet? We lay together, bullet, shrapnel, tumor—a disease seemed even more capricious than a combat injury.

Vic Delgato had been in that end bed on and off earlier in the year. A captain, he had come back from Korea with a persistently sore neck, half wasted, by the time I met him, with cancer. At first he would drop me at P.T. before going on to get radiated; to death, it seemed. Now all that remained of him was one stark cross in the National Cemetery.

Hell, the parallel between Vic and me isn't that far off. He saw the end, the imponderability of it, and had accepted it like a new duty station.

"Man, when I get transferred out of here," he volunteered, poking around in his tray one morning, "you know what's going to be good? No more of these friggin' rubber eggs."

I could see myself out on the streets too, with a future as imponderable as Vic's. I'd gladly do the next twenty years at Fort Polk . . . if only I knew.

Vic had the motivation of pain, mounting daily on a parabola's course, to an intersection with his release. My own curve skewed down off the graph, confounded with hidden variables. I could take control over direction. I believed that now, but it was like being locked in a closet with no doorknob. The choices seemed not to matter when free only to choose which wall to pound on. In a closet for the rest of my life, I thought. What a useless, endless thing.

Father de Ligne, that priest back in Japan, said I should keep open for "possibilities." I supposed I had, for some things—for eyes that worked; for wriggling, naked girls to be dropped into my bed from the heavens like an emergency supply mission. De Ligne had said that prayer would supply the means for the things I needed, but I doubted that my desires were suitable material for it. It'd be a job trying to airbrush blemishes out of Myrna, I thought. It's okay, God, I'll take Miss June from my wall back in Nam to serve it up just the way I like it . . . ri–i–ght.

I thought randomly, hoping to light on something more conventional to pray about. The effort irritated. There wasn't anything else. A gloominess that intermittently shadowed me suddenly suffused like a fifty-weight oil. I slumped on the sheets, motion-frozen in a kinked posture for prayer. I felt like a night crawler finding himself in an evaporating gutter puddle in a hot morning sun. To do nothing would lead to death by slow drying, to become leather by mid-afternoon. So it crawls blindly, in no particular direction. It may mean either certain death in the middle of the street or salvation in the damp grass and loam of another direction.

I recited several prayers with the ease of repeating my Army serial number, generating about as much emotion. Too long out of practice, the Our Fathers just lined up like emblems of my sincerity. It was an insufficient compliment to my seriousness, only filigree to what I wanted to say. It angered me further that my mental groping for religious feeling floundered, like trying to swim in Army boots—much motion, little progress.

"Prayer to me's like chomping on ball bearings and calling them nuts." I got up and stalked about my room feeling predatory and powerless at the same time. It was like staring into the dark slit of the Black Knight's tilting helmet, as he leveled his lance at me and his great steed pawed the ground. I could only reassure myself that my pajamas were protection enough. "But what do I do? What can I do?"

Like a man shooting craps talks to his dice, I began. It did matter, and like that man I knew the number needed was only as far away as the cradle of his palm, but illusory without a little help.

Okay, God, where is this whole thing going? I asked. *If I know which way, at least then I can work it. Are You going to just leave me here in this room? Or some other room? They're all the same room to me anyway. I'm hurting . . . I'm hurting in two ways. I can't see a thing, and I'm alone. I know the first part is a problem, and we won't even discuss it. It'd be like an amputee praying for his leg to grow back. I want to make you some kind of a deal about this loneliness thing because me not seeing screws up trying to find a girl. I can't figure out the exact terms, though, and this going it alone is like smoking on a night ambush. Sure as shit, it will get me wasted. I just don't know when or from what direction. I'm only twenty-four. I've got to do fifty or sixty years of this? Alone? With hookers? With a chick like Myrna? I'll go nuts. Don't you want something better for me?*

What I really want is love, same as anybody, same as I did before all this crap happened. I don't know if I deserve it, and I don't know what I can give you to get it. But there it is.

Look, I have a little faith that it's possible for someone to love me; but I'm afraid I'll use it all up waiting. If love is possible, what's wrong with now? It comes down to whether I matter to You or not. Do I? You know I've got

*no heart to mess with this alone. There. I've just flat
admitted it. I need help to even up the fuckin' odds.*

My contemplative communication with the Almighty
didn't automatically calm my passions. Acid bubbled in
my sternum and cut loose a great rolling burp, mindful of
the relief in privacy. I swallowed an antacid and wrenched
open the door and shot the tip of my cane into the hallway
ahead of me. Someone tripped.

"Carla?" I blurted, in bare recognition of a gasp.

"Oh, Steve. Sorry. I was in a hurry to take these
reports upstairs and was trying to read one on the way.
Hey, how come you're here in pajamas? I heard you had
moved out to the Glen."

"I did, but they said I was a fire hazard. It's a long
story. I had to come back, so I decided to take a nap, and
the nurses always get nervous when they see me sleeping
in my bed with all my clothes on."

"It's not exactly your hospital kind of thing. By the
way, are you doing anything tonight?"

"Nah," I answered, "probably just going up to the
club for a while."

"Fine. I was hoping you were. I've just finished all
my studying for the week. So I'll see you there. We can
have a few drinks together. Okay?"

"Sure. I'll see you about seven." We pushed through
the swinging doors and she hurried off up the long ramp. I
stood there staring at the corridor, thinking, *This is not the
way it's supposed to work, God. The finest nursing student in the hospital delivered to my door! I know you can
do it, but if you do, you're running the thing and I won't
know what the deal is. I ought to be rolling dice a few
times first. Then when I'm ready, I'll call on you to tip one
of them just so.*

I opened the door to Ward One and headed toward the
pit. I mused over the image of a table for three, me, Carla,
and God. *As weird as this world has become, I'm still tied
to it,* I thought. *I'm not lounging on some metaphysical
cloud, and I know damn well stuff that nice doesn't come*

that easy. I'm no better off than I was. I know girls all over this place. How will I know which one is getting the divine push? Or if you're in this thing with me at all? Okay. I said I had some faith.

"Andy, the whole thing's fucked up," the thickening Goal Post air and the galloping sound of "25 or 6 to 4" vibrated my diaphragm and sucked away my words. "I danced slow with her up at the club and I thought I was having a heart attack."

"Why?"

" 'Cause it had to pump so much extra blood, you dope."

"Why's that fucked up?"

"Because I don't want to do the shit I did with Audrey—go down that road only to say bye-bye."

"We all have to do that all the time, though, with whoever it's gonna be."

"What do you mean *we*. I don't see you jumping on anything."

"I'm looking."

"So tell me something about Carla."

"All right." He breathed that sound of the reluctant story. "Secondhand now, but I overheard Hamilton talking to Colonel Blanchard out at the Glen about being blind and whether it's better to lose both legs or an arm too to being blind. You know that old shit. They're kind of new around here and don't know how close we are, so I got drawn into it. Hamilton starts telling this thing about how they were sitting with a bunch of nursing students in the mess hall. You came in and got the guy at the register to help you as usual. That started them talking about your blindness. They were saying what a shame it was that it happened to you. They said they liked you and you were cool, but *they couldn't handle taking care of you*. Audrey was one of them."

"And Carla?"

"Yeah, she was there, but—"

"Let's go!" I interrupted and shoved my chair back. "You remember that real sleazy joint, the one where the girl singer had a pink eyepatch? Let's go down there and get fucked up."

Too many people stood between me and the rear exit, so I made for the nearby front door. We could walk around to the car. Several people were entering, and in the too tight entryway I bumped one of them. He stepped hard on my foot.

"I'm sorry," I said reflexively.

"Watch where the fuck you're going, Moishe." He spat the comment rough, like he needed to clear some crap from his throat.

I stared at his nonface, squinting malevolently. "I said excuse me." His shoe lifted lightly over mine. He was going to do it again. His bulky frame leaned forward. It already touched me. I sensed the matchup. Fifty pounds on me, muscle under fat, shorter by two inches. In a ring I might have danced around him, scuffed up his head, then he'd finally get his punch—that solitary demolition ball.

"You're still in my way, shit-for-brains." His hands jacked up my jacket while the foot pressed downward with a crushing twist. My fist slammed into his solar plexis with every reed of concentration I could summon. No pause, stay with him, I thought. People shouted and grabbed at me. He wheezed with a beautiful sound, and my hands took hold of his ears with my fingernails anchoring in the flesh behind. I shot his head backward and crashed it off the cigarette machine twice. A forearm went around my throat. This happened once in a schoolyard, I recalled. Trying to break it up, they allowed the *other* guy one last punch. Not letting go, they pulled the two off from behind and hauled at me. I kicked his legs out, took him down to the concrete doorway and bounced his head with a knock so loud that everyone around us groaned.

Andy had me, levering my arm back, tearing me from

him. I let go. He pushed me out onto the sidewalk and I could hear Philly roaring.

"He was gonna whip my ass, Philly!" I didn't think he could hear me. Around back I slammed the door and stretched my legs into the MG. Andy did not start the engine.

"I never saw any of those guys before. They won't be back, that's for sure. But what I was trying to tell you before you got up from the table about Carla . . . was that time with Hamilton, she was there at the table when they were talking about you but got pissed off at what they were saying and left."

"Andy, sometimes I need friends to help me with shit like you do, but I don't need anybody to take care of me."

"Sure, but you also don't have to get so crazy that you grab a stranger and half kill him. Man, Steve, that dude was out cold."

"Andy, you didn't see what happened. It didn't have anything to do with that story. He crushed my foot on purpose, twice."

"Okay," he said, turning the key, "when we get to the next place, why don't we just break ends off bottles as soon as we walk in so they'll know where we're at from the start?"

CHAPTER FIFTEEN

Dave Stretton hailed from behind the still swinging doors. "I've got something to tell you." Dave, a clumping quadruped, agile with crutch, leg brace, and casted foot, followed me back into my room. "Up on the Hill this morning I met this weirdo. He wants to come here to talk . . . to interview us."

Dave had been helping a congressman friend who represented their suburban Pittsburgh constituency. Now that we'd hit the NVA in Cambodia, he'd been seeing mostly college students milling around, swelling the protests from all over. I scrunched my face. "So? He wants to check out Walter Reed? Tell him there's a prerequisite, 'Contemporary Vietnam 201.' It's as near as his local recruiting station."

"Hold on, this dude is really weird, head like a lion's mane only bigger . . . all snarls, and sticking out like a giant ball of Brillo that came between two high-voltage terminals. Man, this guy has trouble getting through doorways with his hair."

"Have I got the girl for him. Why do we need a freak to ask us questions, though?"

"Listen. He's the editor of the American University newspaper and wants to do an article on us. He wants to talk to us about atrocities and Calley."

"Don't they all? You gotta think about what they're

207

like. Andy and I went to a big protest rally near George Washington U. There were all these speakers from action groups and coalitions thumping the tub about all sorts of antiwar stuff. Finally they brought out the star, David Dellinger. The introduction about his Chicago Seven fame was a whole separate speech. He didn't talk about the war that much, mostly about revolution and how we 'need a new order.' He has a cool way of feeding off the crowds. When he did talk about Nam, he said that it was a natural extension of American society and Calley is a symptom of capitalism! They ate up that shit like ice cream, and you want to invite one of those guys here for an 'honest discussion'?''

"They're not that bad," he said. "You've just been out of school too long."

"Not as long as you."

"Yeah, but you don't get a subtle appreciation of the campus radical in his native environment at a military academy like the Citadel," he scoffed.

"I was only there two years before I went to St. Anselm's."

"Now there's a hotbed of leftism."

"It's all underground—very deep." I laughed. "At one time I was known as the most rebellious student on campus. Admittedly, though, I don't know much about these protesters here; but it's not because I didn't go to Princeton like you." I added, "Because everything changed so fast, and it all began the year I put on an Army shirt—just four years—and now there's a whole new generation of dudes only that much younger than me."

"That's just it," he said. "Here's our chance to tell our side."

"They don't want to hear our side. They think they already know our side, and that's the reason why they're on their side. They just want more stories about atrocities to support their claim that they are already as common as rice paddies. Your friend there, Electric Lion, will edit out all the good stuff anyway. He'll probably get a nice media job telling people just what he wants them to believe. We'll all come out like junior Himmlers.''

"Then we'll go over and get him," he rasped.

"Okay, Heinrich."

"Anyway, he's coming today," he confessed, "to this room. The pit's too busy."

Our college editor arrived on time and was given a chair between two of the beds. Seven of us, sitting on the mattresses or chairs, formed a relaxed but close cordon. Nervously or maybe fastidiously, he rearranged papers in his briefcase, laying some of them on the bed next to me. Finally he introduced himself again for the last two who came in. His soft-spoken, bookish manner made it difficult to buy into Stretton's wild lion image.

"In case you didn't hear before, my name is Ronsdale Bandicott from American U., and I'm doing an article for the school paper, *The A.U. Eagle*, an article on the war. I want to read this first," he said, quietly contained, and proceeded.

A bandicoot? I wondered. An inchoate recollection from an encyclopedia plate of some furtive Australian marsupial struggled for clarity in my mind. The velvet intonations, almost deliberately meager, obscured for some moments the content of his prepared statement condemning America for our participation in the war. The sins of the Army in conducting it punctuated each line.

"Wait a minute," Stretton interrupted, "I thought you wanted to talk to us about our actual experiences in command . . . in the field."

"I am proceeding on the now common assumption that the war in general can be considered one enormous atrocity perpetuated by this country against the Vietnamese people."

A couple of groans stopped Bandicott. "Did you stop off at the Bulgarian Embassy for a copy of that on the way over?'' Stretton asked with frustration. "It's about that derivative."

"Okay then, let's discuss your experiences with atrocities."

Andy weighed in by explaining First Division rules of engagement as laid down by the C.G. and MACV directives and Army doctrine on land warfare. Problems of their application brought in the others with incidents and anecdotes. The conversation would have drifted into a typical pit session but for Bandicott's frequent requests for clarification. Terms that for us were part of everyday speech beleaguered him. The tools of our trade had significance only in the way they were used. A lot of jargon had crept into the media, and Bandicott was well-rehearsed with the antiwar movement's glossary on Vietnam: search and destroy, free fire zone, napalm; agents used exclusively to kill civilians, especially women and children.

To our ears his "intrinsic crimes" attitude seemed feminine; like trying to explain combat to a girl up at the club. To them military matters seemed incomprehensible and capricious and there was no basis for understanding.

"I have real problems with all of your assumptions," said Cassidy. "The ones about atrocities in particular. We were in charge. We were responsible. We did not do *anything* close to what you're talking about."

"Well, this is precisely the charge," Bandicott rallied. "Maybe you didn't, but you're only one person. In the Army in general it's all been covered up."

"No! Look, none of my unit *ever* committed a war crime; and just because there aren't more Calleys doesn't mean the Army has hidden anything."

"They tried to hide what happened at My Lai."

"I don't know what happened there except that people were killed . . . civilians, and the Army's going to court-martial every commander up to the division C.G. Over there we cared what happened. We did have one incident in our battalion—a lieutenant shot a prisoner out in the field, he was tried, convicted, and is in

Leavenworth right now. I don't believe it even made the news."

"Even if that's so," Bandicott said, "it doesn't affect the fact that the war's still an atrocity."

"I've been back for six months," I said, "listened to every news show on, and I've come to the conclusion the antiwar movement isn't against the war because of Calley or any weapon or bombings. They're against it because commies are the enemy and that's a problem for them. Because of that, to debate the issues is not relevant and this conversation is a waste of time."

"I'm not a communist."

"You haven't told me—a what, then?"

"I'm a progressive liberal," he said confidently.

"I know, there's some distinction. A communist approves of communist atrocities as necessary. The liberal whatever disapproves but usually works up some way of making it our fault."

"I'm disturbed by any atrocity," he defended. "But theirs are trivial compared to ours."

"Trivial," I mouthed slowly, "Tell the five thousand civilians murdered at Hue about how trivial they are. All the journalists had for that one was a great big yawn."

"Anyone studying the history of this war can see that their actions are only retaliation for what we've done."

"Oh sure. What we do is our fault, and what they do is our fault."

"Getting back to Calley, isn't the Army using him as a scapegoat?" Bandicott asked, abruptly turning to the others. He remained controlled and measured.

Feisty, outnumbered, I thought, but win or lose, this guy's taking us all on. So much for the interview.

"No, I don't believe he is," said Stretton, again our spokesman. "Since the story broke, we've discussed it a lot, trying to understand how a thing like that could happen. It's a fact that those people in the village of Xom Lang are dead. Calley not only had command responsibility, but appears to have had personal responsibility . . . in pulling the trigger. There's not much room for a defense. Right wingers are going for the scapegoat bit because they're frustrated with the circumscribed way we have to fight this war.''

"Right wingers think he's a scapegoat!" he exclaimed.

"Sure. The left are more cynical, they think it's business as usual . . . we kill it if it moves. The right has helped throw around the idea that you can't tell the civilians from the soldiers. But it's bull on both sides."

"Haven't you seen that picture of the Vietnamese girl running and burning with napalm? That's apart from Calley, and to me symbolizes our whole conduct of the war."

"Yes," acknowledged Stretton. "It's one of those pictures worth millions of words, but as a symbol it's as illogical as any generalizing from the particular. That picture only says if you get caught by accident in a war, it can be mighty horrible. I don't personally need convincing."

"We drop thousands of bombs. She stands for the thousands of others who were their targets."

"They're not targets," Stretton insisted. "Look, we are all frustrated with the restrained conduct of the war . . . gradual escalation . . . the whole thing. The North Vietnamese are fighting a total war, and we have political handcuffs on us. But even if we did get to fight our way, it would not mean mowing down civilians everywhere we looked."

"But if you can't tell the civilians from the soldiers . . ." Bandicott introspected.

"I can't believe you believe that! Come on. That's what Calley's defenders are trying to say."

Across from me, Stonehouse, a lieutenant we called D.J., sat up as if provoked. He had been lying behind Stretton and Andy. "Look man, when you're out there in the bush and three quarters of your casualties are coming from anonymous mines and booby traps, and Charlie's forcing civilians to help lay them, you began to look real hard at these people; but an officer's got to make sure that you keep making clear distinctions between soldier and civilian."

"Recently I was watching a program where some Vietnam veterans all talked about children throwing grenades. What kind of 'distinction' does that create?"

"Hell, I reckon I'd just drop the kid," drawled Stonehouse. "I ain't going to just stand there. Let me say something, though. You hear a lot of war stories, some of them over and over again. Some pieces play real well, I guess, like kids and grenades. Back in Nam I never heard of it even once. Now that I'm here, dudes talk like it was a daily occurrence. I think it's all bullshit. Some of them swear up and down that it's true. I still think it's bullshit."

"It's not implausible," commented Bandicott.

"I didn't say it didn't happen. Once. But it's not really the way gooks operate."

"Many people have come back from Vietnam who are against the war because of their experiences."

"You got to understand something," Andy shot in, "by now there are a couple million men who have gone to Vietnam, if you include Navy and Air Force pogues. For every swinging dick in the field humping with a M-16, there's thirteen who aren't. When they all get back here, though, you can bet your ass they've all fought in the Great Asian War. Most never even heard friendly fire, that's how close they were. They feel they've been close enough to have an expert opinion, though. But a kind of folklore is developing . . . myth . . . turning it into legend or something."

"The way I see it," interrupted Stretton, "the truth is being bent as far as possible solely because it will get us out of this war faster."

"Yeah, and what I was trying to say was the Army has drafted a lot of guys," Andy said. "Some were opposed to the war and were sent to Nam. Most would have managed to get themselves a job in the rear. They blew grass for a year and came back. What they would have seen probably only gave them more ammunition to oppose the war. They saw a war without an enemy, but now they've got the credibility of being veterans!"

"I want to tell a story," Johnson called from over by the closet door.

"Right," jabbed Andy, "I suppose you want to tell us again about how you put in for a Purple Heart for V.C.-V.D. . . ."

He laughed, "No, about this atrocity stuff. I think it's only natural if you scrape up hundreds of thousands of guys off every street corner in America, give them all loaded weapons, and dump them in some friggin' jungle on the other side of the world to stomp around for a year while getting shot at—a Calley or two is bound to pop up. I hope we don't get our two."

"I would argue about having them there in the first place," retorted Bandicott. "All the killing for a corrupt dictator like Thieu?"

"That's the trap the communists love to put us in," I said. "Whenever they want another country, the alternatives are either hand it over or war. The 'we only want peace' crowd doesn't have a hard time falling in with the commies. The Thieu thing's just icing. Hell, next to Pham Van Dong and his boys, Thieu's about as lethal as some scoutmaster."

"I think the 'peace crowd,' as you say, is only advocating that they work out their problems alone . . . without our bombing them into the Stone Age."

"I don't believe that for a minute," I said. "They want us to capitulate."

"Capitulate?" Bandicott asked. "There is no end in sight for this war. The North Vietnamese aren't going to give up. How can the United States possibly win?"

"If it's up to you, we won't win. I don't mean only you—the antiwar movement—all of you ignore the South Vietnamese; fighting and dying . . . several hundreds of thousands by now . . . because Nixon and Thieu asked them to? Peace? Right, to you it means handing over the South to the North Vietnamese army. Vietnam belongs to the North Vietnamese but not the South Vietnamese?''

"If you keep on helping the South Vietnamese, the argument will never end. How can the United States possibly win?'' This time the question brought silence, that singular unmentionable part of the war that hammered out optimism. Bandicott asked it to our silence and a roomful of distasteful reminders of our compromised efforts in that faraway place. That loaded possibility, couldn't he see so many parts of ourselves gone? None of us wanted to think that we had squandered ourselves on a losing war.

"Or,'' he drove on, "will Nixon continue to expand the war—beyond Cambodia?''

No one spoke. Cambodia, I thought, a minor sixty-day hiccup into the "Parrot's Beak,'' and he knows it as well as any of us. A protest leader's elixir, but not the right question for us. *Will we win? is the question!* Two hundred thousand troops have already been pulled out, with complete Vietnamization not far off . . .

"I don't know,'' drawled Stonehouse wearily. I could almost feel him considering his leg, the one that disappeared midway down the thigh.

"I think we can still win,'' said Stretton, sanguine in tone.

"*Will* the U.S. win? was the question,'' Bandicott asked smugly.

"A lot of Americans are sure as hell working hard to make sure we won't!''

"It's a screwed-up country that would allow it, and that's us.''

"Dudes are dying in the field, while some fuckers kiss Charlie's ass in Hanoi.''

The rancorous exchange dribbled away. It was over. Stretton stood up and, facing our college editor, spoke emphatically. "We will win if we put pressure on the North. People think bombing is the only thing left to us now . . . politically; but I'd like to see the South Vietnamese cross the DMZ. Then we could just hold tight in where we are with the NVA dashing back up the Ho Chi Minh Trail to get home. The North has never felt threatened. It's the way we ended it in Korea. Of course, we had leadership then in the White House and the Army. Now, we sit across the table from the North Vietnamese in Paris, our military *equals*. It's painful to be part of such a thing."

"I can't believe you're saying this," remarked Bandicott.

"It could have been different." Stretton shuffled his casted lower leg around and pumped a crutch a couple of times to move himself to the end of my bed.

"Can I ask you about the hospital? I mean, are you receiving good care?"

We all mumbled or grunted in affirmation.

"Is there anything you need!?" Suddenly effusive, he sounded as if he were ready to zip down to McDonald's for an order if we asked. I realized that he was seeing us as hospital patients in the usual sense—pajamaed, bedded, confined.

"We could use a few girls," offered Andy.

Oh, not for me, for Steve. It floated through my mind in response. *I'll strangle him if he says it*.

"Yeah? I've got an idea," Bandicott blurted, much less of the prim adversary. "The newspaper that I edit has an unclassified section, almost anything goes in there. You could advertise!"

"Right, like 'S & M enthusiast seeks likeminded whatever, preferably pre-med,' " I proposed.

"Well," hesitated Bandicott, "there are a few that—"

"What about 'Wanted, women keen on amputees . . . ' " someone else suggested.

"Keen on their what?"

"Whatever they're keen on."

"You'd better throw in—'skilled in the Oriental arts.' "

"Oriental arts?" asked Bandicott.

"You need floor mats and a couple of Oriental broads . . . for realism. So you mount up with one of them, any way you like; and just before you let out the clutch, she wheels around and karate kicks you in the nuts. Your mind goes into orbit—right over the Great Wall of China,'' joked Stonehouse.

"That's good?'' Bandicott asked innocently.

"It's only for mean bastards like me—with the proper training.''

"Why two girls?'' someone asked.

"Because they're small—you need a spare for a warm-up. Shoot, I know all about that stuff . . . I read *Terry and the Pirates* every Sunday when I was a kid.''

"All right,'' barked Stretton, "take this down, final copy. Leader in bold type or caps, 'Wounded,' no, 'Convalescing Vietnam Veterans' . . .''

"Officers.''

"Shut up, will you? Okay, then . . . 'affluent, free spending' . . .''

He waited for the laughter to stop. " 'Young officers desire female companionship. Call Lieutenant Steve Maguire, Ward Two, Walter Reed, TA9-8700.' ''

"Screw you, Stretton, I've had enough losers lately,'' I said. "Nice of you to share, though.''

"It's not generosity. They'd just never get through to me on the phone. If any call, send them down to the pit sometime after supper so we can check 'em out and divvy 'em up.''

The empty room seemed heavy with cigarette smoke when I retraced my steps out of the bathroom. The indolent air-conditioning ducts above my bed strained as I pushed up the window. It was raining. Disinclined to do anything, I stood there while droplets of water slid along the fluted edge of the window and dove irregularly into a broken chorus line on the sill. A faint fairy-light spray kicked up into the warm humid air that touched my face. Will we win the war? It bobbled in my head like an annoying fragment of a tune. Will we win the war, and who will I be if we don't?

For twenty-four years the world and I had learned to

live with each other, often trading punches, but still in the same weight class. Suddenly a dark jungly thing, it glowered at me, it goaded me, the new me, the pushover—not the me that I knew, but the thing I knew I'd become. Clammed up in a viny locket of a world, listening to a not-so-faraway war . . . and listening to people who said "us" and "we" who were fighting hard against my side.

Outside the window larger drops of water began to plop from their four-story tumble, scattering cool tears onto my face.

CHAPTER SIXTEEN

"Lordy me, Maguire, two lovely ladies come visit you, and you laid up snoozing the daytime away." It was Mrs. Lambert, a nurse, pitching her black accent high in a mock scold. She spoke no other way.

"My watch says it's bedtime," I grunted, not actually taking note of what she'd said.

"Now, I don't know if we going to let you entertain in quite that way." She swept across the room and hauled on the venetian blinds.

"Ladies?" I bolted up, shaking rebellion from my head. *What's she talking about?*

"I'm Susan Jamieson," came a softer voice. "I answered that ad . . . we talked on the phone last Wednesday. I've brought along my roommate, Sharon Kaplan."

My God, her, here, now. All I managed to say was, "Yeah."

Mrs. Lambert left, clucking nonstop that the girls shouldn't except too much from a guy who doesn't come in to go to bed until after she has arrived for work in the morning.

Damn. I pictured myself and swung in a reflex at my table. Glaring at them was my clear plastic globe of a left eye, a grisly display of raw meat under glass, the wide-eyed expression of a dying carp in rumpled pajamas. My hands burrowed through my assorted belongings.

219

"What are you looking for?" Susan asked, coming closer.

"Shit," I hissed, knocking the eyepatch to the floor. I made erratic sweeps for it. I had not told her I was blind. "Nothing," I answered, connecting with the patch and slinging it on in a single motion. I smiled, as if to say all was normal, like putting on a pair of glasses to see better.

"I thought you were coming Tuesday evening."

"I'm really sorry." She extended the tone of forgiving, as my words had come out unintentionally harsh. "But your phones have been busy for three days solid. Neither of us could make it on Tuesday. The switchboard won't pass on messages, so . . . we're here now."

"There's only one extension for the whole ward," I said, trying to be nice, but still sounding gruff.

"I did look for Captain Stretton like you said, but he's not there."

Stretton was supposed to send her on only if she was pretty. I had planned on being ready in any case Tuesday night—good civvies or even my khaki T.W.s—more nearly the recuperated officer than the bed-trussed casualty. Her visit with Stretton was on the pretext that he had no family and was particularly lonely and could use some cheering up. She had commented on my caring. Hell, Stretton was probably shacked up with his girl for the weekend.

I felt ridiculous, standing there in a frowsy half somnolence, unshaven, facing two girls who were thinking God knew what.

"No one on the ward, huh?" I asked, trying to conceive a diversion.

"Well, not in that big room at the other end, but . . . Sharon's brought along her guitar. Maybe we can find some others down here and have a concert."

If a girl could sound pretty, she did.

"Right," I said. "There's two guys in traction. I know they ain't going anywhere."

Walking around the end of the bed, I hesitated so I wouldn't stumble into them. I would have to tell them about my eyes. "Oh yeah, I should take one of your arms. Didn't tell you before that I can't see very well." I had lately been testing this lie, never able to predict when the lean truth, the "I'm blind," would stun. Mr. Magoo could draw a laugh, fun in the chaos of nearsightedness, and that was what I preferred just now.

Quickly both girls looped in at my sides and began tugging gently at my arms, drawing toward the door. I stood still, balking at the implicit helplessness, saying, "Hey, I'm not that bad off. I only need an arm to guide by." I reached for Susan's, but she had turned and I fetched one of her breasts instead.

Another black mark, I thought as I adjusted and took her elbow. "I'm sorry, I—"

"They're so small, I didn't think you'd notice."

"It's a reflex I've picked up from the nurses."

"The nurse that brought us in was in her sixties."

"Oh my God." I put my hand over my mouth. Schtick.

I leaned into the "Crib," named for a couple of adolescent dependents who had once occupied it along with their broken legs. Now a TV murmured softly on the right, McCann's bed. On the other side would be Ray Montgossa.

"Hey, Airborne," I rasped malignantly, "look what I've got."

"Well, come on and join us," McCann responded, sounding a mix of piquant interest and his usual wry self.

"Guests," I continued, "payoff from that newspaper ad I told you about."

"You mean you girls answered that stupid thing?"

"Well," Susan hesitated, "should I reconsider the idea? I wanted an excuse to come over here anyway."

"Too bad you weren't in on it from the start. They're rolling in every day. Scooping them up like winnings at a crap table." I felt a sudden urge to bite my tongue at that indelicacy.

"That's the way it's been?" Sharon cut in soberly.

I forced a wink and smile in her direction. "Hey, Goose, you awake?"

"Yeah, I'm making a puzzle . . . hurt my foot this morning trying to reach something in my cabinet and Mad Mary won't let the nurses give me a fuckin' goddamned thing for it," he answered sourly.

"Strange," said McCann, "that foot ain't bothered me all day."

"Yeah, weird, your mouth is painful to me all the time."

I belatedly introduced the girls to quell a typical flack session between two people long tired of staring at each other in the context of pain.

McCann pried for more about the ad, and I told all of them the truth. There had been only a few calls. The constant busy signal on the ward phone would have put off most. One wanted to know if I was interested in a peace thing—they hadn't any officers and she was sure that there were some that would help, especially ones who had been wounded. Another had recently been in an auto accident and was interested in astrological connections, at least that was the part I understood. The next to last girl called just to tell me that she had been born in Walter Reed. When I asked her, "Recently?" meaning to make a joke, she'd hung up. Susan had been the last; her warm vibrant voice had wished only to meet me.

Women visitors on Ward One weren't unusual. Families, relatives, friends and their friends clustered around this bed or that every day. Off-duty nurses or RAIN students would be around, sitting in on a card game or just talking. Three marriages had recently taken place, a couple more teetered, the fermenting normalities of people in their twenties anywhere. Bits and pieces of some of us were missing, the physics altered, but the chemicals bubbled and flowed the same as before.

Susan and Sharon had to be coaxed to pull out the guitar; but finally Sharon strummed into a long medley of requests, their voices blending with the sound of plenty of dormitory practice. The nurse on duty delivered rounds of cold beer.

Jim McCann still hung in traction because of a broken femur, and was heavily casted on the whole of his right side and most of his torso. Down the expanse of white plaster, painted in water color, was a succession of combat cameos: tanks, APC explosions, fire and smoke, C-119's depositing tiny parachuting forms across the plaster-hard sky of his chest.

The conversation after a time slid unavoidably to the war. The girls were interested, and laughed over McCann's Armageddon-emblazoned soma, his bullhorn cry of "hawk." After three beers he would be wearing a tattered bush hat, his only memento of a bad afternoon in a piece of jungle somewhere. Discreetly, preferring anecdotes to the provocative, I guided the conversation to some of our inexhaustible tales of Ranger school, which had been more physically demanding than Vietnam.

Jim and I had attended the same Ranger class in the winter of '68-'69, barely remembering each other, as we had been in different platoons; but one fuzzy recollection remained. A blanched face emerging upward from the other end of my rope, which disappeared over the dizzying edge of the mountain. I had been belay man at the top of this final exercise in the mountaineering phase of our training. On that mid-afternoon, the temperature had suddenly dropped into the twenties. Fog gripped the summit and thickened, the wind whirling it into clouds that rocketed past us like express train ghosts. It coated the rope and every rock nubbin with an indurate glaze of clear ice. With anguished fingers, I hauled at the stiffened field jacket, pulling it that last yard; above the breast pocket, the name tag McCann. He flopped over on his back and slowly announced, as if grimly contemplating what it would have meant, "I almost fell."

"I hear it's nice up here in the summer," I'd said.

"Yeah, next time I'll be sure to bring a date and a picnic lunch."

A grainy but permanent print of him remained in my memory. We had talked of it the first time we'd met on the ward, and now I retold the story for the girls.

Montgossa was quiet, either busy or asleep. That suited me. His purposely crude language could shorten a visitor's stay. He was supposedly married, although no one had ever seen his wife. On his debut mission in Nam he had piled his spotter plane at the end of a runway, and resented that we joked of it more than he resented that it had happened. He was not well liked on the ward.

"I was supposed to attend an Outward Bound course two years ago, but went to Russia and Poland instead—a student exchange. I'm interested in mountaineering, and if I get the chance, it's something I want to do," Susan said.

McCann seemed to be familiar with this school for wilderness survival training, and it separated us into pairs. Sharon's thick New York accent and encyclopedic knowledge of rock and blues music held a certain fraternal attraction; yet from my opposite side, the amiable conversation of the other two owned my interest. Curious about our lives and what had brought us to such an end, Susan asked many unpretentious questions. Responding, McCann flirted. Susan obviously liked him. As Sharon gently picked on her guitar, fragments of favorites jerked my attention back and we talked some more, although she volunteered little. Was she a natural introvert, I wondered, or coaxed into coming?

"Tell me how officers are promoted," I heard Susan say.

"Ask Steve," answered McCann. "He's getting promoted next week."

"For captain, it's automatic—with a few conditions fulfilled; but for major and above, it's kind of esoteric—it would take some time to explain."

"I don't mind," she said inexplicably.

"I do," interjected McCann with a sigh. "Why don't you tell us about your competitive swimming instead?" I listened impatiently as they traded the minutiae of their

shared interest. It explained the firm arms I'd felt earlier.
There would be a pair of inviting legs as well, I was sure;
and I couldn't avoid imagining her dripping wet.

She laughed amiably, and I could sense his good
looks flashing with each smile. The foursome had divided
as resolutely as an amoeba. The contrast with Sharon
became stark. Susan attracted and did it far beyond the
three beers McCann had drunk. After his four months on
Ward One, I knew him well enough to respect his judgment. Sharon's quiet intelligence was failing to compen-
sate. The woman's mind was not of lesser importance,
only lesser priority; to be discovered later, if there was a
later.

A mordant little problem, wafting from the juices of
jealousy, that nudged me into brooding. Both of these girls
were mine; not as coolly deduced possessions, but as a
whispered pigheaded right. I hadn't brought them to this
room like an open box of chocolates.

The supper trays arrived and the girls decided to go.
They had stayed far longer than they had planned. I
walked them up the hall with the satisfaction of getting the
last good-bye, and their lingering pleased me.

"Three more weeks in traction," McCann issued,
when I went back into his room, "then maybe a week or
so until I get a brace made up. Then I'll be after her. What
do you think, Goose?"

Montgossa made a lewdly guttural sound in confirmation. "I could climb aboard that stuff anytime."

"I know, but that isn't much of a testimonial,"
McCann said to me. "He'd bugger Mad Mary if she gave
him half a chance."

A disagreeable snigger came from the other side.

"I've been keeping my eye on a couple of RAIN
students since I've been here," McCann went on, "for
when I get free. But I'd say this Susan ought to be number
one." He spoke with a convincing certainty, continuing to
describe her in some detail, ostensibly for my benefit.

He changed the subject. "I'm in a slight dilemma.

The doc doesn't think I'm going to have enough bend in my leg to use a clutch. That'll be it for my Chevelle SS, but I've been thinking of something like a Mercedes Benz—something classic, you know?''

His choice of cars? I thought. Who cares? McCann, like Andy Wilson, had been severely wounded, but in time would not come out all that disabled. He'd do most things again, the important things anyway; and one of them would be at my expense. In high school they had the cars and the girls, I had my shoes. Why do I have to live through this again? I asked myself. She's a sheer escarpment of wind-polished rock, without any apparent hand- or footholds. So what! I etched an emerging decision with the bottom rim of my beer can into the wet on the table. Why not me? I would call Susan in the morning. There was one thing McCann couldn't do and that was have her now.

Periodically I dialed Susan's dormitory the following morning, but without success. I conceded that her classes and extra language labs made her absence probable, but winced at one thought—that she might be linked to McCann's phone on Ward One. With all he'd said about her, I couldn't expect him to just lie there and wait for his cast to come off.

I stood in my bathroom and plugged a toothbrush into my mouth, debriefing myself over the events of the previous minutes. A specter from my past had become real, almost from overwork, it seemed. Dwayne Skinner, my point man, whose blunder had triggered that blast. He was here at Walter Reed and had phoned. He claimed he had been around almost as long as me, though he was away from his ward, 39, most of the time.

Mother humpin' Dwayne Skinner, gee-ez. I slid a towel back on its rail. Same familiar Tennessee accent, and as full of bull farts as ever. Deciding to put off shaving for the moment, I shuffled to the bed. I knew what his injuries were that first week together in Saigon, only a bad ankle and some loss of sight in one eye. Yet he was whining as though he'd been wounded a couple more times in the interval.

On the phone he rehashed the events of November sixth and the incident itself, frontward and backward. Listening, I was surprised at how different his version was from my own. It seemed as though I'd been wounded somewhere else. As history closed in on the final moment, I noted a shaky stammer intruding into this speech. He knew, too, of my condition, of its permanence.

I wasn't all that anxious to see him again, except that he had heard more news of my old recon platoon than me and would bring letters.

Skinner arrived late and I was already getting ready to go out for the evening. I didn't expect he'd make it at all. Bouncing a gift of a six-pack on the bed, he introduced someone who'd shadowed him—his girlfriend, an Army nurse on his ward. Female officers were presently his style, he said. He began logging a mini-history of his hospitalization, pausing every so often to confirm if I'd experienced the same indignities. I shook my head, even when I had. In a few minutes he'd talked us back into the Mekong Delta, to the spot of the blast. I listened tolerantly as he went over it all again. Like a small jittery bird pecking among the blades of grass and small plants, he searched for some morsel of circumstance that would exonerate him.

"Look, Dwayne, I told you to go down that trail . . ."

"But we knew it was there!"

". . . to disarm it, as we almost always did," I reminded him, and went on. "No one but me was responsible for my following you, just an instinct to supervise. You know I never liked any of you guys to do anything with explosives. I could really only trust myself for sure."

"I just didn't see it," he was saying in brittle self-reproach, as I wondered if I hadn't made it worse.

I thought of the sequel to Andy's own tragic story.

The day he was wounded, he'd been the one to trigger a very large explosive charge. Several were hit, but the full force had literally disintegrated his radio man. Andy knew him well, knew about his wife, who was nine months pregnant. In his early days in traction, Andy thought of it often, the constancy of his own pain a reminder of his responsibility as a direct lethal agent of the horror in that family's life. He decided it was his grim duty to go and see the wife once he was well. By the time I'd met him, the guilt had slackened; the story had become no more than a sad incident. So would Skinner's.

"Dwayne, we tramped a lot of paddies together, an awful lot," I said, as if we'd been pals. "Heard a lot of shit go bang, but there's more to it than the sound and the smoke. We were touched by it. We weren't just in the war. We were the war, and that's why we're here today." I yanked off another can and sat down for the first time.

"But . . . *why* did you send us down that trail?" He was obviously not finished.

"Because I wanted to," I pronounced coolly, hoping to end it. I excused myself to search for a tie in the closet. His attentions turned to the girl. He whelped an heroic yarn about our small legion, featuring Skinner and his lieutenant to the fore.

In Vietnam, Skinner's clowning led most of our activities when we rested at base camp; but still he'd been more tolerated than liked by the rest of the platoon. My own feelings for him had always been mixed. Although a sergeant, his heedless bravado stymied him as a leader; so I let the point team develop into his thing. Its greater potential for action suited him, as he had often and openly admitted his desire to win a Silver Star and be recognized as a hero. If time and place had conspired to give him the opportunity, it would have come.

I pretended to listen to Skinner's stories but heard nothing. Hell, additional recognition would have come to me if it hadn't been for Skinner. Didn't I once actually think about a DSC? I saw myself in him. I tried to rationalize that a professional officer often had to put objectives or missions ahead of personal safety. The highest purpose was not surviving a one-year tour, but fighting and winning; that is, engaging in some significant reaping of the enemy. Setting for myself the goal of a Silver Star or DSC would have been fairly suicidal. Had I dangled myself out there in front of the enemy, like live bait trying to lure him in? Knowing that my foe was wily and could strip off bait in his sleep . . . or leave it bitten and mangled. Of all the higher medals I had seen that were given and deserved, not one had been the goal of its recipient. Each instance had amounted to a shoot-out in order to escape some desperate situation that had cornered them. Had I actually been in search of a shit storm to throw myself into for the pleasure of trying to escape? The beer cans emptied; the two stood to leave.

"Sir," he said with the hint of a question. The "sir" buzzed my attention; it had been "Steve" since he'd come in. "Could you do me a favor? I'm getting out soon and would like to get promoted to staff sergeant before I do . . . I've brought some papers for you to sign—an efficiency report, backdated, and letter of recommendation. It's all filled out, just have to sign it."

He handed me the papers. Straightening them, I slid them into my top drawer without comment.

"I could take them away with me now."

"It's all right," I said. "I'll see to them."

"Maybe I should take them . . . and bring them back for you to sign tomorrow," he blurted with some concern.

"I *said* I'd take care of it." They'd stay in the drawer forever. Skinner wasn't my choice as a reflecting pool.

Andy met them both on the way out. "Who are they?"

"That, my friend, is Dwayne Skinner, the famous trip-wire artist. Been here five months, but we just linked up again for the first time since Nam."

"I've seen those two before, up at the club. She's a nurse, hefty mama, face like a bunker . . . even pockmarked from a few hits. He looks like Elvis in his early years, you know, hillbilly greaser. You know something, we were in the club and those two were sitting not far away. I almost said something; he stared at you all night.''

''You know, Andy, it's a little bit worse when you get blown away by a hotdog.''

Reluctantly I had to admit Skinner and I were connected by the most profoundly important thing that had ever happened to me.

I sat on my bed and tossed through my things, searching for a smoke; but I'd had my last one on the way in the night before. My mind refocused on the scene and that instant in time. The undergrowth, the pale green line, Skinner's boot, me crouching, a thing of incredibly compacted fury. I supposed that it was only natural that it was a hard thing to shake—that last thing you ever see.

CHAPTER SEVENTEEN

"Steve," called Cotton Ruthbin, a captain from the 101st. Shot up, he'd been hanging in traction for seven months. "We're having a little celebration. Come here and meet a couple friends of mine... John E. Walker and James 'Firewater' Beam."

"What's the occasion?"

"Getting this damned leg cut off."

"Ouch," I grunted with a frown, "give me a toss of the Walker. After all this time?"

"It's not getting any better," he replied with resignation. "It's worse, sort of slowly rotting. We've tried everything, but the pain's increasing. There's just not enough circulation left... so the docs gave me a choice. Stay right here in bed waiting for gangrene to set in or whatever, or get free of it. Not much of a choice really."

"When is the big day?"

"Day after tomorrow."

"That raunchy dude should find its way to the mess hall by Friday," quipped Cassidy from his wheelchair.

"Nice," said Cotton at the arrival of another person.

"... Never notice it in a stew."

"Ever think of calling a taxidermist?" The banter failing to die was jerked from my attention by a female voice, unmistakably Susan's.

"Steve, I heard you over here. I was just going across

231

the hall to visit Jim, but his curtains are pulled and a doctor and some nurses are doing something to him. Nothing serious, I hope.''

"He's getting his shoulder drained," informed Cassidy, "daily routine."

"Yeah, he's full of pus," I said matter-of-factly, hoping the association would stick and wondering if she'd gone to my room first. "We're celebrating," I went on. "They're going to chop off Cotton's leg—that's him." I pointed and introduced her.

"Celebrating?" she asked, as if preparing to behold the act.

"I had to make a decision," Cotton said. "I've given it my best for seven months. Irreconcilable differences— it's a bitch, we used to go everywhere together... Hey Wilson," called Cotton, and I assessed that Andy had just passed by in the hall.

"I've been looking all over for you," Andy said to me with some irritation.

"I've been here. I want you to meet Susan Jamieson. She's the one I told you was with us last Sunday over in the Crib."

"Hello," he said tonelessly, then moving closer to my side, added, "that booze is cool. You said we were going to mass at St. Augustine's College."

"We've got nearly two hours."

"Fifty-five minutes."

"It's only a small one, on account of Cotton's leg coming off. Besides, maybe I'll stay here." I had to do something, and leaving Susan there, ten paces from McCann, wasn't it.

Andy went over to Cotton's bed, and the details began again with another charging of his cup. "When that guy in the black hood brings his ax down... I'm going to be driving out of here in my car... before they've even washed up the blood."

Their conversation went on; but I wanted to talk to

Susan, at least arrange to see her again. I had to talk to her alone.

"Come on, sit down," I invited, and motioned her to sit next to me on the unoccupied bed I'd been leaning against. "I'd like to see you tomorrow night," I whispered. I preferred the telling to the asking.

"Sure," she said without hesitation, "I could—"

"Man, are you coming or not?" Andy interrupted, now obviously perturbed.

"Just a minute." I tried to conceal my own rising irritation and surprise at his impatience. I got up anyway. I needed to know why he was so bothered. We still had plenty of time.

"Could you get over to A.U. somehow?" Susan asked.

"Of course," I replied, having no idea in hell where the place was. "Let's go outside for a moment." I put my arm on her shoulder, but Andy seemed to want me to take his shoulder and just leave her there. It caused a stupidly awkward exit as we went out through the fire door on the other side of the room.

"Where's your friend going? I've only got two seats."

Grimly, I tried to ignore him, while wondering how Susan might be taking this. His reactions were stupid. I had told him all about her; she was hardly a late night Goal Post liaison. Andy dropped into the MGB and began gunning the engine.

"What are you going to do?" I asked her quickly.

"I don't know, maybe see if they're finished with Jim."

"Nah, they wouldn't be," I said dismissively, casually, while my mind sprinted around to shut all the doors. "He's got a lot of infection."

"Oh, then I'd better look in on him. He looked so good on Sunday."

"He'd be out of it ... from a shot. His kind of wounds take forever to heal." Damn, I thought, in a minute I'll make her so sorry she'll be in there holding his hand.

"Got any paper? I'll leave a note at his bedside that I was here."

"I'll tell him for you. Too late for you to go back in now." I flipped open my Braille watch. "Twenty to seven . . . visiting hours are over. You know the Army, eighteen-thirty hours and . . ." Could she still believe me?

Andy switched on the tape deck, and music from The Band erupted from his car. His foot punched out a few more insistent revs. I felt my grip loosening, the ledge retained by splintering fingernails.

"Sorry about Andy, it's on account of his dog. Someone poisoned it. He found it this morning. He's pretty upset." An empty silence formed to my front, as if she had just walked away. "How'd you get over here anyway?"

"I took the bus. It's a long way. You have to make two changes." There was a tinge of discontent in the voice. "Oh, I've gotta ask you something before you go. About a newspaper clipping my mother sent me on a minister named Cory Coggins, an Army chaplain who lost his leg and is supposed to be a patient here. My father's a Methodist minister; and when Cory was a boy, he went to one of my dad's churches. My mother said my dad influenced him into going into the ministry. I'm interested in meeting him. Is he on the ward with the other officers?"

My stomach squeezed into a lump. Cory Coggins, the wheelchair speed fiend, was now walking quite well, playing golf even better. He had a way with women that could dwarf this little problem of McCann. "He's left . . . he's on convalescent leave . . . but don't worry, I'll take care of you. I'll get you a cab."

"I don't have enough for the fare. Anyway, it's only a little over an hour before the next bus."

I wrenched out my wallet and remembered there were only two dollars. Giving them to her, I sprang at the car door. "Give me some money," I hissed.

Andy grumbled something and began sorting through some bills. With impatience I seized the whole handful.

"Hey, that's everything I've got," he protested.

I dealt him half, having no idea of the denominations, then shoved the rest at Susan. As she began to protest, I said, "Go up that corridor—call on one of the pay phones there—and meet him out front." I slammed my door saying, "Seven, tomorrow, I'll call you before I come, okay?" The MGB jerked and bucked as Andy shoved at the gearshift meanly. The small car edged itself narrowly between the closely parked cars in the circular drive.

"You know, Andy," I mused, "cotton dresses on broads sure are nice. I mean, the synthetic stuff is fine for night, like when you go out; but summer days have got to be cotton, short ones too. Not many girls are wearing cotton dresses much anymore, have you noticed? Sometimes you just got to get back to Mother Earth, you know that song?"

"Sometimes I think you need to be up on one of the psychiatric wards getting checked out."

"So how much do I owe you?"

"Thirty bucks."

"All right, okay, so what do you think of this Susan Jamieson?"

"Cute."

"That's all?"

"I said she was cute," he snapped, "you know, cute!"

I sat there for a while not saying anything, but at last I said, "I like her."

"She's too happy."

"You'd be happy too if someone just gave you thirty bucks." I turned to him. "How can anyone be too happy? I suppose you'd prefer the ones doing this bummed-out thing . . . like it was sophistication, 'I've seen it all. The world is a fuckin' hassle.'"

"Hell, this one probably'd say . . . 'trees, yeah, sky, oh wow! Blind guy . . . oh wow!' She ain't your type."

"What the fuck do you know," I grumbled.

"I've spent about every day with you for the last six months, and you're one of the only wild bastards left in this Army. I should say, we are. Broads are great; but if you take them too seriously, they'll have you all fucked up."

"There's been a lot of changes, Andy. Some I've been slow to recognize, and some I still don't want to. The war has been turned into a jungle jug-fuck, and worse, I ain't going back. Wild, hell, I can't even get in a decent fight anymore. I've been thinking lately about our good old Army. What does that leave for me?... The second nicest thing in the world. And that's what I want now."

"You'd go for the first one that came along, and I don't think you know what you want," he added with a heavy breath.

"Not a chance, man," I said angrily. "Look, we've been through all this before. Just because I'm working hard at it don't mean shit."

"You don't need to work at getting tangled up with her... her in particular."

"Maybe I won't," I said, figuring to end the talk by hinting to agree with him, but without being satisfied that I understood his objection. Was he seeing in her something I wasn't? Was he jealous... jealous of the possibility that she could come between us?

Soon Andy would be discharged; and the inevitability of what it meant hacked between us like a well-honed machete. Fateful insignificance; Andy back at the same college he'd dropped out of to join the Army. A student! I'd be out soon enough myself, poking around, a blind combatant, probably a student again myself.

Two unknown soldiers; uncommitted to what they were to be, and uncommitted to lifting the camouflage of self-deception that concealed their animus at these strange demotions. So down diverging trails they'd go, one more likely than the other to remain alone.

*   *   *

"Any news?" Susan asked. Her typical enlivening style of questioning always left little room for my typically negative answers.

"I had the gastroscopy I told you about. I'm going to be operated on for a tumor."

"They found a tumor?"

"Yeah, they found that it interferes with the proper digestion of beer." I smiled at her. "It's a polyp, benign." I took a gulp of air and let out a classic belch to demonstrate. "You don't want me going around like that all the time, do you?"

"Wicked man," she said, "you guys really do get close to the body's functions, don't you?"

"It's something to do. TVs in every room, but no swimming pool. And obviously I've got to have this thing cut out. It's uncomfortable all the time now."

"Changing the subject," she said, "I was wondering if you'd mind me reading to you." She pulled something from her bag. "I found this old paperback *Last Letters from Stalingrad* lying on a table in the school cafeteria. I read it a while ago, but I thought of it again after talking to you on the phone. You know, like it says on the cover, 'The doomed men of Hitler's Sixth Army . . . eloquently reveal their thoughts and feelings as they face certain death.' "

"Thanks a lot, pal. Things aren't great around here, but *doomed*?"

"That's not why I thought you'd be interested. It's the men themselves . . . them facing their fate. You guys are having to do that, like Cotton facing amputation last week. I think the same kind of humor is here. Listen, 'Over eighty men are lying in this tent; but outside there are countless men. Through the tent you can hear screaming and moaning, and no one can help them. Next to me lies a sergeant from Bromberg, shot through the groin. The doctor told him he would be returned home soon. But to the medic he said, "He won't last until the evening. Let him lie here until then." The doctor is such a good man. On the other side, right next to me against the wall, lies a soldier from Breslau who has lost an arm and his nose, and told me that he won't need any more handkerchiefs.' You guys describing things are funnier. I guess you can afford to be. You're not preparing for an unknown death, but an unknown life ahead. You've talked about that before."

"I'd rather have my fate than freeze to death in Russia. I see the parallel, though. The man with no nose. Amputations are always good for a chuckle. There was once this major here who lost a leg just below the knee. He got fixed up with a good prosthesis and they eventually let him go back to Nam as an advisor. He wasn't there a month when he stepped on another mine and blew his new prosthesis to shreds. Lying there, he yelled at the gooks, 'Fooled you this time, didn't I, you bastards.' "

"The humor's in the men, not the wounds."

"You gotta be one cool guy to go back and hump the boonies with a prosthetic leg."

"You seem to have plenty of humor, but I don't think it's connected with what happened to you."

"Yes, it is. It's connected to something called Polish roulette. You lived in Poland once, right? You run through a mine field with your hands over your ears to protect them from the sound of the blast . . . barefoot to make smaller prints . . . eyes closed to protect them from schrapnel . . . I guess I peeked."

"I like the way you're zany and dry at the same time."

"There's a dark side to this thing, but I do joke about it. It helps others put it into perspective. I avoid playing the clown, though."

"We're spending a lot of time together, and I think I understand why Andy enjoys your company so much. Anyway, you want me to read some more?"

I nodded, and she began reading pieces she'd marked, pieces of thought from men with their futures below E and deep in the red . . . haunting bits written to family, friends, lovers; last love letters written by those who knew it would be their last.

" . . . Nobody knows what will happen to us now, but

I think this is the end. Those are hard words, but you must understand them the way they are meant. Times are different now from the day when I said good-bye and became a soldier. Then we still lived in an atmosphere which was nourished by a thousand hopes and expectations of everything turning out well in the end. But even then we were hiding a paralyzing fear beneath the words of farewell which were to console us for our two months of happiness as man and wife. I still remember one of your letters in which you wrote that you just wanted to bury your face in your hands in order to forget. And I told you then that all this had to be and that the nights in the East were much darker and more difficult than those at home . . . ' ''

"The nights do stay in your mind more—especially ambush patrols. Hey, Suzy, I didn't tell you about going over to the colonel's house, my battalion commander from Nam."

"You said he'd gotten in touch with you."

"He's assigned to the Pentagon now. Took me over to his house in Falls Church for dinner and told me all the details of what happened after I left. The battalion moved its fire support base to the Bobo Canal . . . Okay, here's the parrot's beak of Cambodia, that's where they are right this minute." I traced the outline of the border on the wall to demonstrate. "The Bobo was a main infiltration route while I was there. It comes down like this—straight southeast, right into our A.O., Area of Operation. The Old Man said that then the gooks found alternate routes, and there were only a few skirmishes the whole time he was there."

"Meaning, if you hadn't been wounded where you were, you probably wouldn't have been?"

"Unfortunately, my recon platoon got chopped up in those skirmishes."

"Were many killed?"

"Surprisingly none, but almost everyone was wounded. A couple were fairly bad off. One of my squad leaders, Robby Smith, took three bullets in the back. The C.O.

dusted him off with the C & C and no doubt saved his life. They were down to only five men."

"What do they do, just fill the whole platoon back up with new guys?"

"With recon, it's a bit different. They're all volunteers. After that the Old Man could only get a couple, so he disbanded the unit and let his successor deal with it. You know, Susan, the platoon as I knew it lasted about ten months. I was the third of four lieutenants to shape that platoon; the first two lasted only a month or two before they were hit. I lasted almost five. With each soldier having only a one-year tour, any unit is doomed to time; but it hurt to think of it. We worked so hard for something so ephemeral."

"Do you think your commander feels like the boxer who accidentally blinds his opponent in the ring then vows never to box again?"

"I think he feels bad about it, but he could face another tour in Vietnam. So if he feels any futility in the war, he has to keep it as an undercurrent. He's probably like me, though, thinking this war isn't futile in purpose. If you've been attacked, that kind of thinking is a luxury.

"You're misreading me. I understand the pragmatism of war, but for the loser there's an immeasurable futility, and the winner has to honor so many dead."

"The NVA don't talk about futility, I'm sure. They don't really seem to mind losing thousands."

"Steve, are we gonna win this war, do you think?"

"We've got to. Because I don't want fifty-thousand good men to have died for zip. Besides, we should and we can and we damn well better. Hell, these days winning only means *stopping* the communists. Defeating them has been taken from us. We're only allowed to toy with them. At this point though, I'd be satisfied just stopping them. I've given enough. I could be happy with that." I hopped off the bed and went into the closet to fetch a sport jacket. My thoughts were on the win or lose of the war. They weighed on me like a heavy rain weighs on an already sodden hillside. The slippage was not just a portent of a mudslide, but a sign of its inevitability. My army at Walter Reed, with its bureaucrats as generals leading troops of rear-echelon clerks and women majors, had made a long march from the Ranger Department of Fort Benning. The sensation had been one of something slowly digesting me—as if in a monster's intestinal tract. I might balk or cramp, but I could never turn around. I'd been spending so many listless mornings preoccupied with the state of my army, while headquartered in my room, watching Andy Griffith and *Beverly Hillbilly* reruns. Maybe I was taking unfair advantage of Susan's willingness to listen to it all. "Let's go up to the club and get some dinner." I came out and she was standing by the door. "I get kinda intense about this stuff sometimes. It's all I can think about. Of course, the TV and radio don't let me forget, and never fail to tick me off."

"It's okay. I can take it. I am in International Studies, after all. Conflicts are the pivot for half my subjects. I know war is 'the ultimate ratio of international politics, the final and unanswerable divide for producing solutions to conflict, has always been the organized application of violence in the form of war.' I memorized it for a test. My teacher wrote the book, and I figured I'd see that one again. It's funny, for the whole time I've been in college, we've been fighting a war, and I've never met one single person who was in it. I like getting to talk to you."

CHAPTER EIGHTEEN

My cab pitched along, the driver abusing the steering wheel and stomping brake and accelerator as if they were stubborn. Sitting in the rear, desultory thoughts jostled with my body and blended with a warm anticipation for the end of the ride. I ignored the longer outlook, which still remained as inscrutable as the unknown passing landscape.

"How'd your accident happen?" he asked, interrupting a silence that had lasted since our exchanges about the unabating D.C. heat.

"It wasn't an accident, they did it on purpose."

"On purpose?!" he jerked himself around to look at me. "Who?"

"Some North Vietnamese bastard."

"Oh, you mean the war. I thought you meant someone did it to you on purpose."

"Well what else would you think when you pick up a blind guy at Walter Reed in the middle of a war?"

"I dunno. I pick up a lot of problems. I try not to think about 'em. Walter Reed's good, though. Ike was there, ya know. He was there when he died. I'll bet they'll be fixing you up soon, huh?"

"No."

"Can't they do somethin'?"

"No."

The end of a long stretch and we swung through the traffic at Tenley Circle, only a few blocks from the Goal Post, heading toward American University in silence.

"I know what I'd do if that happened to me," he said pensively, as if to someone standing outside his open window, "I'd kill myself. I couldn't take being blind."

It startled me, the directness of it. No one had ever come even close to slinging it into my face, or even my rearviewed image. Forgetting my own impulse for suicide in Vietnam, I had an instinct to defend myself, to defend blindness. "You're talking about going blind; if you really did, you wouldn't have an aversion toward yourself. You'd hate the blindness, but the will toward self-preservation is stronger."

"No . . . man, you can't do nothin' if you can't see nothin'."

I thought of his cab and said "yeah" unintentionally.

"Sure," he brayed, "it would have to be quick, though."

"I'm not aware of blind people knocking themselves off at any unusual rate, are you?"

"Bullet in the head, that'd be the best way, get it over, you know." He tossed his comments over his shoulder like the bits of paper and wrappers that littered the floor at my feet.

"I can't change what happened to me, but I'm not unhappy outside of that."

"What are you going to do with yourself, then?"

"I don't know."

"Yeah, man, like I said before—I couldn't take that."

"I can still come over here to A.U. every night for some ass," I lied, feeling the moment right.

Pulling into a side street, the cab halted like the last frame of a slot machine; the man's head turning, as if pregnant with payoff. "No kidding . . . I'll bet a lot of those broads would feel really sorry for someone who was blind."

I breathed heavily, beaten, and decided to say no more.

"Where exactly you wanna go anyway?"

"Letts-Anderson. There'll be a girl waiting for me."

"Lots of ass around there," he mused.

"They're not so kind to taxi drivers?"

"Nah . . . the little cock bites . . . I get a lot of looking, though. All that pussy, just walking down the street."

"I could kill myself if things got that bad," I retorted.

"Hey, things ain't that bad."

"That was my point."

Susan and I walked slowly, with no particular direction in mind, across the languid evening campus of American U. Other summer school students passed at random, sounding as unhurried as ourselves; they seemed a species apart from their classmates of a few weeks earlier who were crazed to hysterics over the Cambodia incursion. Even the graffiti yawned, bored from insistent Day-Glo roaring at quiescent buildings . . . Free Bobby . . . Angela . . . Huey . . . Weather Underground—no competition for the soft scuffled echo of our footsteps.

Probably it was all just asleep—as if a huge sombrero had been pulled over the place to wait out the heat. In a few weeks bandoleers would be thrown across the chests, shopping carts filled with pelting rocks would again be pushed through clouds of tear gas, and professional radicals would spring onto Ward Circle to hawk revolution like bottles of snake oil.

Susan observed well, neither voyeur nor sympathizer. Her descriptions were always intriguing, particularly those of the life and times of peace rioters. We had been seeing a great deal of each other, often talking far into the night, but not actually dating. That somehow seemed intrusive. Yet I noted my feelings for her growing steadily. By now I liked her far more than I had liked that first impression, my reason for trying to develop the attraction. But she was an enigma. I sensed a vague field between us when we were together. Although her robust enthusiasm and consistent optimism drew me without hesitation, there were invisible spines. It was as if something would be damaged between us if I touched her. The whole relationship hurtled forward like an overloaded airplane, straining every rivet to get off the ground and too far down the runway to stop. It would lift off or crash.

Maybe Andy had been right about her not being my type. I had always preferred another kind, the ones who were just this side of slut. They understood me, understood my impatience. Susan, however, turned everything upside down with her opposites, and dazzled me.

"Why did you decide to transfer from Greensboro, and to pick this place . . . especially now?" I asked, having only talked around it before.

"I wanted to transfer to Georgetown—it's well known for international studies, but my father said, 'You're not going there and get some rotten ol' Catholic boyfriend.' "

"I'd respond, in Latin if I could." She laughed.

"And since here Methodist ministers' kids get a tuition cut—A.U. got the nod. Besides, the School of International Service is good. Anyway, it didn't get chaotic around here until this spring, after Cambodia and Kent State. Kids started coming into Washington from all over, looking for a free place to sleep. A lot of them found one in the hallways, bathrooms, and lounges of my dorm."

"But why are you in international service?"

"Because during my summer in Poland and Russia, two years ago, I became interested in how politics affect people's lives. Before that I was alternately majoring in art and biology. I could never make up my mind which was more interesting. That trip, though, settled the question. I was hooked on international relations."

"On politics or people?"

"Over there it's difficult to separate. But the events that went on around me seemed more important than my mud puddles of amoebae. Like the time I visited the shrine at Czestochowa because the family I stayed with told me

I'd never understand Poland unless I did. I found myself on the next train, without my passport, which was being held by local police. Beating the authorities is the Poles' favorite game. My friends said I wouldn't need my passport there . . . but they didn't tell me the shrine was a couple of hundred miles away.

"When we arrived, everyone was waiting for Cardinal Wyszynski; it was his birthday, and some people had made a pilgrimage to say prayers for him. He was already very late, so eventually everyone went into the Chapel of the Black Madonna. They had found out I was an American. I got pushed up to a place of honor in front of the altar rail—sweating it out, trying to make the sign of the cross in the right direction and attempting to pray in Polish-sounding syllables.

"Afterward, during another long wait, the priest took me and some of the others up to the top of the tower to look out on the countryside because of rumors that troop movements had taken over the roads. He said disruptions were almost always carried out by the Russians around holy days . . . The rumors appeared true. We could see all kinds of troops. Since the cardinal wouldn't get past, we left on foot for a train. It was hours late, and on our way back it was stopped again and again to allow army trucks and tanks to cross the tracks. My friends and the passengers were glued to the windows, watching. They had decided Czechoslovakia was being invaded. They were right.

"Back in Gdansk I had to walk part of the way home alone. It was early morning and very foggy, and I got cut off in a small square where a Russian unit was lining up its trucks. Standing there in the middle of them, I was convinced something big was on; World War Three was about to break in Central Europe, and here I was, already surrounded by the Red Army."

"So that's when you became internationally minded?" I asked playfully.

"They weren't going . . ." She made the sound of a

wolf whistle. "Just looking—staring. I had on a very short dress . . . and would you believe a mini-trench coat, and just then I felt like the hems were as high as my belt buckle.

"So I came here to study and to understand politics and people abroad . . . But the real difficulty I'm having is understanding radical teachers, like one I've got for economics who explains everything by saying *we're* the ones who've got a military-police state. He hates this country. There are a lot more around here like him. Funny, many Eastern Europeans I found either secretly or up front idolize America . . . like on that same train, the one going back to Gdansk. It was very crowded and I became compressed between a mass of passengers and a man sitting on a stack of suitcases. Hearing me speak, he suddenly stood up, saying, 'American, American,' and unfastened the top case. It was full of cherries. He began giving me handfuls—armloads, and when I tried to say no more, he still wanted to give more—saying, 'You American, I give you all,' while showing me that every case bulged with cherries.

"And later on I tried to get some sleep on a baggage rack, but a conductor woke me for tickets and identification. I showed him I had nothing, but gave him my Social Security card. He looked at it, turned it over upside down, then looked at me with an incredibly tired expression saying, 'American,' punched a hole in my card and gave it back."

I chuckled. "Maybe it had more to do with you than your country."

"No, things like that happened to everyone in our group. VIP treatment from everyone—although I do have this girl-next-door face or something."

"The foldouts in *Playboy* have a look like that."

"I don't know. I never got searched or detained or questioned, although with the others it was constant. Anyway, what I've been getting at is that that trip was a watershed for me, like the war must have been for you?"

"I suppose. The war certainly was the most dramatic

thing that has ever happened to me. I've got enough water in my shed to keep me awhile."

"I've come to realize how people's lives can be perplexed by politics. Like, on my last day in Poland. I asked the mother of the family I stayed with if there was anything I could send her. Aspirins was all she wanted. Aspirins! She suffered from painful joints she'd developed in a labor camp during the war. I sent out a few bottles. They never reached her. My letters don't either. I've gotten theirs, but they think I've forgotten them. I'd prefer to forget politics, but I figure a realistic worldview requires an appreciation of the power of it—a kind of loathing respect, maybe."

"Maybe. It makes me think of those protesting students, in spite of how much I dislike them. It seems like people and politics are hitting them directly for the first time in their lives . . . by way of the draft rather than the moral outrage. It's a bitch to think that one of them got us together. Bandicott never did do that article on us guys, did he?"

"No, I've looked every week. You might give him more credit, though. It was a sincere impulse to help you guys out." She placed her arm around my waist for a few moments, and I could sense her approval at what had turned out. Wryly, I envisioned myself standing in front of Bandicott to pin the Legion of Merit on him. We continued to walk, my hand lingering on her shoulder rather than just guiding on it; listening to her voice rather than just her words. Briefly we entered a building, to be mugged for change by a pair of vending machines.

Outside again, she said, "I haven't mentioned to you that I've gotten an offer to train with the Peace Corps, to go to Brazil as some kind of community organizer. Thinking about it now—when I consider working two part-time jobs this fall to pay for bomb-scared and boycotted classes—a couple of years in Brazil could be more worthwhile. What do you think of the idea?"

"It could be a good idea," I answered. About to ask her something, I stiffened as if in mid-brain a small kernel of neurons had seized; me tapping around with my white cane in a V.A. hospital in Connecticut, her in Rio, sitting brown and smiling in a sidewalk café, falling in love with Sergio Mendez.

"But on the other hand," I stammered, "you only have two semesters left. It would be a shame to leave now . . . and miss everything." I noticed that we were no longer following the sidewalks but for a while had been on smooth dirt. Still pensive, I scuffed the ground. "What's this?"

"The track," she answered laconically, and we continued on. "Do you know," she began again, "I'm very good at talking people into things . . . things they might not have thought of, or want to do."

I nodded amiably.

"It's almost dark," she said.

I looked at her, waiting. If she was being catty, the tone was all wrong—like getting propositioned by your sister. "Why don't you try me?"

"Okay. Let's run."

"That's what you think about out here with a guy in the dark?"

"That's what I like to think about. The last time I was here at night, I had come for a walk with a Dutch student after an African drum concert . . . and I had to do more than talk to get him off the idea my panty hose needed to come down."

"But I've got . . . my right knee is still pretty bad. I'd better not."

"We'll go slow."

"Naah."

"Well, I want to stay in shape for swimming, but I never seem to have enough time. You don't mind if I do?"

"I'll sit in the bleachers and toss out a few yahoos each time you come around."

"Oh, come on," she cooed, pulling my hand, "if it begins to hurt, we'll stop."

Twice around and my lungs felt as though they'd

shrunk to the size of walnuts. Next to me loped a machine-like pacer, the kind that wouldn't break in the next ten thousand meters. Another lap and I'd be wheezing on the sidelines. The thought needled me.

"Okay," I grunted between ragged gasps. "Let's sprint down to the next turn." I pulled ahead and yanked at her hand to mark that I was ahead and capable of going faster. Judging we were nearly at the end, I let go and hurdled forward—pitching, twisting in the air into an empty beyond. The ground lurched upward, slamming the track across my shoulders as if judoed into sandpaper. Susan cascaded over me, sprawling in the dirt.

"How's your leg?"

I had knocked out the gnat's breath of remaining wind in the tumble and could only suck at the night air while brushing my pants.

"I was trying to keep you in the middle—someone's been driving a car on the track—and you tripped over a rut . . . You know, you flip just like a cat."

"Yeah," I said dryly, "they see well in the dark."

The moist warm air and the exertion made convincing the rivulets of sweat that ran down my forehead. Yet the real heat cooked from within, microwaved from the fleeting moment when I'd held her damp shirt and tight corduroy jeans as they splayed across me.

We wandered across the field until I found myself on a shotput pad. With melodramatic strain I heaved a few imaginary iron balls downrange while our conversation remained centered on the physical. I told her how I'd once done a perfect score of 500 on the Physical Combat Proficiency Test. It justified bragging, and sparked a demonstration of the low crawl, its most bizarre event. The two of us were soon scrambling across the grass on our bellies like a pair of hungry iguanas hell-bent on some skittery prey.

Susan's complete unselfconsciousness pleased me, and I could almost forget that I wasn't still soldiering.

More stories of my first love were a result. Her absorption in them seemed to come from an understanding . . . I was the natural soldier—exceptional in most skills, better than most in the rest. That had to be the validating criterion—willful success; the motivation; the cause. I could easily spin off a tale of pride to her; of moments of reckoning; of the challenge of annihilistic risk. Men against men to the death. It would contrast vividly with the gloomy crevasse that lately I'd slithered into. Interrupting myself to keep from merging into maudlin nostalgia, I pressed her to talk about herself.

"You mean more stories of red clay and 'Tobacco Road'?" she quipped in a thick accent.

"It's hard to believe that six months up here and you've not only lost your southern accent, you can't even imitate a good one."

"Okay. Are you ready for a few tales of white trash behind the woodpile?" she drawled out, trying again. "Or behind the Ivory Towers . . . ?"

A signal? I wondered optimistically, aware of a near surfeit of desire. A signal of that kind would need heavy confirmation. We sat facing each other on some steps to a doorway in the rear of some building. A huge air-conditioning unit nearby droned with dull huskiness, blanketing all other sounds on the campus.

"Not very convincing," I retorted. "I ain't ready for Aunt Jemima."

"Well, you see, my dad's from New Jersey and my mother's from Charlotte. But I never listened to her—at least that's what she'd say. Some of my closest friends were from the North. And I've moved at least twelve times—inside North Carolina, but I always listened for differences. So altogether it could account for the southern accent I never had . . . Listening?"

I wasn't. The tease of my own thoughts only served to make me attend to something not quite forgotten. "Tell me more about this Brazilian thing."

"I don't know that much. They want me to help out in an impoverished village in the northern part of the country. To find out what a community organizer does, I'll have to tell them I'm interested, then they'll send me the details."

I wanted to know more about her intentions, how definite or tentative her plans were, but remained quiet so as to conceal my own.

"If you're wondering why I want to go, it's because I'd be doing what I'm good at . . . As soon as I was old enough, I had to organize all sorts of activities, projects, and committees. My father sometimes had as many as five rural churches, and being the preacher's daughter, there was no wriggling out. As soon as things got organized, we would be required to move—so it helps, and saves time, that I'm good at judging people."

"You, judge people?" I asked skeptically.

"It's a loaded word when you say it that way. I mean being a good judge of people's characters, knowing who can be counted on, by way of the first few impressions."

"I'd like to hear your assessment of me."

"I don't mean that they're oral assessments, just intuitions."

"I'd like to hear that, then. How about a quick personality scan?"

"I'm not an astrologer," she chided, trying to back off.

"Only holding you to what you said you were good at."

"All right. I think you are an intense person, a man of certainty, precise—concise in whatever you do, preferring to deal with the known. You make it your business to know details important and unimportant. You're practical and resourceful, but very impatient with imperfection . . ."

"So you describe me as a soldier, what about me now?"

"That is you now. I didn't know you before. But you're probably the same; people have their basic natures."

"Yeah, Captain Hero comes home. Watch him before

he fades.'' The words sounded sarcastic, bitter, beyond the mild sarcasm intended.

"You lost your sight, not your nature,'' she shot back, her condescension catching me like a pugil stick to the chin. She slid over beside me, challenging. "You assess me.''

"There are a lot of unknowns running around. I've been trying to put leashes on them since I met you. One gets in my way while I collar another. It's a silly word that comes to me . . . earthy.''

"Yeah, true. You should see my nails after our playing crippled lizard out in the field.''

"You're different from me.''

"That wasn't very difficult,'' she scoffed. "I don't drink, smoke . . . or do the other.''

"I'm prepared to give up smoking . . . Ambiguous, let's leave it at that. But what else don't you do—concerning guys?''

"I don't know, most of the time I try to stay detached. If I'm too natural—they think they're in love with me.''

I felt exposed and made a grunt of displeasure.

"I'm just generalizing, for instance, this guy was tutoring me in Russian and invited me over to his apartment to meet his wife. When I arrived, she was just leaving, and as soon as she shut the door, he practically jumped on top of me, his little child watching from the playpen. I almost caught up with the wife with him yelling out the door 'I love you.' It seems like I spend a lot of time avoiding men. I don't think I'm frigid, I've got all the right feelings, but I want to be loved by someone I love.''

"Oh, I agree,'' I said, wanting to pull off her jeans and pin her, there in the entrance. "It's just because you're cute.''

"Cute?''

"Don't worry. I'm overly disciplined . . . haven't you noticed? You being cute, though, is good . . . fits my trait of liking perfection. But it would be a tough world without a few tolerances—like things that are outside my ability to do anything about. The soldier is used to assessing and reacting to those kinds of external factors."

"What about the internal ones?"

"They always seem to get in the way."

"I don't believe all you're saying. You aren't tolerating the imperfection of blindness, and that's outside your control."

"Oh?"

"I could see that at the Goal Post during your promotion party. Clearly. Trying to be . . ."

"Normal. So what's wrong with that?"

"More normal than normal. Climbing up the drainpipe in back to get on the roof to light those firecrackers . . ."

"I'm still good," I said irritably, "and sometimes I have to do stuff just so the dumb-asses can see me do something they couldn't do."

"But you couldn't see that the thing was rusty at the top and coming away from the building. Does a narrow escape with death gain you immortality or something?"

"I don't know. Many times I've felt more vulnerable, closer to death."

"Could it come from killing—seeing others die?" she pursued cautiously. "Tell me about the first time you ever did. Did it make you feel the way you thought it would in training?"

I looked at her intently, trying to understand her motives and how the conversation had come around to this. I studied my image of her. Someone on the ward had described her as resembling the actress Sue Lyons, only as a brunette. The image squirmed from my grasp. Yes, *The Night of the Iguana*, another vision took life, a killing in color. My platoon, called in to sweep a woodline near a large river. Me, still new "in country," but the mission by then routine enough.

Artillery and gunships had just worked over the area, and several bodies had already been spotted from the air. I put two squads on line, each man about four meters apart; a reaction squad behind. We began moving through the thick yet uneven vegetation. Half the platoon slowed in mud and nipa palm and fell behind, the line becoming annoyingly ragged as men sought firmer ground.

"One down here, sir," someone shouted. Twenty meters away a squad leader yanked and turned over a lifeless khaki-clad form from the muck. The rest of us entered a banana grove, and I crossed a canal first, walking easily along a stand of trees with irrigation canals on either side.

Ahead, facedown in the water—another body. Casually I called the attention of a couple of men to my left while continuing to move forward, then bellowed again for some others to straighten up the line, seeing that they were still dragging ass. I glanced back to the body. It was standing waist deep in water, a pistol drawn from a holster. In a snap of reflex I jerked as if to dodge a bullet, with my CAR-15 banging out a single shot. The man shuddered in place, no more than a shaken statue. My thumb spun the selector and from ten feet I put a burst into him. He flew backward, the impact slamming him into the opposite bank; the outraged slugs virtually ignoring his flesh as they erupted into water and mud. A lone tracer hit hard soil beyond and hurtled momentarily, as if its incandescent tail had sent it into a burrowing frenzy.

His face, even now over a year later, was clear, sharp, and confident; a hint of a smile, as though he knew he would kill me. I remembered my RTO coming from behind, whistling, saying, "Man, you sure zapped that gook officer. He ain't going nowhere." I stood there surging with adrenaline, reading a bluish-pink length of entrail that hung clean, wet, and iridescent out of an obscured hole in his back.

"Yeah," I'd said, walking away as though sandbags had been strapped to my boots, "his whole day is shot."

The primacy of the incident had sharpened the definition, crisp from that moment on, the scene remembered in vibrant hues, with the action slowing down to stop on the strange intimacy of that lone smile. Other times, other corpses now seemed diced by endless chopper blades mixed with an endless green into a caldron of countless missions.

The incident, spoken, was over, and Susan remained quiet; perhaps waiting for more, perhaps stunned.

"I don't think about that stuff so much anymore," I said, softly. "I used to dream about it, but not anymore."

"But the war changed you. I mean changed how you feel about life and death?"

"Yes. Before, I always had the feeling that life was more or less cemented to the body, as if permeating the flesh—reluctant to leave. It was an easy notion to prefer when projecting death from the context of training into the real thing. Maybe it's weapons. They perform so . . . unequivocally . . . Just now thinking of that body count of 'one' makes me think of something I'd once read—Crane . or maybe O'Casey—about the spirit of life escaping through a bullet hole, as if exhaled. That's the way it seemed, like some vaporous thing whiffed out through those holes I'd put in him, and just diffused in the air."

"I would think those sorts of thoughts would work against a soldier."

"That's the paradox, Susan, you reject the possibility from the gut. Me dead? Blind? Not if I can help it—and you believe you pretty much can. In your head you know that on the scale of the whole war, that the numbers are with you—the odds at the onset anyway. You willingly accept long odds that are in your favor. If I'd known what would happen to me, I would never have gotten on that plane at Travis. Fresh, I'd probably take those same odds today . . . and go back."

"Okay," she persisted. "Consider that it did happen—because it did. What are the differences?"

"Screw it." I shrugged. "I've been adventurous my whole life; reckless is probably more accurate, deserving to be hurt with some of the chances I've taken, with real odds that were known to me and ignored. So I know now that I'm not immortal, not even slightly invulnerable. The stimulation of that kind of adventure—what I was telling you about out in the field—its importance is shrinking fast; the problem is now—hanging around, doing jack shit; like being blindfolded, punching out at a guess, ducking on intuition.''

We both stood up, either talked out or mutually suffering from the stiffness of lounging on concrete steps. On an impulse I took her in my arms and kissed her. She responded with a sort of vague hesitancy. A prudent caress and another gentler kiss and she warmed, but not enough to stop me doubting. I needed to say something.

''You're quite a woman,'' I said deeply, yet almost whispering it, and holding her by the shoulders to impress sincerity.

''Thank you,'' she replied, softly, approvingly.

The knowing of her and the idealized image I had crafted repudiated all others. In my mind it was almost bewildering that she could bump aside even the hungriest females I'd ever known, without even competing. But I still needed to hear her say something positive, some kind of affirmation that would cut loose my restrained desire.

''Steve,'' she answered gently, ''wouldn't it have been nice if we'd met a few months earlier, like when I first came up here? I've always enjoyed being with you and talking with you. Everything you've said has been important to me. More than you would know. I'll remember it all, everything.''

I studied her words as if they contained some hidden cipher. Oh yeah, that's me, useful dude. My spirits tumbled, not downward, but as they might in a weightless vacuum. And just like the direction of up, any meaning I could give them, would be arbitrary.

CHAPTER NINETEEN

Andy and I lounged on wrought-iron lawn furniture, casually occupying space between poolside and house. Lank strips of sun succumbed by degrees to neighborhood rooftops. Rubbing one arm's radiant tingle, I wondered if my hospital-white body had absorbed too much or not enough. Wide silences spaced the non sequiturs which passed for conversation.

"I must be out of my mind," I said, "coming to a tacos and enchiladas party. My gut feels like somebody's been throwing in hot rivets." I tossed three antacids in my mouth and washed them down with beer. The glowing brazier in my gut began to quench.

"Vietnam Vet ODs, Antacid Freak," Andy muttered, as if musing over a newspaper.

The party was for Andy, given by a couple of airline pilot friends. He would soon be leaving Washington to return to college. Most of the guests were neighbors, suburban couples who seemed to have little in common with us. They asked standard questions on the war and blindness. They were leaving now; all the other Walter Reed guys already had.

Three stewardesses arrived and we exchanged introductions and a few amiable words as they shimmied from their outer clothes and into the pool. Andy abruptly got up and followed them. I remained behind, preoccupied, thinking of Susan.

The existence of a phone on the glass table next to me suggested a call. While dialing, I thought of apologizing for the night before, because Andy and I had gone to her dorm straight from the Goal Post; we were beyond the courtesies of the hour. She was in bed when we called up for her, but good-naturedly she'd come down. By that time we had gotten ourselves into a wrestling match on a wide expanse of carpet in the TV lounge, horsing of the kind where you don't give in, even to your best friend, until you win. My rowdy, impressive conquest worried me. I couldn't quite remember what impression I'd made—less Captain Maguire gentleman officer than Sergeant Fury, psychopath.

On the phone Susan sounded happy enough to hear from me and we traded a few small matters. About to say good-bye, I told her I'd just called to hear her voice. "When we see each other again," she said suddenly, "we need to talk about something important, I have to tell you . . . something in person." Her tone became careful, uncharacteristically grave, and I felt a touch of alarm.

"About what?"

"Us."

An ominous thought . . . the big dump. How had I missed it coming? I retraced the last few days in an instant, as if clues would quickly emerge: not the wrestling thing . . . she'd just mentioned that it was funny. The river before that . . . after lunch in a Georgetown restaurant, we'd strolled along the Potomac, arms across each other's backs in a half snuggle. It had unfolded into the kind of afternoon that women often take as romantic, the kind I had never appreciated in the same way, until lying side by side, mottled in shade with the sun speckling flecks of warmth on us through tussling leaves. Resting my head on her thigh, a myriad of dowsing receptors from some verdant reservoir had gone off. Feelings as strong as that, and she'd have to be feeling them too, yet this swaggering horror was about to happen. How could I be such a fool? I wondered. But damn it, if it were going to happen, let it happen now, I thought recklessly—but aware that some of the others had rejoined me on the patio, I softened. I'd have more impact face-to-face and determine whatever, then.

"About us?" I pursued, barely hearing over the garrulous chatter of Andy and the others. "Is it good?"

"Yes." She wavered with just enough hesitation, just tentative enough to confirm intuition. Feeling that further talk was inappropriate, I said good-bye. We would meet the next day in the hospital.

Andy and I changed seats so I could tell him in private what had happened.

"I can hear it now," I told him. " 'I like you Steve, I like you a lot, but I can see you are getting too serious, and I'm not ready for that yet.' It's like saying I like you . . . up to a point."

"Don't think I'm gloating," Andy snickered, "but I did warn you."

I sent a puff of air through my lips dismissively. "She says it's good for us both. Man, she's rationalized the whole thing already."

"She didn't say a whole lot."

"Ten-to-fucking-one she's putting the boot in," I grumbled, liking the flavor of pessimism.

"Eight-to-five is the best I can do. I've seen the way she looks at you. She likes you."

"Right," I drawled mockingly. "Thirty-two to one on Duke Wilson and 'I like you . . . but I just want to be friends.' "

"How about 'you're coming on too strong.' I've gotten that one more times that I've wished."

"That sure as hell wouldn't be true this time."

"Or try this one," he added. " 'It's not that you're blind . . . I just don't want to be tied down right now.' "

"That's my ol' snatch twenty-two, and a mean one at that. I avoid thinking about that possibility."

" 'You're too good for me,' ever hear that one?''

"Nah, anyway, a girl would have trouble saying it with a straight face."

Andy and I continued swapping the banal clichés and joking over them. Inside, though, I was surreptitiously being dismembered, drawn from within, or imploded, over the sheer viability of them, because I would actually hear one. I had fallen in love. Finally I told him for the first time, and his humor became like mine, half-hearted. He understood.

"What do you do now?" Andy asked.

"I've been in love twice before," I said, leaning back in my chair, trying to gild nonchalance onto my mood. "I walked out both times. I was immature or naive enough to have chosen those two in particular, but smart enough to have done what I did. Getting cut out is nothing . . . but when you're in love . . .''

"You didn't answer my question."

"Have my stomach operated on at once," I orated. "The pain as a tangible purging; a sacrificial piece of myself, sliced out . . .''

"Right, and sent to her. How about a piece of your frontal lobe instead?''

"There are things I could do. Let me tell you about this friend I had once. He got sent up to Enfield, the state penitentiary, and when he first got there, he wrote to every girl he knew, reasonably well anyway . . . told them the circumstances of how he had gotten where he was. He never claimed to be innocent or anything, just offered a real rending hard luck version. But most important, he told each girl that she was the only one capable of helping him, like if she would write to him, he'd be able to get it together while he was still on the inside.

"He called it sending out flyers . . . 'The girls that responded will get you through without your going batshit, and you don't start at zero on the day you get out.' When you've got three-to-five to do, obviously honesty is not that important." I paused. "I never told you this, but when I came back from Nam, I sent out some flyers of my own, like this blindness thing was a sentence. At the time I wasn't all that sure it was permanent. Hell, I even got my own sister to help me compose it. The mail was nice to get in those early months, I let them run out . . . except for one.

"She was one of the two that I had once loved. Since then, she's been through a marriage, got a two-year-old son, lived with a dude or two—did drugs in the meantime. Combine that with all the minuses that brought me to leave her in the first place. You could call me stone-ass crazy if it weren't for those positives. We've talked a few times on the phone. Man, you wouldn't believe how those rationalizations Ping-Ponged around in my head, how easy: cab over to National, quick flight up to Boston, whole weekend in a nice hotel. Susan came along and sat on the other end of the seesaw. It stopped that craziness."

"But now that she's getting off?" Andy asked.

"I won't deny there's no temptation in something easy, something that luscious. Yet it seems to go against everything I believe now; I've only been able to reason it all out because of Susan."

"Look," he shot back impatiently, "I'll pick up another semester in college while you get out of the hospital then dump all these bitches around here. I'm nearly as tired of them as you. We could drive the MGB all the way down to South America, screw every Juanita from here to Pata-fucken-gonia. We could even go to Africa."

"Yeah, capture giraffes."

"We could make a pile of money doing cool shit."

"No, Andy. I've spent a lot of time getting my head out of the Army thing, and that's the Army all over again. I've got to recognize and accept that I just can't live on my physical wits anymore . . . and that's what your idea would take."

"You know what to do," he demanded, "and you know how to do it."

"But I can't actually do it."

"You pinned me in wrestling and I'm nearly thirty pounds heavier."

"So I still have one or two things. It's just not enough. Hell, I could still parachute—at night even—but where do I go when I hit the ground? We've fantasized over ideas like this before. Damn, I always carried the assumption with me that if the Army ever failed me, I'd take up the soldier-of-fortune approach: Selous Scouts. Anything from hunting ivory poachers to freelance soldier. By the time I'd absorbed the skills required for that kind of work, I was out of it. In some perverse way, I intended that shuffling around the hospital, being called captain by everyone, would make me feel like I was still in it."

"Hold it Maguire," he said abruptly. "Do you expect this girl to replace the Army or something? Gives her an awful lot of power over you. You aren't able to replace it yourself, so you've enlisted a broad to do it for you."

"Better a weak plan than no plan at all," I poked. "Put it this way: my attractability of females is less today than it was—so blindness has made me less of a man . . . to that extent, that amount of my gonads is automatically in the hands of some female for reconstructive purposes. Masculinity only has meaning in the intimate company of females—they're the ones who confirm it."

"You were a man in the Army without any reference to females."

"What I know and what I feel are different. Maybe one affects the other. Maybe you can't completely feel yourself a man amongst women until you are a man amongst men."

"So you want some cunt to tell you that it's still all right," Andy cooed in sarcastic consolation.

"That's right ning-nuts. And she can do it, but only on my terms—and love is it. And I have to admit, Suzy is capable of making the Army irrelevant."

"You're talking like the back end of a bull on a straight prune diet. Why does it have to be her?"

"It didn't have to be, but it does now . . . I'm in love with her. Besides, this one understands the Army and me. There probably are other ones I could love, and get loved back too. I've had to believe that."

"So get another, then."

"Man, it's hard work sorting through broads."

"Expensive too." Andy suddenly got up and growled imperatively. "Okay Ranger! Into the water."

I gave him a sardonic look and got up. "Okay junior birdman, into the sky." Following his plunge, I crossed outdoor carpeting to wooden planking, then finding the edge with my foot, sat down to think. I had to answer Andy's question: What do I do now? I had reconciled little and all my ideas were fouled and kinked. Sure it was risky, narrow, stubborn; so what? I coddled the notion of Andy and me spinning through South America, gathering up ass in one country after another, collecting them like philatelists. I would present Susan with my Brazilian triangles and they would all be stamped.

I slid spiritlessly off the side, sinking with the despondent resignation of a man in cement shoes. The water and gloved pressure aroused a curious sensation in me, as if let loose in a viscous depth. Susan ebbed from my mind momentarily . . . but she was a competitive swimmer. I pushed off, downward from the sloped side, and cruised the bottom with dull, deliberate motions, like some great cartilaginous beast.

Maybe I would have to sink even deeper, for a long time, immersing in an underworld of suffering, to be restored. My meditating conformed more in that moment to the airless liquid than to my attempts at prayer. Girls had addicted me by my being male, and like some fabulous candy could give tooth decay . . . of the soul or salvation itself.

God knew what I wanted, but what would I do if His answer was no? Panging for oxygen, I twisted and shoved upward from the vinyl sea bed, grazing someone as I thrust for the edge of the pool.

A pair of arms serpented my neck. "You finally decide to join us," she said, "and you go straight for the bottom . . . of the pool, I mean."

"I'm a bottom feeder," I breathed, she was only an inch from my face, ". . . and I don't mean the pool's."

Her stewardess legs floated upward on either side of me, as if from natural buoyancy, ankles crossed behind my back, snug.

"Then it's dinnertime at marine world. Are you hungry?" She kissed me, her tongue a hot eel.

"Yeah." I frowned, sluggish; her clinging pubic-float was bringing me up fast with sexual bends.

I had been behaving as though no one else was around, as if there was no party at all. But now, so elegant was her attack, that I almost doubted it. Had she been watching me since she arrived? Attracted by the purple scars adorning me like football lacing? Or to me, without the eyepatch, one plastic orb looking at her in a shameless inanimate stare?

"Come on," she whispered. "We need to go into the house." She pressed my hands against her breasts as an appetizer, and pulled herself out of the pool. I trailed at her behind; a stray, lean enough to follow any promise.

Another errand of mercy, came a taunt from my head as she towed me through the kitchen and down a hallway. *Don't listen,* instructed another, *you're wounded. This kind of help is just what you need.* Yeah, first aid, I agreed.

"I've forgotten your name from before," I said.

"I'm Susan," she moaned, as if from studied practice.

I squenched my eyes at the words' impact.

"Something wrong?"

"Nah, maybe too much sun out there today."

We stood in a bedroom, sound muffled by bed, drapes, carpet. Having shed her swimsuit, she pushed her wet body against me to let me know, and the dank despondency raced from me like goblins from a torch.

"Come on," she called, jumping beneath the covers. "It's cold."

I stood in a trance; maybe I'd run across easier bitches in my life, but I couldn't recall any.

"If you're worried about Tom, it's okay. I asked. We can stay all night."

"How about his wife?"

"She's gone—she doesn't live here."

I chucked my bathing suit and got in. She was a lovely girl, almost as tall as myself, and I felt her curved length with satisfaction. The warmth and evaporating damp wafted muggy pheromones that excited. We kissed with like-minded greed and I sank my hand into the warm kitten between her legs. With a gentle squirm her thighs hinged open, knees lifting, and I imagined steam pouring through my fingers. Sliding a leg over her, I pushed to get on top, but she stopped me with a "No." I had anticipated that she was about ready to gobble me whole, but kissed and caressed longer.

She worked herself against my body, grinding, as if trying to feel as much of me as possible. I stole upward, then got between her thighs . . .

"Don't, we can't."

"Can't? Can't what?"

". . . Can't let you . . . I'm a virgin."

"So am I," I said huskily, a tease, "but just this week I was thinking of giving it up. It's our chance." My mind centered only on pouting pudenta. I moved her knees farther apart.

"No, please, I'm not fooling." She stiffened. "I just wanted to hold someone . . . you, that's all."

Confusion wallowed in the remnants of perhaps too many drinks. At the last moment had I mistakenly turned into the wrong bedroom, boarded the wrong stewardess? Was Susan lying next door, arched in lordosis, by now terminal with coital starving?

I drew nearer, with the mentality of a lower organism closing on its opposite. Again "No." This time a tremor in the voice. She was apprehensive. I touched my lips to her cheek and relaxed to the side.

"You really want to, don't you?" she asked sympathetically. My head went up and down, a boy of four mutely nodding to the offer of an ice cream cone. Below, my balls were as latent as a pair of cookin' off grenades.

"Are you afraid of getting pregnant?"

"Yes."

I preferred this reason, it lent gravity to the moment.

"You make it difficult. Going this far—I want to, and I don't even know you."

"I like you," she said. I had rolled over, but now I wanted to tell her about this other Susan and of how I was in love and never been nearer than a kiss, and how I was about to be dumped and of how a delicious bit like her could help me, and of how at that moment, somehow it would betray that love, regardless that the love was just exhaling its last breath, neat as a blown kiss.

She had stopped me all right. Nothing else would have. Stopped me from mauling my own sensibilities, from nearly pulling the tubes on something that would be dead in less than a day.

Would she be interested in hearing from the naked man lying next to her of how love would surely die without fidelity, and hear it from someone proclaiming a love subordinated to body functions and appetite alone? I could teach her how a manifestation of love could replace love, if she wanted to use me as much as I did her. But there wasn't any reason to tell her anything, it was becoming clear enough; sex would never satisfy me unless I did it intent on love.

"I'm sorry," she breathed, nuzzling me from behind. "We could do some other things."

I smiled. A dreamy sequence perforated with her words; my stewardess serving me from the aisle, lifting her dress, straddling the seats, coaxing, begging, forcing those other things, the things dreams are made of. I was asleep.

*   *   *

"Geeze, Steve, you look awful." Susan gingerly dumped a couple of items on my bed, seeming almost cheerful—either pleased to be ready to unburden herself, or poised like a discus thrower to unwind with the mood swing of her life.

"I could hear those stewardesses having a good time over the phone. That must have been some party. But look, I don't want to say what I've got to say if you don't feel up to it. Should I come back tomorrow?"

I rubbed my face, as if to kneed some blood into it, and thought of how I'd looked the first time she'd seen me. Hung over then, hung over now. A neat circle. "I feel great," I said coolly. Remaining seated on the bed, I lit a smoke, a screen between this girl and me . . . this girl whose characteristic penetration of my states of mind were for the first time failing her. It would serve to conceal my emotions, get them to mimic my hardened exterior, and not let her know.

"Okay, shoot," I said.

She didn't move closer, sensing my need for distance. Smart, avoiding counterattack by not cornering the victim. How had I allowed things to go this far, I thought reproachfully, without checking to see if it was mutual? I could be reproachful because I did it on purpose. I'd never been reluctant on taking a chance with Suzy. With her it had been impossible to think of risk.

"I rehearsed a lot of things to say . . . or how to say them, even though between us it's always been easy . . ."

"If it's so easy, just *say* it. You said this was going to be important and about us." I thought of how trite those standard clichés sounded, mulling over them again.

"It is, but Steve, I've never done anything like this before." She was unflustered. "You might not realize that in our time together I've told you things no one else has ever heard. I kept a diary since I was eleven. I've stopped keeping it since meeting you. I didn't need it anymore. You know more about me than anyone."

It appeared simple. I got to know her, I fell. I grunted an acknowledgment, still rummaging for the right mask—serene detachment? Weathered unconcern? "I *thought* I did know you."

"Yes, but this is the hard part—not one person I know has approved of my liking you. All my friends warned me off. Even your friend Cassidy. He got me aside once and said, 'You don't know what you're doing. Leave him alone—he's *blind.*' When I told my mother I had a friend at Walter Reed, she went down a checklist, 'Has he got both legs? Both arms? Both eyes?' I told her you'd lost one, and didn't say you couldn't see out of the other. She didn't even like that. Your best friend, Andy, doesn't exactly like me. Plenty of others, everyone, seems to be protecting me or you from me or you. So it's taken a lot of thinking to come to the conclusion that I have."

I didn't want this to be the reason; it didn't suit her, capitulation to the one thing I couldn't change. But the finality of what she had decided was clear, her tone itself a natural announcement of some firm and immutable judgment. The scythe was coming around.

"Unanimous disapproval of my existence," I said flatly, preparing to draw some blood on my own.

"Yes, but that was okay. It made me think about us even more and separate out what your blindness meant when I was away from you. When I was with you, I wasn't ever conscious of it. Being discouraged by everyone allowed me to see something that was important, because you were letting yourself go further than just friendship."

The smoke thinned over a cratered landscape, artillery lifted. I had crossed that thin red demarcation line alone, then only yards from the summit—gunned down. Letting myself, I thought, hell, I was on the other side, overrun, taken . . . and now she was about to stake me out in the sun. "Your effect on me has been hard to control."

"I was pressured and confused by my feelings for you," she continued. "I've never been attached to anyone. When I was a kid, my family moved every year or two, and every time we did, it was as if everyone left behind had died. You know I'm not unsociable. I like people—it's not that—but I've always been able to leave them. Friendships and memories of them are not the same thing. I've always been going in the end. Time and distance take care of whatever emotions remain, and it's always been inevitable.

"Another thing I have to admit was that loneliness was always with me . . . and just before I met you, I prayed for help in finding a man I could love. I felt it was you, but rebelled against that."

I thought of a student nurse friend who had broken up with someone in favor of her career. She had decided that nursing and romance were mutually exclusive, valuing not so much the career, as its aspiration. The trouble was, she'd been pining for him ever since. Susan—off to Brazil, I thought. Will she think of me? Big deal, what consolation is that? Going off to Brazil because American University was a bore was hardly a career aspiration. But it did seem in keeping with what she just said, always moving on, never enough time to get close. This all seemed neurotic, which Susan definitely wasn't. Her life seemed more substantial.

Susan's words floated in my head, purposefully detoured into unraveling platitudes and heard as if in a half sleep. They had gone on too long; anger accompanied the return of focus. I wanted this girl more than anything I ever wanted, but if it was gone, it should go. "Look Susan," I snapped, "if you've come to repudiate all our time together . . . then cut the crap and go—to Brazil—or wherever." I flipped open my watch. Maybe I should go down and get some ice. Have a drink. Get loose, consider the near future after she'd gone.

"Steve!" she exclaimed. "I haven't said anything about Brazil! I'm not going there or anywhere. I'm not repudiating our time together either. I'm *just* trying to explain how confusing it's been for me. All those negative things people were saying about you being blind. People who don't really even know you. After a while my not feeling sorry for you seemed strange. Was I blind to something everyone else could see? I decided that I knew you better. I realize that you can take care of yourself. You can figure anything out—the way you sort out details. You've got more sense and intelligence than any of those who are observing you. You know that I'm your type of woman and that's why I feel the way I do. I love you."

My head jerked involuntarily at those last words, so quick and confident. They sprang up as if flushed from the dark in front of me, then scampered into silence. My mind reflexed to grab after the darting syllables. In my abdomen some organ or length of bowel shuddered, a visceral twitch as physiological response to a library of emotions. Thick-tongued with the blue bile of stupidity, I began to speak of contrition.

"Susan. I've been making a big mistake here." I got up and held her shoulders. "I thought something else was going on. I thought the worst because I've come to expect the worst. I thought you were going to reject my feelings for you. I was in dread because I'm in love with you."

"I know," she said warmly, "but you did have me confused. I came in and you were coiled up on the bed like a snake, cold—just the opposite of the normal you. I've never known you to get so distant."

"It's a good example of how I felt, expecting to lose you."

"That's impossible with what I see in you."

I relaxed back on the bed, pulling her hand for her to join me. She put her arms around my neck and kissed; slow, savored, unambiguous kisses. I found myself lying with her, not caring that at any moment one of the ward staff would swing through the door and find me hugging amid a welling, dizzy joy.

"It seems like a long time, Suzy, a bitch of a long time since anything went the way I wanted it to."

"I can make a few improvements there," she said,

having good reason for confidence. My pessimistic thoughts were now only dark puddles before the breaking sun.

"Your face feels hot," I observed.

"I suppose that's how love feels."

"Like malaria?" I smiled, and she kissed me again. That word love. From her lips it still scattered like small birds tumbling around a steeple in a strong spring wind, but so were my spirits, high-blown in a blue sky.

CHAPTER TWENTY

The close and sweet hemp-threaded air of the Cellar Door seemed almost fresh against the leaden summer heat outside. The D.C. night was the warm belch of a derelict wino. We stepped onto the sidewalk unmotivated. Tim Hardin, with the help of a comedian, had tried.

"Just existing in this city is like taking a toke off a tailpipe."

"You should have been here a hundred or so years ago," Susan remarked, "mud-filled streets piled with steaming dung . . . behind the White House there was a big swamp that supplied scads of mosquitoes. Sometimes in July or August it got so hot that most of the government would just leave."

"Got so hot and bothered, we had a civil war."

"A little known fact. America survives as a nation primarily because our government buildings are air-conditioned."

"What's all that noise?" We swung around to face it. Down the street a rolling commotion grew louder, spilling boisterous incoherence from the next intersection.

"Looks like another protest riot."

"Let's cut around to Wisconsin," I directed, "before the police bust out a lot of tear gas." In thick profusion the protesters seemed to accost the pavement and facades all around us.

273

"They're breaking windows, setting all the trash cans on fire and kicking them over." We rounded the corner into Wisconsin, hoping to grab a taxi, but instead found a much greater mob directly in front of us. A great glass mower, it churned straight for us, engined by hoots and hollers. Large sheets of plate-glass clanged unmistakably as they broke and crashed to the sidewalk and into storefronts.

"Pick a doorway and head for it," I shouted. We sprinted several yards and darted into a recessed doorway between display windows. "Get behind me," I ordered, and stood astride, arms folded. A length of pipe ricocheted across the pane parallel to the street. Voices howled and the pipe whanged again with bursting glass tumbling, chunks smashing.

"There's hundreds of them," Susan whispered from behind my ear.

The one with the pipe seemed to stumble from the crowd and lurch into our entrance. Instinctively I thought of taking him—go low, shoot the knees. The pipe wouldn't do much in close . . . slip behind, finish him off. But somehow I didn't sense true malevolence. It seemed almost frivolous, a mayhem party.

"Take out these two, man." I jerked both thumbs outward. The two huge panels could divert some pipe energy . . . away from our heads. Thong! It glanced mightily, and a thin sliver keeled out and thudded on the rubber mat.

"Fuck the pigs!" he yelled, and swung the pipe from one side to the other, left and right. Splintering shards of glass crashed back into the display window, some falling and breaking at my feet. The random smashes muted quickly, echoing against the next block. A few stragglers trotted by with ripped-off items to regain the security of the crowd. A siren or two whooped and howled against the distant sky as if confined to one-way streets that were taking them farther away.

"They've broken almost every store window for as far as I can see," she commented. The sidewalk was a slippery strewn mosaic; thick pieces of glass crunched under foot as we walked in the other direction.

"Venting their rage? Suzy, I can't see the rage. I cannot believe that guy with the pipe cares about anyone dying in Nam right now. It's just too out there for them. We're supposed to be seeing it all on TV. Still, it's just some journalist's rendition, his script, his edited footage, his selective attention. It's like a weird western with big guns."

"They do have that element of self-interest."

"I have my doubts about that too. With the lottery everybody knows for sure where they're at. Andy and I asked a bunch, and it's like everyone out there had a safe number. I didn't see a lot of northeast college types dying in the mud."

"A lot of the ones we just saw are still in high school."

"It fits, everyone around here seems juvenile. Did you notice how that comedian only had to say a few four-letter words and the audience went into spasms? When he did that thing about masturbation, I thought some of them might stop breathing. Maybe if they were in junior high or something I could understand. It's that they're supposed to be big-city hip and they're paying good money to hear some guy say nasty shit."

"Hmmmm. They may have some possibilities for you."

"Fuckin' A, right . . . hey, I'm only a few years older, same age as some, and I don't recognize a thing anymore."

"Steve," she said as she held my hand firmly, "I recognize something. You make me feel more secure than I've ever felt before. I'm not insecure . . . but you don't even think a close call's a big deal, do you?"

"It could have gotten a lot closer, but you mean because we didn't get gassed or something?"

"No!" she laughed. "The A.U. campus is gas city. I'm used to it. I mean I feel secure all the time. Because of the way you are. On campus, a lot of guys act quirky on purpose. Personal hang-ups are 'in.' Maybe it's an existential wounding. I suppose you have to pay your dues somewhere to get credibility. Sometimes they don't even pay—appearances are just as good. Some are even into this idea that men have to be more like women.''

"Right, so to rebel you sought out some ass-kicking Ranger... who still knows what men and women are supposed to do."

"It wasn't a conscious rebellion."

"About those rioters. They'd claim they're fighting for peace. No doubt this rioting stuff gives them the feel of a fight, but they'd be hard put in a real fight. As we grunts used to say—'in the shit,' or even worse, 'in the bad shit.' You understand my frustration?"

"Yes, it's part of why I love you."

I flashed her a quizzical expression and took my hand from her shoulder. "I'm happy to hear it again, but it's hard to..."

"Hard to believe, huh? You don't have that low opinion of yourself."

"No, it's just that I have such a high opinion of you. C'mere." I pulled her close to me and kissed the side of her face. "You may not know it, but I'm shaky about things. There are times when my losses are too frustrating for me to believe in anything. Times when they seem worse than death. I'm real good at night navigation, but a lifetime of it?"

"You don't show it."

"Look at us, walking. Half the guys in the hospital have Corvettes, Camaros... whatever. Who could ever think you could envy an amputee?"

"Nobody. What started all this?"

"Us walking twenty blocks."

"Do you hear me complaining? So there are nice cars around, but what do I do with the guy when he's parked it in the garage? They're not worth anything to me compared to what you're like. So shake it off. Buy a car and I'll drive it."

"All right, I will. I still feel exactly the same way I always did, still think the same, but I have this instinct that people see me as an object of pity. It's the barrier that I can't seem to get a hand on. That bothers me. Those who already know me by some chance or another are inside the barrier. Everyone else is on the outside, and I don't know how to move them to the inside."

"Strangers do stare at us, but just name one person who knows you who pities you. It's the people who don't . . . who can't think any further than how awful injuries like yours are."

"Most people who I don't know, seem to want to protect themselves from the idea it could happen to them, by keeping some distance between us. Remember the cab driver I told you about? That bothers me. You know, for a long time I've been worried, to put it mildly, that I have lost the ability to be attractive to girls. I suspected that if there ever was one, she'd be mighty desperate, someone I really didn't want."

"Jesus Christ, are you talking about me?"

"No."

"I understand you found your way upstairs in the Goal Post with some poor desperate things."

"Who told you that?"

"Philly D. He even pointed one out. Pam, I think." Her voice cast away, toying. " 'Mighty desperate' is not the way I would describe her."

"Suzy, I'm trying to explain my darker feelings. A girl could be attracted to me, but it's been easier to deny it on some grounds or another, and easier to worry about the next one or be jealous about the one someone else had. Hard as I try, I can't see this stuff objectively.

"I've been touched by this war. Well, that's obvious . . . but I mean *really* touched. I suppose I mean by degree. I will never see another thing, never you, never even a lonesome glint for as long as I live. It's a hell of a sentence for just some insignificant moment in Nam. Then there's this other weight. I'm afraid we might not win this war. It seems like everywhere I turn there's people working hard making sure that all our losses will be for nothing. Working hard to make sure we lose. That I lose. My losses . . . If we win, I could at least think I've traded my sight to save a country. It's a fair swap. But if these people have their way. Man! I keep hearing about the war as some great big corrupting process, especially for officers. The values ingrained in me—courage, honor, discipline, devotion to duty—are being ridiculed. Here I am an object of pity . . . an object of ridicule.''

"Regardless of that, what are you gonna do? Reject yourself? Reject me?''

"No. I understand what you're saying. That I appear to be doubting that you could possibly accept a guy like me. I know you accept me; it's me that doesn't accept me, and I haven't been able to separate where the war ends and I begin.''

"Look, I noticed a kind of hierarchy among you guys. You respect the ones who had it the worst. You can't do that if you're not ready to apply it to yourself.''

"Being in the next bed . . . you can't help making comparisons. A guy comes in with a foot blown off—we yell, 'Hey get some wounds, will ya!' Coming from a dude who's a double amp has got to make him feel good.''

"You know, you're pretty high in that hierarchy.''

"That's the problem. It's a judgment passed completely on the future. Getting your leg torn off is no joke, but I've seen too many. A good prosthesis and they're packing their bags; the bad stuff's over. Remember the Goose? He just got accepted at Georgetown Law School. I remember him when he was crying in his oatmeal.''

"Have you and Andy talked about these things?''

"No, but we've talked about everything else. He never had to, he understands.''

"What did you mean about the future?'' she asked.

"It doesn't matter how bad a soldier's hit, his future has everything to do with how limited he's gonna be in five, ten, twenty years. We don't talk about it now, but eventually all the others will go in any direction they want . . . Andy too. Sure they'll still have bad memories of a time they wished hadn't happened, but it will be all behind them."

"And all in front of you."

"For as long as I live."

"I was hoping you had thought about it all being in front of us."

"This conversation has turned into a woe-is-me thing. I'm sorry, because it's not really me. I feel so comfortable with you that I just have to say this stuff. I've thought about it so long alone. A big part of love is comfort."

"I understand." She looped an arm around me and pressed my hand again with an energy that drew me close.

I stopped and held her tight. "You're quite a woman."

"I've paid close attention to you guys and that hierarchy, but it isn't as important as something else I sec. You're tougher than the rest. You've handled it better than most of them did with whatever they got. Your strength means a lot to me. Strength in hardship can't be put on."

We had reached the rear steps of the Goal Post. Before going inside I halted, wanting to come to some resolution in the conversation.

"It's hard to talk about these things without drawing too much attention to being blinded. One of the great things about you is that you understand that I've just about killed this injury. It mostly happens up here," I pointed to my temple, "but I guess I put it to rest by slow strangulation. People ask me, 'How did you adjust? Must have been hard, huh?' At least they sense I'm on the right side of sanity, but what's hard is getting the answer right. I can't say, 'Yeah, it was a ball buster,' or 'Nah, it wasn't nothin.' What's true is that I've largely made it. I think it's like assessing the terrain around me where the widest open spaces are inconsequential. Either it's close or not very relevant. Excess. Redundant. A huge rock ledge, like one that's incredibly intimidating, is no more than the extent of my next reach. I can do that much, and then that much again.''

''Not long ago you told me that blindness was like some dark jungle thing. That analogy for life seems intimidating enough . . . but not out of your control.''

I smiled and pulled her toward me, then kissed forcefully as the familiar overheated blood began flowing around my body. ''That's right, I forgot to tell you about my fondness for jungles.''

Suzy and I entered the Goal Post through the narrow passage in the rear. I did not receive my accustomed catcalls from the bar. It was as if I had just sauntered into some bar across town where nobody knew me. I tried to focus my attention on one or another of the many undirected voices that garbled on my right. We edged along the wall behind several standing men. ''Is Philly here?'' I quick-checked over my shoulder to Susan.

''Yeah, he's there.''

''There'' meant on the single stool at the right end of the bar, that sole promontory for observing everything and everyone in the place. ''Get us over there; we'll tell him the news.''

''Hey, Philly D.'' I spoke gently, seeking acknowledgment.

''Finally gonna join us, huh? Too good for us last night.'' He snorted the words acidly. They notched up my eyebrows. I was startled but not really sure whether he was starting into his next joke.

''I'm here, I'm here!'' I said, searching for some silly way to fend off this curious greeting.

''I said last night.'' His voice barked mean, no joke. ''We had the whole Anheuser Busch yacht sitting out there in the Potomac waiting for you—and what? You take off with *her* without a word to nobody.''

''Whooah, hold it, Philly. I was in my room all night, waiting to be picked up.'' I bristled at the unfairness. ''I even gift-wrapped a six-pack of Schlitz for the skipper. You know I really wanted to go.''

"Right, go with her. Andy went over there and couldn't find you anywheres. He held the whole thing up thinking you would come, by some other way."

"Other way? Andy's the only one who knew where. Where is Andy!?" Philly got Eddie the bartender to fetch him from a table at the far end. "Andy! Where were you last night? Philly thinks I took off with Susan, and I was waiting for you the whole time. Sat in front of the tube. I can prove it . . . the news, Carol Burnett, Dan August, a documentary on—"

"I came by and you weren't there," he cut in evasively. I could almost feel him looking away.

"What time?"

"About five."

"Right. You said you were coming at six. You know I always go to the mess hall at five." I spoke hurriedly, wanting a quick acquittal from this nonsense. "Even a dud would have checked the mess hall."

"No way, pal. I just figured you ducked out with Susan . . . again."

"You sure as hell didn't need to eat," Philly cut in. "I told you there was going to be a whole goddamn boatload of everything."

"Damn it, Philly. I told Andy Susan was studying. Hell, I told him I would be waiting, just like I was."

"Come on," Andy scoffed, with snide condescension. "Who knows where you are anymore? You're always with her."

Frustration curdled in my chest; it distilled in a rush. "We're going to get married." I planted the words like a flag, skewered into the ground on a hilltop. "That's why we're together a lot, but last night was set aside for you guys."

"Aw, 'set aside,' " Philly echoed with derision, "you just need a little nurse to take care of you. Give you a little nookie once in a while when you've been a good boy."

"Fuck you, Philly," I hissed.

"I let you got upstairs with her, didn't I? Ain't that just for my special friends?"

Susan squeezed my arm. "There's more pollution in here than outside, Steve." I turned and we moved toward the front door.

"You don't need to do nothin' for pussy. You want it, you just tell me when and who and it's yours. You let *me* take care of you."

Susan and I stalked up the street to a languid standstill, both of us hoping to catch a quick cab. Something slowly evacuated my limbs, and in a pair we leaned on the windowsill of a store. Fixed in a torpor, we gazed blankly across Wisconsin Avenue.

"Gads, Steve, they're not into our happiness, are they?"

"That crap was incredible. I expected that the announcement would launch a big celebration. Hell, when I got promoted to captain we had a wicked blowout."

"Steve," came a voice. I looked up with surprise.

"Julio?" I really didn't know Philly's Peruvian kitchen boy, but we'd spoken a thousand times, one each for every time I passed on the way to the toilet.

"I am sorry."

"Julio, you don't have to be, we—"

"No, I am very sorry. I watch you here for a long time. You are a great man, and you and this woman have a great love. I see this. They do not understand. Your marry is good."

"Thanks, Julio."

"I quit my job now."

"Over what just happened?!" I asked with astonishment.

"Yes, but it is not the first reason. It is the last. I will get work at the Black Greco. You know this place?" I nodded. "Maybe you can come there . . . and your woman."

"We will," Susan offered. "Thanks, Julio."

"I will be a waiter." He shook her hand and mine almost in unison, then walked off down the street. We listened to his footsteps until Susan turned back toward me.

"Why's Philly so bitterly against me? I gave him more credit than that, didn't you?"

"Yeah, I guess he probably thinks you're the type that'll keep me away from here, like the wife of this other blind guy who used to come down here nearly every night before he got married. Like me, before I met you. His name was Tommy Ballard. He's a big-time disc jockey here in Washington. I met him once. Doesn't come anymore except maybe to say hello at Christmas. Philly often complained to me about how Ballard's wife stole one of his friends. He's painted a picture of some shrew who wouldn't even let the guy out for a couple of beers. Philly can't see that the guy's got a family now and a lot of things going on."

"Why does he think I would be like her?"

"He doesn't know anything about you; probably not Ballard's wife either, but when you're off at school, whatever—not around the place —he sees you as willfully not being part of the old gang. Besides, he's vaguely suspicious of anyone who doesn't drink. It's his own little clubhouse. You do it his way or go down the street."

"I still love to come here, though. I've had more laughs in the Goal Post . . . especially you and Andy together . . . that's what's bothering me. Why is *he* so hostile toward me?"

My answer was interrupted by a sudden thudding accompanied by curses to our left.

"It's Andy," she said. "He's in the phone booth. He just ripped out the receiver!" A huge familiar crash followed. "He just bashed the front window of the drugstore with it." Urgent ringing from an alarm spit into the night, seeming to issue from buildings across the street. "Shouldn't we talk him down or something? Come on, we need to do something."

"Andy! What the fuck are you doing?" I screamed.

"I don't think he heard you. He's gone back into the Goal Post."

"Shit, I'm not going back in there again." I took her by the hand.

"What about Andy?"

"Don't worry about him. I'm just not going to forgive him too soon for his screwing up. He's the kind of friend who doesn't expect forgiveness when it isn't called for. We'll always be friends. He thinks like me."

"You think like that? The two of you ought to be down in Georgetown with the other window breakers. Blood brothers all."

"There's a difference between us and them. Tomorrow, guaranteed, he'll pay for that mess, the window, the phone. He'll—"

"Last night I ran across this quote in U.S. history," she interrupted, "something like, 'It's easier to fight for principles than to live up to them.'"

"Living with you is going to be like living with James Madison."

"So? The point is, fighting the war might seem easier than sorting things out with Andy."

"He'll be gone in a week. It's strange, I always thought that I'd be the one who'd be alone at some point . . . but I'm not and he is, and he's going back home to Ohio for no other reason. I went home and it was a mistake. With all that has happened to us, we're just too old to do that thing again. Tell you what, I'll call him a lot, tell him what's going on down here. I'll bet you he'll be back by the end of the semester."

"I've noticed him becoming more tense lately."

"There's more going on than you know. I understand him."

"Understand him or not, you would *never* have done what I just saw him do."

"Nah, I would have used a pipe."

She put her arms around me, a somatic alchemy turned right. I held her to feel the slow accretions of love.

EPILOGUE

The end of this story, there back in the summer of '70, was of course only the beginning. I wrote it because many really did ask me, "What was it like?" The war as I knew it truly was a grand spectacle, of men and weapons of every variety, stirred in a caldron of mud and jungle and blood. To have been cast into this, and to have had a hand in orchestrating a chunk of it, made an indelible impression. To have left behind a significant piece of anatomy sharpened and intensified that impression like nothing else could. Today, I look back on Vietnam with a kind of loving nostalgia. In part, because it was the last thing I ever saw, and those images need to be cherished; but also because I have squeezed out the pain and anguish. Like a rucksack full of rocks, I dropped the emotional perturbations as a useless burden, stone by stone.

When I returned to college, on my retirement from the Army, the war was still going on. Teachers turned my captive classrooms into forums for their antiwar politics. It was agonizing, but I cocooned myself in my studies. The results were salutary, I had let go my first stone. In April of '75, when South Vietnam fell, my obsession with TV news coverage became pure masochism. It had come as no surprise; events had been lining up in that direction for a couple of years. Yet the finality of it was so abject. All our losses literally went up in smoke. Defeat, in black pajamas, stole into my living room, to find me hog-tied on the couch. My invective distilled the epitaph, and I blamed anyone who had ever, even for a moment, thought positively about such an end. I wanted to leave America.

Work on a doctorate in psychology, in Cork, Ireland, was a genuine antidote. Another stone was pulled from the ruck. There, with Susan and our three children, I created a new life, and it was as far from the war as the South China Sea is from those rain-sodden, shamrocked shores.

In the late seventies a great many books began to appear on the subject of Vietnam. The urge to read them was too tantalizing and with help from Recordings for the Blind, at the Library of Congress, I devoured them all. Most only frustrated me. A common thread seemed pervasive, that of the protagonist having prescience on the outcome of the war. Authors never failed to inject their characters with a weighty sense of futility. It did not ring true. They had succumbed to the temptation of screwing their post-Vietnam heads on to those of their soldiers. The essence of thought and emotion in combat is complex and has been the subject of countless books, but one aspect is undeniable. When you are in the shit, perspective is lost. All becomes an intensified tunnel of undistracted sensation, with you at one end and your foe at the other. In that world, compressed into a jungle clearing, with your wits pitted against high-velocity, slugs aimed directly at you— or bouncing Betties, primed to blast you into a future as an invalid, no one has time for geopolitical clairvoyance. We had fought the enemy and beat him on every occasion. Both I and those around me believed that those successes would win us the war.

In January of '82 I took on an opportunity to work for the U.S. Army, as a civilian. Our growing family and I moved to Kaiserslautern, Germany, where I became clinical director of an Army drug and alcohol treatment center. Although I was, by education and experience, well suited to the task, my subliminal purpose was to somehow recapture that unrequited love for the military. Several issues conspired against me from the start, however. I did not find myself among combat troops, but rather in the largest support and material base in the European command. I had nurtured some vague anticipation that my Army accomplishments, my medals, my exploits, would be recognized in a way that they previously hadn't. It proved a silly expectation. The Army had changed. It had become minorityized, feminized, and peacetimeized. The REMF had always been a target for the grunts' condescension, based solely on their being bombproof. Now, safer than ever, they swaggered around in camouflage between chow hall and office as though they were Commandos.

After three years I changed my professional direction, by taking a job as an administrator of a pediatric clinic for service families with developmentally disabled children. An office in a large Army medical center did have its ironies, as few may hold affection for eighteen months of hospitalization; yet I did. Although Army medical personnel are certainly rear echelon, they make fewer pretenses about it. In spite of this, however, and with a job that was both challenging and absorbing, I still felt some pangs over the Army around me. I continued to harbor, or even husband, inchoate expectations. At one point, after seventeen years out of uniform, I attended the commanders' annual affair for his officers. Resplendent in my dress blues and bedecked with awards, I searched for something that was not there. I even returned to the Mess a couple more times, perhaps for good measure, but on the last occasion, I appeared to make MacArthur's adage about fading away come true. No one spoke to me. I put my uniform in a bag, at the very back of my closet, and dropped the last stone.

I returned to the States in late '89, with Susan and our six children, to live in New Hampshire and continue working with developmentally disabled persons. Although the rucksack is empty and stowed, with no residue of the vexing twinges that pestered me, there is an unavoidable sadness. Maybe I cheated a bit and discounted those small pebbles in my pocket. It is as hard to describe, as it is to conceive of sixty thousand dead soldiers.

The images come back to me in odd, random moments, though. One among many: Harlan Wilkenson, a kid from Omaha, in the shit for just a single week, lying on his back on a paddy dike. Me and one of the medics, bug-eyed in the dark, frantically ripping open bandages with our teeth in maddening desperation, trying to press his life back in, while finding ever more horrifying holes. In vain . . .

For most of us who came of age in the sixties, the Vietnam War was the defining event of our generation. For some of us that abattoir was the consummate experience of our lives. For myself, the war still exacts a moment by moment personal sacrifice. Fortunately, the confidence, self-discipline, and ideals the Army developed in me, the ones that played a role in causing my sacrifice, are precisely those needed to strengthen me day by day. I live comfortably with that irony.

Andy Wilson is still my best friend, the best I ever had. He married a girl, Nancy, whom he met at a pit party on Ward One. They and their three children live in Virginia. He is a successful business executive and runs his own financial services firm.

THIS _____ VIOLENT CENTURY

Bantam War Books Tell the Story
of Military Conflicts Throughout the World

1918

April 21   Baron Manfred von Richthofen's career comes to an end. *A History of the Luftwaffe* by John Killen.

1919

Jan. 1   More than a thousand Soviet troops attack American soldiers entrenched around the village of Nijni Gora in northern Russia. *The Ignorant Armies*.

1927

Oct. 18   HMS *L 4,* a British submarine under the command of Lt. Frederick J. C. Halahan, R.N., rescues the crew and passengers of the SS *Irene* from Chinese river pirates. *Submarine Warriors* by Edwyn Gray.

1932

Dec. 26   Chesty Puller drives off sandinista "bandits" who are attacking his train just outside El Sauce, Nicaragua. *Marine! The Life of Chesty Puller* **by Burke Davis.**

1937

April 10   German bombers attack the Spanish town of Guernica. It is the town's market day and 1,600 civilians die. *Full Circle* **by Air Vice Marshal J. E. Johnson.**

Aug. 17   Having missed their fighter escort, eleven out of twelve Japanese carrier-based attack bombers are shot down over Hangchow by defending Chinese fighter planes. *The Ragged, Rugged Warriors* **by Martin Caidin.**

1939

Sept. 14   The author, a young British aviator, is called to active duty. It is going to be a very long war. *Tale of a Guinea Pig* **by Geoffrey Page.**

1940

April 7   HMS *Sealion* in the middle of the German invasion fleet on its way to Norway watches the ships sail past. Rules of engagement prevent an attack. *Submarine Commander* **by Ben Bryant.**

May 10   The Phony War is over. German troops invade Belgium and Holland. *Churchill and His Generals* **by Barrie Pitt.**

Sept. 15   The critical day in the Battle of Britain. The Luftwaffe is beaten back from her daylight skies and Stanford Tuck, one of Britain's greatest air aces, shoots down a German Me 100. *Fly for Your Life* by Larry Forrester.

Nov. 11   British Swordfish torpedo bombers attack the Italian fleet anchored in the harbor of Taranto. *To War in a String Bag* by Charles Lamb.

1941

March 15   A hunter killer group commanded by Captain Donald MacIntyre sinks a U-99 and captures its captain, submarine ace Otto Kretschmer. *U-Boat Killer* by Donald MacIntyre.

April 16   Egyptian liner *Zamzam* sunk in South Atlantic by German surface raiders. *The German Raider Atlantis*, Rogge & Frank.

May 24   "I turned around to look for *Hood* and stared and stared and stared. It was clear to the horizon and *Hood* was no longer there. She'd had a crew of nearly fifteen hundred. Three of them survived." *Heart of Oak* by Tristan Jones.

May 27   German battleship *Bismarck* sunk. HMS *Hood* is avenged. *Pursuit* by Ludovic Kennedy.

July 4   The 10th Gurkhas with the 2nd Bn. of the 4th in reserve attack Vichy French and Syrian troops defending Deir-es-Zor, Syria. *The Road Past Mandalay* by John Masters.

Aug. 9   Douglas Bader loses a leg as his fighter plane is shot down over France. Fortunately it was one of his two artificial ones. *Reach for the Sky* by Paul Brickhill.

Oct. 31   U.S. destroyer *Rubin James* sunk by German submarine. *Tin Cans* by Theodore Roscoe.

Nov. 22   Major Robert Crisp fights his "Honey" tank against Rommel's panzers at Sidi-Rezegh in the North African desert. *Brazen Chariots* by Donald Crisp.

Dec. 7   Japanese carrier-based aircraft attack the U.S. fleet at Pearl Harbor. *Day of Infamy* by Walter Lord.

Dec. 24   The gallant defenders of Wake Island are overwhelmed by a Japanese amphibious landing force. *The Story of Wake Island* by Brig. Gen. James P. S. Devereux.

Dec. 27   British and Norwegian commandos attack the German garrison at Vaagso, Norway. *The Vaagso Raid* by Joseph H. Devins, Jr.

---

1 9 4 2

Jan. 27   Lt. Commander Joe Grenfiel, commanding USS *Gudgeon*, sinks the Japanese submarine *I-173* near Midway Island. *Combat Patrol* by Clay Blair, Jr.

Feb. 8   From the embattled fortress of Corregidor the submarine USS *Trout* loads two tons of gold bars and 18 tons of silver pesos for transport to Pearl Harbor. *Pig Boats* by Theodore Roscoe.

Feb. 11   Three German capital ships are making a run from the French port of Brest up the English Channel toward a safe haven in Germany. *Breakout!* by John Deane Potter.

March 6   Operation Nordpol commences with the capture of a British radio operator in Holland by Abwehr personnel. The problem now is to turn the agent so that he sends false messages to England. *London Calling North Pole* by H. J. Giskes.

May 8   British commandos blast their way into St. Nazaire harbor so as to destroy the Normandy dock. *The Greatest Raid of All* by C. E. Lucas Phillips.

June 1 Captain Frederic John Walker, R.N., in *Starling*, with *Wild Goose* and *Kite* in support as a hunter killer group stalk Captain Poser's *U-202*. This German submarine is hidden 800 feet below them in the depths of the Atlantic. *Escort Commander* by T. Robertson.

June 4 Nazi General Reinhard Heydrich dies of wounds received on May 27 when his car was bombed by Czech OSS agents. His side had neglected to develop penicillin. *Seven Men at Daybreak* by Alan Burgess.

June 16 Sub. Lt. C. L. Page captured and then executed by the Japanese. He'd stayed behind as a coastwatcher to radio intelligence reports on Japanese troop and naval movements from the Tabar Islands to Australia. *The Coast Watchers* by Eric A. Feldt.

June 21 Rommel captures the British North African fortress of Tobruk. *With Rommel in the Desert* by H. W. Schmidt.

June 27 Russian submarine *K-21* fires a spread of four torpedoes at the German battleship *Tirpitz*. *Russian Submarines in Arctic Waters* by I. Kolyshkin.

July 27 Special Air Service jeeps destroy Rommel's precious Ju 52 transport planes at Sidi Haneish airfield in North Africa. *Stirling's Desert Raiders* by Virginia Cowles.

Aug. 7 U.S. marines land on Guadalcanal. *The Battle for Guadalcanal* by Samuel B. Griffith II.

Aug. 8 Wounded and nearly blind, Japanese ace Saburo Sakai nurses a shattered Zero fighter over five hundred miles of ocean after attacking the Americans on Guadalcanal. *Samurai* by Sakai and Roger Pineau.

Aug. 9 British bombers lay mines in the Channel to block the *Prince Eugen* from the Atlantic. *Enemy Coast Ahead* by Guy Gibson.

Aug. 15 The American tanker *Ohio* finally docks at the besieged island of Malta in the Mediterranean. *Red Duster, White Ensign* by Ian Cameron.

Sept. 13 Over the North African desert, German ace Hans-Joachim, "The Star of Africa," with 158 victories, dies as he fails to successfully exit his burning Me 109. *Horrido!* by Raymond F. Toliver and Trevor J. Constable.

Sept. 17 Admiral Donetz secretly orders his U-boat commanders not to attempt to assist or reach the survivors of their attacks. *The Laconia Affair* by Leonce Peillard.

Oct. 4 British motor torpedo boats in battle action against German convoys off the Dutch coast. *Night Action* by Peter Dickens.

Dec. 11 British commandos who had paddled their fold-a-boats through sixty miles of German-occupied territory mine and sink several large German merchant ships tied up in the French harbor of Bordeaux. *Cockleshell Heroes* by Lucas-Phillips.

1943

Jan. 31 General Von Paulus surrenders the German 6th Army at Stalingrad. *Enemy at the Gates* by Walter Craig.

Feb. 7 Commander Howard W. Gilmore, wounded on the bridge of the USS *Growler*, gives the order, "Take her down." He dies but his ship survives. *Sink 'Em All* by Charles A. Lockwood.

Feb. 26 British agent Yeo-Thomas, "The White Rabbit," parachutes behind German lines into occupied France. *The White Rabbit* by Bruce Marshall.

Feb. 28 Norwegian commandos sabotage the heavy-water plant at Vemork, Norway. *Assault in Norway* by Thomas Gallagher.

March 30   Upon landing in Norway, his unit is destroyed by the Germans and this Norwegian commando, Jan Baalsrud, embarks on an incredible journey of survival. *We Die Alone* by Horwith.

May 12   The German Afrika Korps in Tunisia surrenders. One unit, the 164th Light Afrika Division, fights on until the following day. *The Foxes of the Desert* by Paul Carell.

May 16   Lt. Machorton returns to Imphal from the jungles of Burma. Wounded, he had been left to die. *The Hundred Days of Lt. Machorton* by Machorton and Henry Maule.

May 17   Guy Gibson and Squadron 617 destroy the Moehne and Eder dams. *The Dam Busters* by Paul Brickhill.

May 30   Although American troops have secured the island of Attu in the Aleutians, individual Japanese defenders still lurk in the surrounding hills. *The Thousand Miles War* by Brian Garfield.

July 8   Rudel's cannon-firing Stuka takes part in the biggest tank battle of World War II, Kursk, Russia. *Stuka Pilot* by Hans Ulrich Rudel.

July 11   Allied troops invade Sicily. *One More Hill* by Franklyn A. Johnson.

July 11   General George Patton is very much there too. *War As I Knew It* by George S. Patton.

July 27   The German city of Hamburg is consumed by a firestorm. *The Night Hamburg Died* by Martin Caidin.

Aug. 17   British bombers attack the German doomsday missile development base at Pecnemünde. *V-2* by Walter Dornberger.

Sept. 9   Fresh from his triumphs in North Africa, Popski along with his jeeps is landed in Teranto harbor by the USS *Boise* so that his private army can commence its invasion of Italy. *Popski's Private Army* by Lt. Col. Peniakoff.

Sept. 12   Colonel Skorzeny rescues Mussolini. *Commando Extraordinary* by Charles Foley.

Sept. 14   Russ Carter parachutes into Paestum, which is just south of the Salerno beachhead. *Those Devils in Baggy Pants* by Russ Carter.

Oct. 11   Running on the surface in La Pérouse Strait, one of America's greatest submarines fails to survive an attack by Japanese aircraft. *Wahoo: The Patrols of America's Most Famous World War II Submarine* by Rear Admiral Richard H. O'Kane (Ret.).

Oct. 14   The Schweinfurt Ball Bearing works were the target. Sixty B-17s failed to return from it. *Black Thursday* by Martin Caidin.

Oct. 29   Three British POWs escape from Stalag-Luft III. *The Wooden Horse* by Eric Williams.

Nov. 2   American destroyers in battle action against the navy of Imperial Japan at the Battle of Empress Augusta Bay. *Admiral Arleigh (31 Knot) Burke* by Ken Jones and Hubert Kelley.

Nov. 5   Donald R. Burgett wins his paratrooper wings. *As Eagles Screamed* by Donald R. Burgett.

Nov. 13   The Japanese battleship *Hiei* goes to the bottom, sunk by marine and navy airmen. *The Cactus Air Force* by Thomas G. Miller, Jr.

Nov. 20   American marines land on the Japanese island of Tarawa. *Tarawa* by Robert Sherrod.

Dec. 2   Bari, Italy. German bombers sink twenty Allied merchant ships, and a deadly, secret cargo is released. *Disaster at Bari* by Glen Infield.

1944

Jan. 3   "Pappy," after chalking up 25 victories gets shot down over Rabaul. *Baa, Baa, Black Sheep* by Gregory "Pappy" Boyington.

Feb. 1   American and Filipino guerrillas launch an offensive against the Japanese. *American Guerrilla in the Philippines* by Ira Wolfert.

Feb. 22   Heinz Knoke shoots down a B-17 Flying Fortress over his home town of Hameln, Germany. *I Flew for the Führer* by Heinz Knoke.

March 5   Brig. Tom Churchill takes command on the island of Vis in the Adriatic Sea. *Commando Force 133* by Bill Strutton.

March 18   Chindit units battle hand to hand with the Japanese invaders of Burma. *Fighting Mad* by "Mad" Mike Calvert.

March 20   USS *Angler* surfaces off Panay Island in the Japanese-occupied Philippines to rescue 58 refugees. *Guerrilla Submarines* by Ed Dissette.

April 13   Over Hamburg, Germany, an FW 190 becomes the author's 25th aerial victory. *Thunderbolt* by Robert S. Johnson, with Martin Caidin.

June 6   In the first minutes of this day the green light goes on in a C-47 flying over the Cherbourg peninsula. *As Eagles Screamed* by Donald R. Burgett.   *D-Day* by David Howarth

June 9   Normandy beachhead. Keith Douglas KIA near Tilly-sur-Seulles. *Alamein to Zem Zem* by Keith Douglas.

June 22   An American pilot uses a 1,000-pound bomb to cure a long-standing rat problem in his old barracks now occupied by the Japanese. *Into the Teeth of the Tiger* by Donald S. Lopez.

June 24   Marine General "Howlin' Mad" Smith relieves Major General Ralph Smith from command of the 27th Infantry Division on the island of Saipan. *Coral and Brass* by General Holland "Howling Mad" Smith.

June 25 German ace Robert Spreckels shoots down British ace J.R.D. Braham in air combat over Denmark. *Night Fighter by J.R.D. Braham.*

June 26 The French port of Cherbourg falls to Allied invasion forces. *Invasion: They're Coming!* **by Paul Carell.**

June 29 An SS squadron in Russia on the Mogilev-Minsk road is shooting German officers found to be moving toward the rear without proper written orders. *The Black March* **by Peter Neumann.**

July 18 The city of St. Lô is finally secured. *The Clay Pigeons of St. Lô* **by Grover S. Johns, Jr.**

Aug. 15 Operation "Anvil," the Allied landing in the South of France. "The best invasion I ever attended." *Up Front* **by Bill Mauldin.**

Sept. 15 A young marine goes ashore on Peleliu Island which was one of the most bitterly contested of the Pacific island landings. *Helmet for My Pillow* **by Robert Leckie.**

Sept. 17 Disguised as a slave laborer, British Sgt. Charles Coward, a prisoner of war in Germany, has just spent the night in hell, locked inside the Auschwitz concentration camp. He now knows the secret of the camp and has vowed to tell it to the world. *The Password Is Courage* **by John Castle.**

Oct. 3 A young infantry captain enters Germany. It is 11:15 A.M. and the war in Europe is a long way from being over. *Company Commander* **by Charles MacDonald.**

Oct. 25 Lt. Seki successfully crashes his plane into the USS *St. Lô* (CVE-63) and sends this escort carrier to the bottom. *The Divine Wind* **by Roger Pineau.**

Having attacked a Japanese convoy with unbelievable ferocity, *Tang* fires a final misfunctioning torpedo which turns back and sinks this famous submarine. *Clear the Bridge* **by Richard O'Kane.**

Nov. 26   If you have ever wondered where some of our best writers are. Flying a P-51 on an escort mission over Hanover, Germany, Bert Stiles is KIA. *Serenade to the Big Bird* by Bert Stiles.

1945

Jan. 4   The 761st Tank Bn. attacks the town of Tillet. It is just to the west of Bastogne. *Hit Hard* by David J. Williams.

Feb. 3   Convoy JW-64 sails north from England on its way to Russia. *A Bloody War, 1939–45* by Hal Lawrence.

Feb. 23   U.S. marines raise the American flag on the peak of Mt. Suribachi. *Iwo Jima* by Richard Newcomb.

Feb. 28   Company K attacks the town of Hardt just to the west of Düsseldorf, Germany. *The Men of Company "K"* by Leinbaugh and Campbell.

March 15   Bob Clark, Clostermann's No. 4, flying a Hawker Tempest, shoots down an Me 262 piloted by Walter Nowotney, one of the Luftwaffe's greatest aces. *The Big Show* by Pierre Clostermann.

April 1   The Japanese island of Okinawa is invaded. *Okinawa: Typhoon of Steel* by Belote and Belote.

April 16   A German steamship with 7,000 evacuees aboard is sunk outside of Hela, Prussia, by a Russian submarine. There are 170 survivors. *Defeat in the East* by J. Thorwald.

April 26   Adolph Galand leads a flight of Me 262 jet fighters in one of the last air battles of the European war. *The First and the Last* by Adolph Galand.

April 29   General Patton climbs down from one of his tanks to liberate the American POW camp of Mooseburg in Germany. *Prisoner of War* by Kenneth W. Simmons.

April 30 British "Crocodile" flame-throwing tanks take up positions outside the German town of Oldenburg. *Flame Thrower* by Andrew Wilson.

May 3 American armor overruns Jagvelband 44 at Salzburg-Maxglan, Germany, and the war is over for this squadron of futuristic German fighters. *Rocket Fighter* by Mano Ziegler.

May 8 German ace Erich Hartman chalks up his 352nd and final aerial victory. *Horrido!* by Raymond F. Toliver and Trevor J. Constable.

May 8 On a leave train bound for the South of France, the author learns that the war in Europe, at long last, is officially over. *To Hell and Back* by Audie Murphy.

June 2 The USS *Tinosa* recovers the crew of a ditched B-29 just south of the Japanese island of Kyushu. *Sink 'Em All* by Charles A. Lockwood.

June 21 The Japanese commander on Okinawa, General Ushijima, commits suicide. *Marine at War* by Russell Davis.

The U.S. high command declares Okinawa to be secured. *With the Old Breed* by Eugene B. Sledge (April 1991).

June 22 With her last two torpedoes, and just before heading home, USS *Crevalle* sinks a Japanese destroyer. *Hellcats of the Sea* by Lockwood and Adamson.

July 25 U.S. carrier aircraft raids Japan's Kure naval base, destroying or damaging most of what was left of the Imperial fleet. *Combat Command* by Frederick C. Sherman.

July 30 Japanese submarine *I-58* sinks the USS *Indianapolis*. *Abandon Ship!* by Richard E. Newcomb.

Aug. 17 A German U-boat commander surrenders to the Argentinian navy only to be accused of having brought Hitler to Antarctica. *U-Boat 977* by Heinz Schaeffer.

Sept. 2   General Wainwright, recently released from a Japanese POW camp, is present on the deck of the USS *Missouri* as the Japanese formally surrender. *General Wainwright's Story* by General Jonathan M. Wainwright. Edited by Robert Considine.

Sept. 11   After three and a half years of imprisonment, Australian soldiers and American sailors liberate the Kuching prison camp in North Borneo. *Three Came Home* by Agnes Newton Keith.

1 9 5 0

June 25   The North Korean army moves south and the world is once more at war. *This Kind of War* by T. R. Fehrenbach.

Dec. 10   Their breakthrough is now completed, and the marines who fought their way down from the Chosin Reservoir are finally in the clear. *The March to Glory* by Robert Leckie.

1 9 5 1

April 22   In the Battle of Solma-Ri, waves of Chinese infantry engulf the British Gloucester regiment. The survivors fight their way out to the south. *Now Thrives the Armourers* by Robert O. Holles.

1 9 5 5

Jan. 4   On the Foum-Toub-Arris road four men are ambushed and burnt to death in their jeep by Algerian rebel forces. *The War in Algeria* by Pierre Leulliette.

1956

Oct. 10   Dedean Kimathi, the most wanted Mau Mau terrorist, is taken by four Kikuyu tribal policemen. *Manhunt in Kenya* by Sir Philip Goodhart and Ian Henderson.

1958

April 5   A 28-year-old police constable accepts the surrender of Hor Lung, the last of the top level Chinese Communist leaders at large in Malaya. *The War of the Running Dogs* by Noel Barber.

1963

June 11   A Buddhist monk burns himself to death on a street corner in Saigon. *The New Face of War* by Malcolm Browne.

1964

Nov. 24   Belgian Paras and the Lima One Flying Column of mercenaries save the lives of a thousand hostages in the Congo. *Save the Hostages* by David Reed.

1965

May 15   *SR-71*, the legendary recon U.S. aircraft, sets an 80,000-foot Mach 3.12 record. Twenty-five years later the *New York Times*, on February 24, 1990, reports that the air force will retire it. *Air War Vietnam* by Frank Harvey.

June 17   Navy Phantoms shoot down the first MiGs to be destroyed over Vietnam. *The Story of Air Fighting* by J. E. Johnson.

Dec. 18   Air cavalrymen are going into a hot landing zone at Ben Khe, Vietnam. *Year of the Horse—Vietnam* by Col. Kenneth D. Mertel.

1 9 6 6

Jan. 17   A B-52 collides with its KC-135 tanker and a hydrogen bomb is lost. *One of Our H-Bombs Is Missing!* by Flora Lewis.

Oct. 13   A navy flyer's wife receives a telegram listing her husband as MIA. His plane was seen to explode over enemy-occupied territory. No parachute was observed and no radio distress calls were received. *Touring Nam* by Greenburg and Norton.

1 9 6 7

Sept. 15   The Brown Water Navy's Force 117 goes into battle along the Rach Ba Rai against the 263rd Vietcong Main Force Bn. *Seven Firefights in Vietnam* by John A. Cash, John Albright, and Allan W. Sandstrum.

1 9 6 8

Jan. 29   The Tet offensive starts and a marine doctor has no clue as to what the next two days will bring. *12, 20 & 5, a Doctor's Year in Vietnam* by John A. Parrish, M.D.

Feb. 25   Khe Sanh. A marine patrol is ambushed. One third of it returns to the perimeter. *Welcome to Vietnam, Macho Man* by Ernest Spencer.

July 3   A long year starts for an American soldier who has just landed in Vietnam. *One Soldier* by **John Shook.**

Nov. 15   Near Binh Tri village a scout dog finds a Vietcong mine. Casualties: dead 1 dog, 1 PRU, 12 others wounded. *The Advisor* by **John L. Cook.**

1 9 7 0

Oct. 10   There is a patrol just outside the village of Truong Lam, and the word is "Incoming!" *Platoon Leader* by **James R. McDonough.**

1 9 7 2

April 1   An EB-66 meets a SAM 2 just south of the DMZ and the co-pilot punches out at 30,000 feet. *Bat-21* by **William C. Anderson.**

Join the Allies on the Road to Victory
BANTAM WAR BOOKS

Two heart-stopping historical events that shook the world. Walter Lord vividly recreates the drama and terror of the moment.

DAY OF INFAMY

❑ 26777-9 $4.95/$5.95 in Canada

A moment-by-moment, behind-the-scenes look at what actually happened on one of the most infamous days in American history: the hours leading up to the Japanese attack on Pearl Harbor. Based on eyewitness reports and supplemented by twenty-one pages of photographs and maps.

A NIGHT TO REMEMBER

❑ 27827-4 $4.50/$5.50 in Canada

This is the true and incredible story of the "unsinkable" Titanic, going down on her maiden voyage. "All the drama, horror, tragedy of that grim, heart-breaking night are here, never before presented in such superb narrative style!"
—*Chicago Tribune*